A Requiem for the
American Village

American Intellectual Culture

Series Editors: Jean Bethke Elshtain, University of Chicago, Ted V. McAllister, Pepperdine University, Wilfred M. McClay, University of Tennessee at Chattanooga

The books in the American Intellectual Culture series examine the place, identity, and public role of intellectuals and cultural elites in the United States, past, present, and future. Written by prominent historians, philosophers, and political theorists, these books will examine the influence of intellectuals on American political, social, and cultural life, paying particular attention to the characteristic forms, and evolving possibilities, of democratic intellect. The books will place special, but not exclusive, emphasis on the relationship between intellectuals and American public life. Because the books are intended to shape and contribute to scholarly and public debates about their respective topics, they will be concise, accessible, and provocative.

When All the Gods Trembled: Darwinism, Scopes, and American Intellectuals
   by Paul K. Conkin, Vanderbilt University
Heterophobia: Sexual Harassment and the Future of Feminism
   by Daphne Patai, University of Massachusetts at Amherst
Postmodernism Rightly Understood: the Return to Realism in American Thought
   by Peter Augustine Lawler, Berry College
A Requiem for the American Village
   by Paul K. Conkin

Forthcoming Titles:
Modern Inconvenience: The Social Origins of Antifamily Thought
   by Elisabeth Lasch-Quinn, Syracuse University
Academic Politics: The Colonial Colleges and the Shaping of American Intellectual Culture
   by J. David Hoeveler, University of Wisconsin, Milwaukee
History and Public Memory in America
   by Wilfred M. McClay, University of Tennessee at Chattanooga
Integrating the World: Cold War Intellectuals and the Politics of Identity
   by Christopher Shannon, the George Eastman House
A Pragmatist's Progress? Richard Rorty and American Intellectual History
   by John Pettegrew, Lehigh University
Ralph Waldo Emerson and the Problem of Democracy
   by Peter S. Field, Tennessee Technological University
The Murder of Joy: Paul Goodman and the American Battle over Maturity
   by Robert Oliver, University of Wisconsin, Madison
The Public and Protagonist: Tocqueville and American Intellectuals, 1835–2000
   by Matthew Mancini, Southwest Missouri State University

A Requiem for the American Village

Paul K. Conkin

ROWMAN & LITTLEFIELD PUBLISHERS, INC.
Lanham • Boulder • New York • Oxford

ROWMAN & LITTLEFIELD PUBLISHERS, INC.

Published in the United States of America
by Rowman & Littlefield Publishers, Inc.
4720 Boston Way, Lanham, Maryland 20706
http://www.rowmanlittlefield.com

12 Hid's Copse Road
Cumnor Hill, Oxford OX2 9JJ, England

British Cataloging in Publication Information Available

Library of Congress Cataloging-in-Publication Data

Conkin, Paul Keith.
    A requiem for the American village / Paul K. Conkin.
        p.   cm.—(American intellectual culture)
    Includes bibliographical references and index.
    ISBN 0-8476-9736-3 (cloth)
    1. United States—History. 2. United States—History—20th
century. I. Title. II. Series.
    E178.6.C675   2000
    973—dc21   99-40922
                                                                                CIP

Printed in the United States of America

♾™ The paper used in this publication meets the minimum requirements of
American National Standard for Information Sciences—Permanence of Paper for
Printed Library Materials, ANSI Z.39.48–1992.

Contents

Foreword *by Ted V. McAllister*   vii

Acknowledgments   xiii

Introduction   xv

1. History As a Discipline   1
   The First Historian   2
   Local History: A Mirror for American Values   7

2. Creating New Communities   19
   The Cooperative Commonwealth in America   21
   Arthurdale Revisited   37

3. The Road to a Regulatory and Welfare State   51
   The Last and Greatest Depression   54
   The Great Society: The Climax of Policy Reform in America   63

4. First Principles of American Government   73
   Liberty, Property, and Expressive Freedoms   75
   Democracy   87

5. The Dilemmas of Cultural Pluralism   97
   Revolt of the Village   99
   What Holds Us Together?   110

6. American Religion   121
   The Scopes Trial Revisited   122
   American Religious Pluralism and Public Policy   134

7. The South   147
   What Is a Bright Southern Boy to Do?   148
   Hot, Humid, and Sad   161

8. Communal Memory and Historical Piety   175
   Now Let Us Praise Famous Men   176

9. Scholarship   187
   Students and Scholars   188

10. Endings   197
    Good-bye   198

Index   201

About the Author   207

Foreword:
The Cosmopolitan Provincial

Paul Conkin is enigmatic. This is, at any rate, what I am told by the historians who discover that I was his student. To this day most historians I meet relate some anecdote (usually gathered secondhand) about Paul that I'm expected to explain in light of my more intimate knowledge of this man. The task is more daunting than they suppose, and I will attempt no such explanation in this introduction. I hope, instead, to provide the reader with some orienting information about his career, followed by a brief description of a dominant tension in the man and scholar that is amply expressed in this volume of essays.

Conkin's books are widely known but not widely discussed, at least judging from the periodical literature. Part of the explanation for this is that he does not limit his work to one field, which might allow him to develop important connections with others who work regularly in a particular subject. Rather than becoming a historian of the Founding period, Conkin played the interloper with his book *Self-Evident Truths*. The same might be said of all his books, with the exception, perhaps, of his recent trilogy on religion in America (*Cane Ridge, Uneasy Center,* and *American Originals*). Indeed, he may now be best known as a religious historian, though he is also a political historian (*Big Daddy from the Pedernales* and *The New Deal*), an economic historian (*Prophets of Prosperity*), a Southern historian (*The Southern Agrarians*), a historian of religious or utopian communities (*Two Paths to Utopia*), an institutional historian (*Gone with the Ivy: A Biography of Vanderbilt University*), a philosopher of history (*Heritage and Challenge*), not to mention his self-designation as intellectual historian

(*When All the Gods Trembled* and, most notably, *Puritans and Pragmatists*). This partial list of works hints at the range of the scholar, but it also tells us something about the nature of the scholar.

Conkin feels the need to be part of the profession, to do his part in a collective effort that for him has great moral import. To this end he works tirelessly on university and historical association committees, serves dutifully his administrative tours, and labors mightily to be a good citizen of these professional institutions. But this professionalism runs counter to his constitutional inability to cede any portion of his autonomy—it runs counter to his self-understanding as an outsider. This tension is evident in nearly every aspect of his work. Perhaps no historian quotes less frequently than does Paul Conkin. Even as he tries to give voice to the beliefs of Lyndon Johnson or Mary Baker Eddy, Paul must speak for them, translating their often contradictory or vague statements into a precise set of statements. He systematizes and then analyzes the claims of others. Conkin almost never debates with other historians, and he rarely cites them—though he has always read their works. He wants to tell his story, his way. The professional requirements that govern most historians, such as the convention of devoting space to exploring the historiographical terrain and then locating one's particular work within this field, strike Paul as wasteful, even as such formalities tend to get in the way of the story. In these ways he will not play the game. Those deeply involved in the game do not know what to do with him.

It may be, however, his style of storytelling that makes him most difficult for fellow historians to comprehend. Two seemingly opposite qualities characterize his works—those things historians see as related, Paul makes distinct; those things that appear unconnected, Paul ties together. Underlying these tendencies is a passion for semantic clarity and an inordinate devotion to logical rigor. Because he employs more frequently than most the precise language of analytical philosophy, and because he seems to be perversely innocent of the works of other historians (this is especially true with regard to the labels or categories that become standard among historians—labels such as "liberalism" or "republicanism"), and because the very form his arguments take don't fit the expectations of his fellow historians, Conkin's works occupy a kind of no-man's-land. His books include neither the specific jargon of the specialists nor the broad generalizations for a large, public audience.

Perhaps for these reasons Conkin has not developed a clear audience for his work. This is unfortunate. As the essays in this volume demonstrate, Paul has a distinctive, hard to categorize, perspective. The singularity of his style and perspective may hamper our ability to understand or appreciate his deeply moral examination of our culture. Understanding and engaging with Conkin's idiosyncratic perspective is no easy task, but the challenge might be made easier with an understanding of the under-lying philosophical and moral claims that inform his history—or, rather, the way historical inquiry functions in his work as a means of philosoph-ical and moral exploration.

* * *

What am I to do? is a question that makes sense only in the context of the more basic question, Who am I? For Paul Conkin, therefore, the search for moral injunctions sends him to history. In our contemporary intellec-tual environment the old markers of identity—always themselves teth-ered to historical storytelling—that emphasized either the gods to whom we belonged or a universal "human nature" are no longer satisfying, the gods having died and Nature having dissolved into process. Or, at least, this is Conkin's plight, and it leaves him in a most exciting (never debili-tating) paradox: Humans are radically free and yet enslaved by their (mostly forgotten) past. The moral challenge embedded in this paradox is that humans cannot escape responsibility for what they do and who they are—this is a responsibility borne by the individual—while one's very identity springs from a historically textured life one did not create oneself, but to which one is necessarily beholden. There are a few places in this book—look carefully—where Conkin shakes his fist at fate for giving him this terrible freedom but so very little power. If humans have no nature, then they have only history to tell them who they are, only history to give them some idea of moral strictures that should govern their lives. For Paul Conkin, storytelling is a calling.

The aim of this history is to gain understanding that frees us from the constraints of the past, understanding that supplies the necessary means of controlling our own identity—collective and individual. Rigorous and truthful accounts of our pasts allow us to reaffirm for ourselves the values and purposes that get encoded in the cultural habits and customs that we inherit and inhabit. These accounts may also give us the power to repudi-ate parts of our heritage, a heritage that in ignorance would still govern our lives though we had no direct part in creating it. Because humans are accul-turated beings, whose most essential characteristics come to us through culture, which must be passed down through language and, in part, story-telling, their very humanity depends upon having a remembered past. But this dependence need not lead to fatalism. For Conkin a rich and textured understanding of this past gives a people ownership of it, and the ability to affirm selectively what they wish to perpetuate, who they wish to become. But, to Paul Conkin's credit, the moral inquiry contained herein and made possible by this understanding of human existence is complicated nearly beyond comprehension, full of tensions, and tamed by a rare piety. Appropriately named after the Christian apostle, Paul Conkin emphasizes human responsibility and freedom even as he notes human weakness, the dependence of all humans on conditions they cannot control.

Wonder and melancholy animate these essays much more than the analytical rigor and clinical distance that some readers associate with Conkin's work. He adopts and adapts key Christian doctrines—original sin, grace—to explain the human (and his own) condition. Language made us human (the forbidden fruit), and being human means to be without an ontologically fixed role. We aspire to be gods (and Conkin gives humans a certain godlike creativity, emphasizing that they are creators rather than creatures), but the freedom of this open-ended creative life brings a strong sense of homelessness and alienation. Still, this "fall" from a fixed nature to humanity is a form of grace, and in his own way Conkin expresses, in word and in deed (for those who know him), a deep piety toward the reality that he experiences. This piety is expressed most fervently in his irrepressible and childlike wonder. In this way Conkin bears a closer resemblance to Socrates than to St. Paul. For Conkin, every day is a miracle and an opportunity to explore, to try to understand, to learn for oneself the truth. Nonetheless, the freedom of the human condition leads to the search for truth, beauty, and goodness—and to existential loneliness. The wonder of a free life (this sort of freedom unknown except to humans) comes at the expense of comforting solidarity.

It takes a rare spiritual stamina to be alone. Note what Conkin writes about himself: "I am one of these solitary intellectuals. I am not part of any cohesive community or sect. Solidarity . . . frightens me. . . . Familial labels—brother, comrade—make me nervous. I do not want to surrender my autonomy, my independent voice." He is not a joiner, but in important ways he belongs—belongs to family, belongs to the village of his youth. From these sources of himself Conkin cannot leave finally; they help constitute his identity. How could he leave? Why would he want to? As is evident throughout this book, Conkin's values, his sense of purpose, and, most important, his affections are bound up in this provincial beginning, this village life. Like language, like the natural world, these affections are part of the givenness of his life—Grace (undeserved, just given). So, while he is the "solitary intellectual," he is still "Harry Conkin's boy"—the latter shaping the former.

But, of course, he is more than his father's son, and as someone who left the village in body and in spirit, Conkin has a sense that he understands the villagers even if they can't understand him. The widening scope of experiences and the new perspectives open to Harry's son made him critical of the provincialism of village life, though they never erased the understanding of the special comfort that comes from what Conkin likes to call "totalitarian" communities. In a special sense, then, Paul Conkin is again alone—he understands and even appreciates the villagers' ontological and moral commitments but can neither accept their values nor be understood by them—he is an outsider in his own home. But it is also clear from these essays that Conkin is still too rustic to be comfortable, finally, with intellectual communities. He has to explain his people to his fellow intellectuals.

The histories he writes and the life he lives testify, beautifully, to these tensions, especially to the moral challenges of a privileged life from humble beginnings. In good equalitarian fashion his stories have no heroes or villains. With an almost Christian sense of human frailty—but without the possibility of supernatural help—Conkin provides sympathetic, almost loving, portraits of his subjects. He understands the complexity of human existence, expects humans to falter, and relishes in their (usually) earnest efforts to make sense of their lives. Conkin sympathizes with losers, though rarely with lost causes. He pays homage to his subjects by telling the truth about them. He explains them relative to their own belief systems, which he systematizes for them. He holds them accountable to their own beliefs first, then to his. Conkin also fights odd battles. He struggles with editors who want to turn "esthetic" into "aesthetic," which for him is putting on airs. He worries that he lives in an upscale neighborhood, emphasizing that he lives in the most modest house in the area. Some of the values of his village live on in the sophisticate.

The stories in this book are meant as an exercise in collective self-interpretation—that is, they tell us something important about who we have been and who we are becoming. Conkin's choice of topic, his way of telling these several accounts of the assault on the village and on certain kinds of provincialism, tell us much about the author's moral strictures, however ambiguous and complex they may be. He is often the preacher. But far more interesting and revealing are the intellectual, cultural, and moral tensions out of which Conkin constructs his stories. These are revealed here more than in any of his books. In ways he did not anticipate, this book exposes the scholar who wrote it—a scholar who is greatly misunderstood by his colleagues. The subject of this book is close to Conkin's heart and speaks directly to his own dialectical exercise in self-understanding. In it we find the pious unbeliever, the liberal communitarian, the moralistic latitudinarian, and especially the cosmopolitan provincial. Ultimately, Conkin's moral search, his demand for universal principles, never squares with the needs humans have for community, much less the necessary intolerance that helps foster community. Reading this book from a scholar caught betwixt and between allows a glimpse into something far more important—the soul of Paul Conkin.

Ted V. McAllister,
Pepperdine University

Acknowledgments

All or parts of five of the essays in this book have been previously published. In each case, the publishers have kindly granted permission to reuse them in this book. For these permissions, I am deeply grateful. The University of Southwestern Louisiana gave permission to reprint selections from two of its books: the chapter in this book, "The Last and Greatest Depression," is part of a chapter entitled "Images of the Last and Greatest Depression" in *Louisiana Gothic: Recollections of the 1930s*, edited by Glenn R. Conrad and Vaughan B. Baker (Lafayette, 1984). My chapter entitled "The Cooperative Commonwealth in America" is a slightly amended copy of a chapter entitled "Three Authors, Three Books, and Three Colonies: The Cooperative Commonwealth in America," in *France and North American Utopia and Utopians: Proceedings of the Third Symposium of French-American Studies, March 4–8, 1974*, edited by Mathé Allain (Lafayette, 1978), pp. 33–44. Arthurdale Heritage, Inc., has granted permission for me to include, in this book, the chapter entitled "Arthurdale Revisited," which is a slightly amended copy of the chapter "Arthurdale Revisited: When Subsistence Farming Made Sense," in *A New Deal for America: Proceedings from a National Conference on New Deal Communities*, edited by Bryan Ward (Arthurdale, West Virginia, 1995), pp. 45–64. The University of Georgia Press has granted permission for me to include, in my chapter "What Is a Bright Southern Boy to Do?" excerpts from a chapter entitled "The South in Southern Agrarianism," in *The Evolution of Southern Culture*, ed. by Numan V. Bartley (Athens, 1988), pp. 131–45. The *Journal of Southern History* has granted me permission to use a very slightly modified version of my presidential address for the Southern Historical Association. "Hot, Humid, and Sad," which appeared in volume 64 (February 1998), pp. 3–32.

Introduction

In 2000 I will retire after over forty years of teaching. During those years I have spent at least half my time and energy researching and writing articles and books in my field of history. In the same years I did what is normal in such a career—every year I presented several lectures or conference papers to a wide variety of audiences. Unfortunately, I never kept a record of such presentations. But I have found, in two file drawers, copies of over a hundred such speeches. These, of course, join with copies of classroom lectures, saved from at least fifteen different courses I have taught over the years. At times the two have overlapped.

What I have collected here are seventeen of those speeches, or history from the lectern. They are not necessarily the most representative of essays I have written for oral presentation, but they do relate to one rather elusive theme—the multiple challenges to the survival of close-knit communities or villages. I have written most of these essays in the last decade, but one or two go back twenty-five years. Only four have been previously published, two as part of the procedures of conferences, one in a historical journal, and one as an introduction to a book of photographs. Most reflected the themes in books under way, or just completed, at the time of delivery. In each case I tried to write essays that were appropriate to a listening audience. The form, and the language, are different from texts written with the expectation of publication. The essays are less formal, more self-revealing.

My scholarship has embraced many topics and fields of history. I have refused to specialize. At the time I wrote these essays, along with many others, I was not aware of any common theme, and in a strict sense they do not reveal such a unity of content. Yet, in going through a stack of past lectures, I found some interesting and unexpected continuities. Clearly, my youth in a small rural community; the bitter experience of the Great Depression; my father's unwanted transition from farmer and independent proprietor to factory worker; and the gradual erosion of communal bonds in an age of pluralism and cosmopolitan values, have all helped shape my scholarly work. Such themes abound in the following essays, even when the overt subject is the nature of historical inquiry, American religion, the development of a regulatory and welfare state, the dilemmas of cultural pluralism, the problems of the South, or the foundational principles of American government.

The title—*A Requiem for the American Village*—is impressionistic. A requiem is a song or dirge for something lost or dead. It implies sadness. In this case I do feel that the small, reasonably autonomous communities—or, figuratively, the villages of the American past—are all but gone. They are inconsistent with a centralized and collective economic system and with a type of inclusive cultural pluralism. Villages, at the very least, have lost most aspects of political and legal hegemony, most cultural independence, most religious autonomy. But villages or tight communities have always been, to some extent, exclusive and repressive. Even as I commemorate their former role in America, and with a sense of loss, I am aware of what Americans have gained from a modern social order, in wealth, in the leeway for free expression, in the accommodation of minorities, and in more uniform standards of due process. In other words, I am ambivalent about many of the themes that I stress in the following essays.

The essays are largely published as written and delivered. I have made some minor changes when the language seemed unclear. In many essays I had to delete sections that closely duplicated parts of earlier essays. To an extent that was almost embarrassing, I often returned over and over again to certain themes. Some repetition remains, but only in cases where the duplicated content is necessary to the logic of an argument. Each essay reflects my understanding, my outlook, at the time I wrote it. On some issues I have changed my mind. But—and this was a pleasant surprise— I was rarely embarrassed by what I said even a quarter century ago. Most of it still makes sense.

1

✢

History
As a Discipline

Throughout most of my career I have been fascinated with the analytical philosophy of history. This interest led to reviews, articles, and the second part of a widely used text. Roland Stromberg wrote the first half, a brief history of historical writing, and I wrote a final five chapters on the major issues in the philosophy of history. The second, and current, edition of this book is *Heritage and Challenge: The History and Theory of History* (Arlington Heights, Ill.: Forum Press, 1989).

I wrote the following, very short and whimsical, essay as an introduction to a Mellon Foundation seminar on the philosophy of history, offered here at Vanderbilt during two different summers. It reveals the possible clan-based origin of historical thinking. The second essay is a keynote address that I delivered at a conference at Appalachian State University in Boone, North Carolina, in 1978. It emphasizes the tensions between national and local history, and thus broaches some of the central themes of all the essays in this book. The theme of the conference, attended by local historians in Appalachia, was identical to the title of my paper: "Local History: A Mirror for American Values."

The First Historian

He lived thirty thousand years ago. Except in the summer, he lived with his clan in a cave in what is now southern France. He was an early Homo sapiens, a Cro-Magnon man, although of course he did not know that. The categories are ours, not his. Given the self-indulgent complacence we often give to the label Homo sapiens, he would rightly have relished it. His name until the time of this story, translated into English, was Short Legs. Subsequently he would gain the name of Tall Tales and would be known for miles around his home cave.

Short Legs and his clan, sometime in the rather recent past, had developed a true or symbolic language. They were not aware of this. They did not even have a name for "language." But they already had a working vocabulary of over a thousand words and had come to accept some complicated syntactical conventions—although they were not aware of these. They as yet had no grammarians. Gradually, during a past that stretched far back beyond their memory, and in a sense even beyond the reach of the type of verbalized memory they now possessed, the clan had elaborated upon a complex system of signals, richer and more varied and keyed to more types of conditioned response than even those of the crow. Thus they had developed an amazing ability to produce modulated sounds. In a process so gradual, so incremental, as to be beyond any awareness, even when they gained the linguistic tools for such awareness, the signals, keyed in each case to a specific response, began to take on more nuanced roles. Sounds became words, or symbols standing for objects—at first only specific objects, such as individuals, but gradually for whole classes of objects. Instead of a name for each bear, they began to refer to all such animals as bears. As the symbols became richer and more encompassing, and as the people augmented their language with words that referred to action, and qualified their symbols with other words that modified the meaning of class terms, the clan gained immense new power over their world. What we call language, and puzzle about endlessly, was not yet a puzzle to them. It made them self-conscious, able to distinguish themselves from the now named objects that surrounded them; but not

2

for a long time would they make the tool—language—an object of contemplation, with all the wisdom, and all the foolishness, that such language awareness invites.

As sounds became symbols, language facilitated the success of the hunt and, on rare occasions, the outcome of battles with other clans. Evolving language was a wonderful tool for coordinating actions. It allowed a hunting party to relay detailed and nuanced instructions about the placement and movement of each stalker and of the prey. The kill grew exponentially. More important, it allowed the hunters, around the campfires in the evening, to plan the next day's hunt, to make specific assignments, gradually to work out specialized roles for each participant. It allowed them to evaluate the hunt of the day before, to home in on critical mistakes, to evaluate new options. It even led to more subtle details in their cave-side drawings, by which they now recorded heretofore unnoticed aspects of the hunt or unnoted details about the prey. Thus language began as a tool. It was justified by its success, as is any tool. If the reports about the past day's hunt enabled the clan to improve its kill, then they accepted such reports. We might ask questions about the truth of such reports, but not our ancient progenitors. They accepted language as a given.

Language soon served new uses, uses never anticipated or even remarked by those who enjoyed or suffered them. All animals have an imagination (they entertain fleeting images), but with language imagination took on a new, verbal form. In moments of repose, or even in dreams, the people of the clan began to rehearse new scenarios for the hunt, to imagine new ways of doing things, to entertain fantasies about themselves and other people. They began to ask why and to imagine answers to new questions. They began to people their world with hidden actors and agents, to see intent and purpose in the wind and the storms. They created spirits and gods to explain what happened, particularly in those areas where they were most helpless. They knew awe and suffered from new fears and insecurities. They became morbidly fascinated with self and, as an adjunct of self-awareness, began to suffer both shame and guilt. They gained a conscience. They also agonized about death. They became human.

Short Legs had a handicap. His legs were indeed dwarfed, and thus he was incapacitated in war and in hunting, although he tried to do his part. He seemed odd to his comrades, but he was not thereby stigmatized. Everyone assumed the gods had planned it this way, and they often stood in awe of him, particularly his talking. Language seemed his game, fantasy his compensation. As he grew older, he seemed to talk all his waking hours, droning on at times even when no one was listening. One evening, as the hunters ate their meat, and as the women and children hovered about, the young men began to talk about their exploits over the last few days and, of course, to boast about them. At this point Short Legs interrupted. In effect, this is what he said:

You have little of which to boast. The great hunts all took place in the distant past. I am an old man now. When I was a boy, the great hunts were not so remote. My father's father was then still alive, and he told me about the greatest hunt of them all. As a boy, he was part of it, and joined in the feasts that went on all winter and well into the springtime. This was the most successful hunt that our people ever enjoyed or, I suspect, that any people anywhere ever enjoyed. Nothing close to it has happened since, and most likely it never will. Your success last week was nothing compared to the great hunt. See there on the upper wall. That is the record of that great hunt. My grandfather helped draw all the figures you see every day but do not comprehend. I doubt that any of you know what those drawings mean. To you they are only marks on the wall, or pictures of bears and deer like those in all the other drawings on the wall, such as the one you boastful young men drew this evening. I know better. I can tell you what every detail in those drawings means. Gather round the pictures and listen to me as I interpret them for you, for I am going to tell you about the greatest hunt that ever happened and about the numerous ways that great hunt changed our lives, even all the way down to the present.

The people gathered around and were quiet, even the children. Short Legs was in his element. He told an elaborate story, with frequent references to subtle details in the drawings on the wall. They came alive for the audience, made sense, documented an epic story. Maybe Short Legs was not a careful historian. Maybe he added details never told him by his grandfather, or inferred much more than the drawings justified. But he claimed, and his audience believed, that the events he described had actually happened, and thus they gained all the import and significance he ascribed to them. He assumed the obligations of a historian, not just those of a storyteller. He had been telling stories for years, but he made them up. Most were fantastic. He had great skills in the telling. Other members of the tribes had recounted past exploits, drawn from personal memory. What was new in this case was his attempt to recover a past lost to immediate memory, a past evidenced by oral accounts and a complex drawing, and a past he now so interpreted as to display coherence and significance. Short Legs claimed to tell the full story of the great hunt. He deceived himself. He had to select and arrange the details of his story and, as a gifted storyteller, probably did this very well. He promised to extract the long-term significance of the great hunt, and this again had to involve a selective interest in only certain aspects of the subsequent history of the clan, whereas these subsequent events, in turn, helped determine what Short Legs included in his story. But such selectivity is a necessary aspect of any history, and Short Legs was naive only in not recognizing this.

Short Legs invented history. This turned out to be a momentous achievement for him. People who had laughed at his earlier stories now took him seriously. His purportedly true stories seemed terribly important. They helped give to his clan a great sense of confidence and pride. They now knew themselves to be heirs of those who conducted the greatest hunt of all time. Some of the young men now boasted of this and grew arrogant. Everyone wanted more such true stories. And in his own way Short Legs obliged. He had found his role in the clan as a much revered man of wisdom, one who alone could penetrate the lost secrets of the past. But Short Legs soon ran out of such stories. He found no other drawings with such potent meaning, could not find in his memories other such accounts from a grandparent. Such limits did not deter him, and thus he told more and more stories, claiming each to be true. He kept returning to the great hunt but, with each retelling, ventured new interpretations, each more imaginative than the last but at the same time more far-fetched. Soon he failed to persuade, and in his last years people began to refer to him as Tall Tales, in part out of respect for his ability as a storyteller, in part out of their contempt for his unjustified truth claims.

Short Legs invented history. He did not invent historiography. This innovation sprang from the skepticism of a young girl, Sweet Doe. She was not given to fantasy and simply found the tall tales of Tall Tales unbelievable. One evening, as everyone listened to Tall Tales pontificate about all the events leading up to the great hunt (he was still the best entertainment in the cave), Sweet Doe interrupted. In effect, she said the following:

> I don't believe it. It ain't true. It could not be true. No one today can do some of the things you attribute to the great hunters. If no one can do such wondrous things today, then how is it that they could do them in the past? It makes no sense to me. And why should I believe you? Who else has such memories? I hear no such stories even from the elders who are as old as you. Why not? Why did they not hear the stories you tell? And what about the drawings? For your recent stories, you rarely refer to records on the wall. And even when you do, you interpret them in such fantastic ways as to leave me confused and unpersuaded. I think you have made up most of your stories. Unless you can find other old men who can vouch for your stories, and unless you can point to wall drawings that clearly and directly support your stories, I think you should shut up, or at least admit that your stories are untrue, entertaining as they may be. I have had my fill of Tall Tales.

With Sweet Doe the critical philosophy of history was born. We owe a debt of gratitude to Sweet Doe. Unfortunately, her clan never appreciated her skepticism. Of course, they knew that Tall Tales exaggerated or made up much of his history. But they treasured the identity that he had helped them fashion for themselves. They wanted to keep alive the story of the greatest hunt of all time, for it gave a special dignity and importance to their lives. In a sense, they were willingly living a lie, assuming an importance not justified by actual events. No matter. Sweet Doe, in her innocent doubts, began to puncture this self-image. The clan soon fell into bitter debates about the past, or what we might call interpretations. At the center of it was the "Tall Tales thesis." Able young men soon had competing theories about the past, and the intellectual game went on without resolution, to the despair of the ordinary people, who were simply confused. Poor Sweet Doe. The clan leaders blamed the conflict on her and seriously considered banishing her from the cave. As you would expect, they had long since changed her name to Sour Doe.

Local History: A Mirror for American Values

My sermon text comes from Ortega:

> Man is not a thing . . . ; man, in a word, has no nature; what he has is . . . history. . . . Man is not his body, which is a thing, nor his soul, psyche, conscience, or spirit, which is also a thing. . . . It is false to talk of a human nature. . . . Man is no thing, but a drama—his life, a pure and universal happening which happens to each one of us and in which each one in his turn is nothing but a happening.
>
> Man is what has happened to him, what he has done. Other things might have happened to him, or have been done by him, but what did in fact happen to him and was done by him, this constitutes a relentless trajectory of experiences that he carries on his back as the vagabond his bundle of all he possesses. (Scattered excerpts from *History As a System*)

Our identity, as individuals or as communities, is ever fragile, open, in flux. Its only firm component is the cultural residue of our past, which lives on in us but which we may or may not recognize. Either way, this past conditions our development, our endless creation and recreation of ourselves. When our past is unknown, its influence is dictatorial, inescapable. When known, our multifaceted past confronts us as a suitor, often beguiling in its solicitations, all but magical in its revelations, yet open to critical evaluation. When we have correctly discerned our past, when we know ourselves, we feel most free, even though we can no more change that past than we can alter the laws of physics. The existing script allows judgment but not editing. The early chapters must remain just as they are. But, fortunately, the drama remains incomplete. We are composing additional chapters. And the better we understand the earlier chapters, the more we justifiably feel that we are the self-conscious arbiters of what we now write.

Man is not a thing. He has a symbolic language. He talks to others and endlessly to himself. We call this thinking. He lives in a world of meaning,

7

which conditions practically all that he does. Unlike things, which often occur in clusters, or other animals, which often live in ordered societies, man alone lives in communities. That is, he lives in groups united by shared meanings and shared purposes. These meanings develop and endure through time. They make up a cumulative heritage. Because of language, humans endlessly but never conclusively define themselves in a context both of memory and of hope. Things also have histories. They endure through time. But they do not gain their identity from their past. Thus, only humans *are* their history. Their identity is always their peculiar heritage of memory and hope, of beliefs and preferences.

Because of language, humans *do* live in a world of things, and they are enormously blessed by this privilege. In a sense humans even fashion the objects of their world, although they do not create the experience from which they successfully abstract such objects. Out of the welter of experience, out of the vast, vague, nonspecific out there that they literally bump into, humans select various repetitious qualities and give a name to them. From vast globs of greenness they select some features and call them a "tree." These features are the essence or nature of any tree. Such objects are eternally just what they are. A tree is a tree is a tree. Therefore, trees are peculiarly manageable, predictable, as are all things. Because we have abstracted objects out of the richer continuities of experience, we have been able to establish many invariant relationships. We call the most systematic of these relationships sciences, and they are very useful. Only acculturated, language-using, concept-inventing subjects can create such sciences and order so many things. But obviously, logically, the human subject, the one who continually works out new concepts and thus identifies new things, cannot be a mere thing. A creator cannot be a creature.

This leads to an obvious lesson. Strangely, it is one that Western intellectuals no sooner learn than they forget and thus have to learn all over again. The lesson: There can be no science of humanity. Remember, humans have no defining nature, but only a history. For each person, that defining history is slightly different from all others. At any refined level of subtlety and detail, any history is quite local. Of course, any history of a rock is slightly different from that of any other rock. But the history of a rock does not define a rock, does not give it its identity. As if we were external gods, we have bestowed that identity. But as vulnerable subjects, we have to work endlessly at our own identity. The task is never done.

I do not mean by all this that nothing unites or relates humanity as a whole. Literally, almost all things relate to humans as a whole. Every thing—that is, every object with a set, defining essence or nature—is open to every person, although selective choice leads some people to objectify aspects of experience ignored by other people. A tree is a tree however many cultural barriers we cross, and however many varying linguistic codes communicate the image we intend by our English word "tree." Likewise, a human may be a part of many of his own objectifications— such as an ever more carefully elaborated world of matter, or an ever more precisely classified organic world. Thus, people everywhere have a common physiology. They also join other mammals in certain patterns of learning, tied to a common neurological base. This alone assures that people everywhere share similar constraints and similar animal needs. They share the frustrations of not being able to fly, short of technological props. If they are to continue to live, they all must eat. If their species is to survive, many of them must procreate.

Note the hypothetical, the "if." Already we confront meaning or culture. Some people, in the context of a cultural heritage, in their continuous creation of meaning and identity, choose celibacy and elevate it to a noble ideal. And a few people have willingly chosen death; they have sacrificed their life in behalf of an ideal. Culture can always override biological imperatives. People have few if any governing instincts. Their adult behavior is all learned. Much of the behavior of other animals is also learned. But only human learning involves shared meanings, cultural continuities, and self-conscious purposes. Without an instinctive base, without the sure guidance even of biological need, human behavior is open-ended, but open only within the limits of the possible. In both the physical and social sciences we chart those limits, the many boundaries set by things. But in so doing we never find any laws, any invariant regularities, that fully determine the path of cultural development in an individual or a community. It is quite possible that all the people on earth share a few common beliefs and preferences and thus exhibit the same culturally conditioned behavior. Their common biological equipment, plus the often similar circumstances that condition their behavior, suggest at least the possibility of such commonality. But no human nature necessitates it, and nothing necessitates that the common beliefs of today will remain common tomorrow. Indeed, most of us must eat. But we do it very differently, and even our eating can have enormous and variable cultural content, as in the rich, symbolic meaning of the Christian Eucharist.

These quite general comments may seem only a diversion from my topic. They are not. To confront the challenges, the possibilities, and the uses of local history, one must appreciate the unique subject matter and the unique uses of any human history. I have so carefully denied any distinctively human nature, and any science of humankind, in order to avoid a completely mistaken understanding of history, an understanding possibly suggested by one interpretation of my assigned topic. Recently it has been fashionable to view even local history as a means of testing purportedly general propositions about humans or their behavior. If a person were a thing, with the predictive behavior this allows, then local history could serve as a laboratory-like test for our social sciences. Armed with a hypothesis about normal and predictive political or economic behavior, one should be able to confirm it by numerous local cases or falsify it by a few local exceptions. (For example, many people in Boone clearly do not try to maximize their income, and thus we cannot assume income maximization as natural to humans). Indeed, I am persuaded that rigorous local histories will sooner or later falsify any and all pat theories about human nature, and thus any purported necessities in the area of culturally conditioned action (I obviously do not deny physiological regularities that are indeed open for generalization). If you are particularly offended by any presently fashionable theory about human nature, you might well launch a local inquiry for the expressed purpose of helping prove it false. But such a historical purpose—to falsify some general theory—rarely leads to any rigorous or carefully nuanced history. I cannot think of a weaker excuse for doing local history.

Then, you might ask, of what possible use is historical knowledge? Because historians do not explain, in the sense of laws and prediction, the behavior of things, their work might seem supremely useless. And, indeed, historical understanding leads to no new technology. It does not tell us how to do anything. It helps cure no diseases, bridge no rivers, produce no food, except as a history of past human effort may contain, quite incidentally to the purpose of the story, some information about medicine, engineering, or agriculture. Only the generalizing sciences concern things and thus tell us how to manage things. These sciences are doubly moral. They arm our purposes with power, even as they discipline our hopes by clarifying the possible. Historical knowledge clarifies not techniques or practical possibilities, but only who we are. History is the one empirical discipline that relates most closely to problems of identity and not to those of instrumental mastery—to ends and not to means.

Identity, I insist, is a vitally important issue. We literally look for ourselves in our past, or, by contrast, in the traditions of very different people. With such understanding we become more self-conscious and responsible actors on the human stage. In our present, unthoughted habits, we act out the conscious choices of our progenitors. So long as we remain in historical ignorance, we do this blindly. When influenced by mistaken caricatures of the past, by bad history, we indulge self-deceit and think we are who we are not, or we cast impious and unfair imprecations against our misunderstood parents. But with historical understanding we know the ends and purposes implicit in our daily acts. We therefore bring more and more of our conduct within the sphere of critical judgment. Historical understanding is thus a tool of moral discourse. Above all else, that is what it is for. By historical knowledge we may gain an added appreciation for our heritage, come to treasure our roots, and thereby deepen our commitments to existing beliefs and values. Historical knowledge is then very consoling. At times such a deepening or revival of our commitments is necessary even for sanity itself. But to know is to risk critical evaluation and repudiation. As we come to understand ourselves, as we compare our habits to what we now experience as good, we may not like much that we find. So be it. Our agonizing penance, which usually involves our parents' as well as our own transgressions, cannot help them, cannot erase the past, but it may be redemptive for us.

All human history is communal history, tied to the particularities of time, place, and culture. But some communities include millions of people—for example, all of us in the eroding but still recognizable Judeo-Christian West probably still share some common beliefs and pursue some common goals. That is a big community, yet spatially and temporally specific, local, parochial. At the other extreme is the individual. The most local history will always be biography. Most of us struggle with communities that stand somewhere between civilizations and individuals. I want to look at the problems of historians who move back and forth between two intermediate communities—that of a nation and that of a neighborhood. By the elusive and less than exact word "neighborhood," I refer to a reasonably distinct arena of primary, one-to-one human relationships, or, next to the family, the one most homogenous form of community, the one in which people share the largest number of meanings, beliefs, and values. In America we cannot apply this definition very easily. Our landscape now includes a mosaic of overlapping neighborhoods. Fellow church members often send their children to different schools, vote in different precincts, loaf at different stores, work in different factories, mingle their remains in different cemeteries. It was not so in my youth. I grew up over in the next big hollow, in a community reasonably well defined by a Cumberland Presbyterian church, a nominally public but operationally parochial two-room school, and a single country store. Such distinct neighborhoods are now rare, and so-called local historians usually devote their attention to larger and less homogenous groups—as in a town or a county. But I can better clarify some crucial issues by keeping our focus upon such an ideal neighborhood.

In a trivial or truistic sense any neighborhood in the United States almost has to mirror some widely shared American values and thus, loosely, exemplify aspects of an American culture. All conceivable local beliefs or preferences, by occurring within America, help constitute the totality of American values, or at least the values affirmed by Americans. But such a compounding of all individual values confronts us with an unmanageable and nondiscriminating complexity. At another equally unpromising extreme, by "American values" we might mean only those literally shared by everyone in America. Any expected belief not present in a local neighborhood would reduce by that much the content of the label "American." Soon we would have no American values at all. The quest for such completely common values suggests a junior version of the social science game, with the neighborhood once again as a test case. I doubt that literally all Americans share even one carefully defined belief, or exemplify any one clear preference. Futility has so far marked our efforts to find some fully encompassing American culture or one clearly defined American character. I can think of no more puerile task than contriving one local inquiry after another to shoot down one or another purported American value. Here I am again objecting to strained and dubious claims of cultural generality, to assertions that all Americans do anything, at least anything not specific to their physique, such as sneezing and belching.

I find it more useful, although still perilous, to use the label "American" for *typical* American beliefs and values. Actually, historians usually deal not with generalizations but with types. Some types are representative (John's beliefs are typical because he believes what 95 percent of Americans believe); some express a median position (Joan's beliefs are typical because they stand midway between two extremes); some are ideal (such as the perfect Calvinist). In either case we have to confront, as honestly as we can, the exact claims we make in our appeal to the typical. Loose quantifiers are the bane of precise cultural analysis (the use of words such as "few," "some," "most," "many"). Generally, the representative type is a historian's substitute for true generality. Such types are highly predictive of individual belief or behavior and often justify our ignoring a dissenting few when we are dealing with large aggregates. But because the dissenting few may dominate our local neighborhood, we can never predicate a large whole on the basis of any local inquiry. Median or average types are treacherous, hard to vindicate empirically, and in no case predictive for any given individual or group of individuals.

The ideal type entails no empirical claim and offers no predictive assurance. It is a reference point, a valuable conceptual tool in one's search for clarity. But such ideal types usually help us only when they relate clearly to the actual beliefs and preferences of real people. If many Americans had not professed Calvinist beliefs, the ideal type would scarcely fit the needs of a historian. The neighborhood, as I earlier defined it, is an ideal type, because it is possible that no such neighborhoods now exist. Such a type is as useful in local history as in other fields of inquiry, but one must not confuse it with actualities. Your village may have plenty of professed Presbyterians but no ideal typical Calvinists.

Even this analysis of types opens up some fruitful perspectives on local history. A local historian may do little more than describe what has happened in her neighborhood, with an eye for a few continuities or genetic links. I hope even then that she tells the truth—that she is precise in her use of language, meticulous in her logical inferences, and rigorous in her use of evidence. If so, she may bring a valued form of self-understanding to her local audience, may deepen local pride or suggest areas for critical evaluation, but she will necessarily leave the home folks as parochial as before. But such honest and detailed local histories, because they do include even without identification much that is unique and particular, can provide outside readers with an array of suggestive comparisons and contrasts, making more subtle their consciousness of self and more sensitive their awareness of others. What such parochial history precludes is comparative judgment. Is this or that belief distinctive to the good citizens of Dogpatch, or fully shared by their neighbors in nearby villages, or by most Americans, or even by most Christians? At one moment a person may express a purely local peculiarity and thereby testify to his membership in a restricted and uniform neighborhood, and at the next moment spout some of the most conventional wisdom of the whole West. Our audience rightfully expects us, as historians, to distinguish the unique from the conventional. And that is not easy. In fact, I suspect this is the most difficult challenge facing local historians.

Usually (I started to say typically), local people make horrendously mistaken judgments about the extent of a community of meaning. They may claim the authority of all humankind for a very parochial religious conviction, even as they confidently and quite mistakenly insist that only people in their own valley correctly follow the phases of the moon in planting certain vegetables. The historian thus must know a great deal more than his subjects know, or he becomes captive to them. For example, in an excellent anthology of oral sources, *Our Appalachia*, the editors completely fail this test—they take the judgment of their interviewees and accept some quite local peculiarities as characteristic of central Appalachia as a whole.

For most local historians the nation is the most convenient comparative reference. I recommend it. Comparison among many small neighborhoods risks an enormous amount of unproductive effort. Few of us have the breadth and versatility to set our neighborhood in the context of all Western civilization, although at times, as in religion, we may identify some more encompassing commonalities. Thus, the United States as a whole is a good focus of comparison and one most easily open to us because national history has attracted so much historical effort. And, clearly, the representative type is the most likely focus of our comparison. If we can become conversant with the wider, more broadly shared aspects of the American experience, we then can use local history to exemplify, in a specific and concrete way, some of these almost common values. Conversely, an awareness of what is most conventional in the beliefs and values of a neighborhood helps clarify what is most exceptional.

The next level of refinement requires us to sort out what is regional and not just local. This is a problem that especially plagues efforts to understand southern Appalachia (what cultural content is distinctively Appalachian, what merely southern). But the hazards in either a national or a regional comparison are obvious. How can we know what beliefs are really consensual among 90 percent of Americans? How can we be sure that the various values reflected locally really mirror American values? Maybe we come to our local history with completely distorted images of what is American. Maybe the secondary sources we use for national history are all wrong, too rarely informed by detailed local histories. Maybe our working images of what are typical American values are either too loose and vague to have any content, or really express only certain verbally celebrated values that do not come close to guiding the actual conduct of Americans.

This leads me to a final, elusive, but possibly most promising interpretation of my topic—local history as a mirror of national values. Again, by a value I mean a personal preference, what object or conduct a person believes to be either good or desirable, what he approves, or what he wants or craves. Just as most behavior is habitual, so most of our preferences are so well established that we do not have an occasion to dwell on them, think about them, or evaluate them. They lie revealed in our choices and in what we do; we are most likely to recognize and defend them only when they face frustration or challenge. Let us call these living preferences our operative values. They usually overlap, but do not exactly duplicate, what I will call official values. I know the label is slippery. What I mean by it are evaluations, of objects and of behavior, that receive at least verbal endorsement by community leaders, by major opinion makers, or by those who claim or exert moral leadership, such as clergymen, teachers, and judges. One context for such official values is a church. A good Baptist knows that, as a Christian, he is supposed to love his god more than anything else. In an opinion survey he might even verbalize such a preference. At least in the context of worship, many people give verbal assent to such an overarching, if often vague, value. But are such normative values operative? Do they actually guide conduct? Surely not always. Many Baptists act as if they love spouses, or children, or even things more than their god. I hope this makes reasonably clear what I mean by official values: those that set the most publicized norms for a community.

We seem to have an array of such official values at the national level. As in ancient Israel, these values are at the heart of our sense of national identity, of our participation in not just American society, but an American community. Some even conceive of these official values as tenets of a civic religion, with its scripture in such foundational documents as the Declaration of Independence and the Constitution, its symbol in the flag, and its liturgy revealed by such civic holidays as the Fourth of July. Unfortunately, it is not easy to discover the exact content of these official national values, for the words that express them are always ambiguous. It is equally difficult to determine who honestly accepts these values, or who gives to them their authoritative status. Often they seem simply to float about our society like ghostly apparitions. At the level of verbal statement, it is easy to list some of those values: equal protection of law, due process in all criminal procedures, equal economic and educational opportunity, no governmental favoritism to any religion, the right to free speech, press, and assembly, government by law and not by personal influence, majority rule. Not only are these stated values not very clear, but by many understandings they often directly clash with each other. The rule of law, of established procedures or limits, often conflicts with the will of majorities.

To make the already elusive even more elusive, the effective meaning of many of these hallowed prescriptions is always in flux. Today they often identify very different values from those of the late eighteenth century, when at least the wording gave a highly moral tone to our war for independence and to our early governments. Americans, of course, are not distinctive in attributing a moral content to their nationhood. People in other countries endorse very different national ideals. They, as we, seek the same sense of moral rectitude in our country as in ourselves. And for a reason. We have to live with our nation's policies and suffer endless agony when these are morally repugnant to us.

In a sense the very elusiveness of such official values helps make them the most significant comparative perspective available to local historians. Such a comparison can respond to a range of very important questions, questions whose answers reveal a great deal not only about the local community but also about America as a whole. Did the past residents of a local neighborhood give verbal consent to these official values? Which ones? Was there local dissent? How did local people understand these values? How did such understanding change through time? Did such change precede, or lag behind, comparable shifts in meaning among national opinion makers? And, most important of all, did people locally go beyond verbal assent, beyond the conventional and expected cheerleading, and internalize such values? Did they make them operative, actually live by them? For example, I doubt that many people in homogenous neighborhoods, in the past or even close to the present, ever understood the implications of religious neutrality on the part of government, let alone demanded it of their local government. Reaction to the prayer decision, or continued and endless controversies over Christmas programs in schools, suggest how widespread is the resistance to such neutrality even by people who continue to affirm the separation of church and state. We already have abundant proof of how seldom any level of government has really offered equal protection of the laws to all people, and we suspect that very few local people have really wanted their police or courts to treat everyone equally. Community histories, for parts of Appalachia as much as for ethnic enclaves in large cities, over and over suggest that local politicians gain office and power by practical, legal, or extralegal services rendered, by jobs given, relatives aided, laws bent, and not by any adherence to principle or even to party platforms.

These examples support a suspicion of mine—that a significant tension exists between official national values and one crucial, if usually unvoiced but overarching, value that still seems to have strong local support. This is a preference for neighborhood homogeneity, for the opportunity to limit primary contact to people of similar beliefs and values. Some call this a sectarian impulse. It supports local exclusiveness, a comprehensive and often legalistic standard of acceptable behavior, large penalties on dissent or defiance, and at least a very insensitive response to outsiders. I do not want such characteristics to seem pejorative; if you so interpret them, you perhaps thereby reveal how fully you have internalized some presently official American values.

I want to come back again to the problem of identity. To function effectively, even to avoid insanity, we have to be someone, have some firm beliefs and commitments, come to terms with the continuities of our own past. These define us and set us apart from other people who do not share them. Given a sense of identity, and a developed ego, one has to judge others; whether one voices one's opinion or not, one either approves or condemns what other people do. In the same sense, a community is constituted by the shared beliefs and preferences of a group of people, by what they affirm and what they condemn. One who rejects some of those beliefs and preferences thereby separates oneself from such a community. The United States may approximate a community. That is, almost all Americans may share a few beliefs and preferences, and these commonalities justify the concept of a national community. But it is not a tight community, for the sharing touches only a few areas of political belief and commitment. Local communities are different. They are more total and thus more totalitarian. Again, I do not use the word in a pejorative sense, but descriptively. There the sharing may encompass all one's most basic beliefs and all one's important values. When it does so, it can be as comforting and supportive as a family, but also as repressive and exclusive. The narrow range of comprehensible, as well as permitted, dissent makes such a community frightening to outsiders. Yet for such a community to embrace complete tolerance, to accept any and all differences, literally to treat everyone equally, would be for it to commit suicide.

In this perspective most official national values at times threaten local communities. For such national values, even though not truly universal, are quite encompassing, now fitted to a very pluralistic society. They prescribe the same treatment for people of different beliefs, values, modes of life. They proscribe types of favoritism, preclude forms of discrimination. Yet favoritism and discrimination are prerequisites of a total community, as essential to Dogpatch as to a Chinese commune. In our early history both national commitments and federal law stopped short of most local differences. Only the federal government had to be neutral toward various religions; several states not only favored Christians but in New England gave taxes to one Christian sect. At the local level governments variously and unselfconsciously upheld all manner of local biases, and in laws and courts endlessly favored their own folk. Thus, at the national level we early embraced a degree of pluralistic equality, but often in order that local communities could remain exclusive. Since the Civil War we have altered course. In its aftermath we invented national citizenship and slowly extended federal protection to various local minorities, blacks being only the most conspicuous. Through laws, and in the courts, we have broken or weakened most legal forms of local favoritism and discrimination. Through effective education, dispensed by various communication media, opinion makers have also persuaded more and more local people to affirm the universalist themes of our civic morality. This has aided local minorities, but sometimes also eroded the formal and legal bases for secure neighborhood identity, for the very particularities—call them biases or prejudices if you wish—that in the past helped sustain tightly knit communities.

The tensions remain. I wonder how fully people of local communities even yet reflect official national values, not just verbally but in their behavior. Surely those of you involved in local history are the ones to search out those answers, for even when posed in a present context they beg an understanding of historical continuities. I recommend to you this very difficult task. To do it well, you must develop a sympathetic understanding of your subjects. You must catch the meaning, the coherence, the integrity, even the beauty of local systems of belief and value, and only then try to compare them to national values. Professional historians such as myself often lack a needed openness to local realities. We are mobile people, long since pulled away from any local neighborhood, even if we once lived in such a parochial context. Ironically, the strongest communal identity we feel beyond the family and perhaps our profession is the national one; the common beliefs and preferences that must bind us to other people are the near universal themes present in our official American values. Otherwise, we are all alone, a community of one. If we have contact with more local and total communities, it is usually as an outsider, as alien intruders, often more sensitive to local bias and repression than to the exact truth.

I have largely worked with national themes, or with people who identify principally with a national community. Thus, I am increasingly aware of how easily such people assume that official national values are all pervasive, and how horrified they can be when they find this is not so. National historians err when they move from some fashionable perspective on national values to easy assumptions about the parts, just as much as local historians err when they extrapolate from local actualities to generalizations about America as a whole.

Historians face a catch-22 situation. They must know larger wholes fully to understand the part. They must know the parts to understand the whole. Some refer to this as the hermeneutic circle. The escape takes not only time and effort, but an interactive dialogue between very local history and broad synthesis. Each has to mature together. Each has to check and enrich the other. If humans were things, if we could pin them down by their fixed nature, if we could grasp the laws that control them, our task would indeed be easy, and we might best approach human understanding from a purely local perspective. But as it is, we have to keep moving back and forth between large communities and small ones, continue seeking the complex relationships between them, and accept the hard fact that these relationships are not static but ever changing. Our task can never be completed. It could be only if humans were things. But who would have us give up our humanity, who would have us be mere things, just so we could get our scholarly work done, just so we could write the final chapter of human history?

2

Creating New Communities

In a sense my first scholarship involved the difficult task of creating new and more perfect communities. I never made a choice to work in this area but stumbled upon it. I decided to do my dissertation on the New Deal community program, and on the agencies that developed subsistence homesteads, resettlement communities, and greenbelt cities. A large fund of idealism, and often unrealistic hopes, lay behind about one hundred reasonably coherent colonies or communities. I told this story in *Tomorrow a New World: The New Deal Community Program* (Ithaca: Cornell University Press, 1959).

While teaching at Southwestern Louisiana in my first position as a historian, I became interested in a socialist colony near Leesville, or the Llano Colony, which had moved from California to the pine woods of Louisiana in 1918 and struggled on into the mid-thirties. Many of the colonial buildings were still present, and I was able to interview the long-term director of the colony just before he died. Soon I decided to pair Llano, as a socialist colony, with some religiously motivated communal colonies, and in searching for an appropriate comparison became familiar with the Hutterites, by far the largest and most successful communal group in American history. From this interest came my second book, *Two Paths to Utopia: The Hutterites and the Llano Colony* (Lincoln: University of Nebraska Press, 1964). Because of these first two books, an increasing number of historians fascinated with intentional communities, or utopian experiments, expected me to maintain my interests in that field. Even yet I meet historians who know only these two books. For reasons I try to explain in the first of the following two essays, I moved away from this field, never to

19

return. Yet on two occasions I accepted an invitation to speak about my first scholarship. Each case involved a nostalgic return to topics that already seemed remote.

The first lecture is the oldest speech included in this book. I was invited back to the University of Southwestern Louisiana in 1974 to present a paper to a symposium on "France and North America Utopias and Utopians." The first essay in this section is a copy of that lecture, as subsequently published in the proceedings of the conference. I do not have my original paper, but I know that it very closely matched this published version. Twenty years later, in 1994, I was privileged to attend, and to present a lecture at, a conference with the rather awkward title of "A New Deal for America: A National Conference on 1930s, Arthurdale, and New Deal Homesteads." This was, for me, a type of homecoming, for I began work on Arthurdale, the first of the New Deal communities, in 1955. I think my essay well expresses my pleasure at being able to look back, from a distance of thirty years, to my first book, which I had not read for two decades.

The Cooperative Commonwealth in America

Briefly, elusively, I want to tell the story of the cooperative commonwealth in America, from its literary birth in 1884 until its final communal expression in the pine woods of Louisiana in the depression thirties. In its theoretical expression the cooperative commonwealth challenged reigning American ideals, ideals I want first to describe as a backdrop to my main story.

These ideals accompanied America's national beginnings. In brief, colonial visionaries and revolutionary idealists aspired to nothing less than a new political order that would encourage men to be free and protect them in that freedom. Subsequent priorities—on voting, on such expressive freedoms as speech, press, and assembly—have almost completely obscured what these visionaries meant by freedom. In the view of a Jefferson or a John Adams, Americans had escaped the major impediments to freedom—priests and mandatory tithes, feudal lords and quitrents, corrupt placemen and all manner of political privileges, mercantilistic regulations and restricted entrepreneurial freedom, and above all workshops and factories and thus a dependence on others for wages and livelihood. To them freedom meant economic autonomy, a lack of servility of any sort. This required easy access to land and other means of production, and exemption from feudal obligations or arbitrary taxes. Property was the single most important clue to freedom—real property, not such pseudo-forms as money, speculative investments in stocks and bonds, or mere consumer goods. Property entailed, above all else, the right to use a part of nature, a nature that God gave to humans in common and that no one had a right to monopolize. This right of access and acquisition, listed in early bills of rights, was logically prior to rights to retain possessions. Note the import of this conception of freedom—that each man would aspire to, and have the widest possible opportunity to become, an artisan or entrepreneur, dependent on no one for a living, and as free as any artist in the management of his productive property and the disposition of his labor. In such individual freedom he could do his own thing, find his own unique fulfillment.

This individual entrepreneurial dream remained far from fulfilled. Slavery and tenancy blighted it in agriculture. Even when individuals attained real property and managerial freedom, they often betrayed the moral vision by a single-minded and vulgar grab for capital gains, for wealth and power, conveniently ignoring the expected artistry, the intrinsic goals, the communal responsibility and good citizenship that were supposed to spring from economic autonomy. But the most pervasive concerns of the nineteenth century related not to a vulgarization of the entrepreneurial ideal, not to some of the moral problems inherent in individual enterprise and open competition, but to the manifold threats to the ideal, to such a foreshortening of opportunities that many Americans would have to give up individual ownership and become wage earners and thus mere employees. The devils were many, but the chief among them were special privileges for such un-American institutions as corporations and factories. The most typical reformers tried to prevent or discipline centralized, collective enterprise, with its restricted managerial elite and its mass of wage-dependent, nonpropertied workers. Our first labor unions reflected the desperation of free artisans losing control over tools, prices, and hours worked. Yet by the Civil War a majority of Americans probably worked for other men, although a minority in factories. In partial compensation for their economic serfdom, these employees received such substitutes as a broadened franchise, more expressive freedoms, free public schools, rising wages and more consumption, and in our day a wide spectrum of welfare benefits. Most of us are now part of a new feudalism, however well fed, however benevolent our corporate or governmental lords.

Henry George was the most radical and last great spokesman for the old ideal. He wanted to socialize rent in order to restore opportunity, to open up a foreclosed nature that had driven landless and vulnerable men into wage employment. Thus, he tried, in effect if not legally, to abolish private property in land in order to regain the values that once attached to property.

The three major advocates of a cooperative commonwealth went the opposite direction. They saw a collective future as inevitable and celebrated its possibilities if it took the form of a selfless and fulfilling community. Their vision touched only a few themes from the American past—the puritan idea of a commonwealth, the longing of detached and lonely American farmers for a closer society and more fellowship, the growing acceptance and assimilation of corporate production, and the sentimental appeal of brotherhood and altruism. But they also dared try to transform

American ideals: Instead of individual artistry, they celebrated solidarity; instead of autonomy, they stressed discipline and efficiency; instead of personal ambition, they desired communal pride; instead of localism, they applauded complete centralization; instead of a free market and open competition, they valued state ownership and planning; instead of government by political choice, they celebrated government by a competent elite.

Lawrence Gronlund first inspired Americans with the glorious prospects of a cooperative commonwealth, although he wrote as much of an economic treatise as a utopian scheme. Gronlund was born and educated in Denmark, coming to America in 1867 at the age of twenty-one. With a university education and training in law, he came to Milwaukee to gain experience in American law, then settled in Chicago, moving from law to journalism, lecturing, and socialist advocacy. He eventually moved to New York, participated in radical circles there, and there published his one masterpiece—*The Cooperative Commonwealth*—in 1884. Even then latent religious impulses mixed with a near orthodox Marxism. In a second edition in 1890, and in the wake of the popularity of *Looking Backward*, he veered toward Christian socialism and American Fabianism and even described the cooperative commonwealth as the kingdom of heaven on earth. In later years he also welcomed the ameliorative reforms he condemned in 1884. In his final book, *The New Economy*, published in 1898 (a year before his death), he advocated a generalized, moralistic reform socialism, with little of the pungency, acute analysis, and angry passion of his masterpiece.

Gronlund's *Cooperative Commonwealth* was, and in my estimation remains, the most persuasive popular presentation of a generalized Marxist theory to an American audience. On essential points Gronlund adhered closely to Marx's historical and economic analysis but took away some of the apocalyptic urgency, some of the prophetic denunciation. He called his position not Marxism, but scientific or German or modern socialism, as digested by an Anglo-Saxon mind free of vindictive feelings against any person or class. In his opening chapters Gronlund offered, with almost academic rigor and quality, a critical analysis of the American economy, but in the later chapters he sketched the probable details of the wonderful new socialist society. He insisted that this preview was not utopian, that the details of a cooperative commonwealth had to grow out of realities, that it could not be imposed by dreamers or by social architects. His account was only a plausible prediction, or what he expected to take place.

In 1887 Edward Bellamy published *Looking Backward*, the most read and most influential utopian novel ever published by an American. It seemed a sequel to Gronlund, but we have no firm evidence that Gronlund exerted direct influence on Bellamy. Born in 1850 in a small Massachusetts town, Bellamy was the son of a Baptist clergyman and came of old puritan stock. He studied law, only to reject it with the same vehemence as had Gronlund. He also entered journalism, although of a more conventional variety than Gronlund, working with established newspapers in New York City and in Springfield, Massachusetts. He had some modest literary success before *Looking Backward* and continued to publish successful articles and books afterward, including a more detailed economic treatise entitled *Equality*. Because of tuberculosis he moved west in a vain attempt to regain his health and died there in 1898, a year before Gronlund.

Most people have read *Looking Backward*. It is a political novel with a precious, oversentimentalized love story, some clever uses of biblical images, and enough diverting romantic details to soften the economic description. I give you a brief plot line: Julian West, a nervous, affluent, insomnious young Bostonian of 1887, seals himself in a vented, underground bedroom, after calling upon the services of a neighborhood hypnotist—his version of a sleeping pill. As we later learn, the hypnotist leaves for another city, the house burns during the night, and all his friends conclude that West perished in the fire. Not so. He remains in a deep trance, without aging, until dug up in 2000 and revived by later inhabitants of Boston. West awakens in a glorious new America and spends the book recounting all its wonders. Whereas Gronlund helped prepare the way for a cooperative commonwealth, Bellamy had the unique opportunity to explore it, using this future to draw a sharp, almost overwhelming contrast with the dismal America of 1887. At the end, in a rather contrived literary trick, West seems to reawaken in the old Boston and explores it with all the insight of what now seems a utopian dream. It is hell, and after vain attempts to communicate his new insights, West breaks down in tormented, inarticulate cries of despair. But this is only a prelude to awakening back in 2000. Hell was a dream, heaven the reality. At the end he plans to marry an unbelievably perfect Edith, a descendant of the Edith to whom he had been betrothed in 1887.

William Dean Howells seems a strange member of our trilogy. By 1894 he was the dean of American letters and our foremost literary critic. From a modest Ohio family, Howells moved to Boston, married well, edited the prestigious *Atlantic Monthly*, taught at Harvard, and moved among the highest social classes. Yet in 1888 he moved to a new editorial job in New York City and there further developed his reform sentiments. Thus, in 1894 he wrote the first of two utopian novels—*A Traveler from Altruria*. He used the novel to express some of the pervasive concerns of many fellow intellectuals—the fear of class conflict, a mixed fear and envy of the masses, a fascination with Fabian socialism, and deep anxieties about the new industrial system. From a literary standpoint I find *Traveler* a failure, not at all comparable to *The Rise of Silas Lapham*, for example. Howells was not a good utopian; he was too ironic, too lofty and detached, too willing to suspend judgment, too self-conscious, too inclined to dwell on nuances of character.

The plot of *Traveler* is thin: A Mr. Homos (Howells plays with names throughout) travels to America from a distant country, Altruria, a recently discovered island lying somewhere off the coast of Antarctica. He comes to visit a country purportedly like his own, for he has read our Declaration of Independence. His host, and the narrator, is a Mr. Twelvemough, a heavily caricatured romantic novelist who becomes the butt of Howells's cleverness.

The host and guest meet at an unnamed New England watering place, where gather the affluent and successful businessmen and professionals from Boston and New York. They make up a world unto themselves, hardly speaking the same language as the rural youngsters waiting on the tables, or the surrounding impoverished farmers whom they refer to as natives and who have no social contact with the resented summer visitors. Howells, a student of manners and social forms, skillfully uncovers the contrasting values and perspectives of the top and the bottom. The Altrurian is a mild, open, generous, disarmingly honest man. He assumes that America is like Altruria, that we believe in and practice equality, and he acts on this assumption, to the unending embarrassment of his stuffy host. Mr. Homos helps the porter, greets the waiters as equals, even helps a shoeblack shine his host's shoes. Over two-thirds of the book records his incredulity as he finds out the horrible truth about America, usually as a result of the trusting but embarrassing questions he asks.

By this strategy Howells lays bare the irrationality and moral shortcomings he finds in his class and his America. It is an America of useless, upper-class women who flirt with illness brought on by enforced idleness; of a society in which affluent men, caught up in practical affairs, in earning money, are almost illiterate boors and vulgarians, while their women are refined and cultured, yet neurasthenic and allowed no role in politics; of a working class ignored by polite society, yet still heralded in the hypocritical folklore of politics; of respectable churches without a single working-class member; of work bereft of all joy; of sideshow arts as window dressings of an ugly society; of men who are completely dependent upon others for employment and even subsistence; of a country in which every man seems out for himself, and in which a gentleman such as Mr. Homos must suppress all his humane instincts in order to preserve propriety and the existing social order. Mr. Homos eventually meets the local farmers and, in a final speech, gives a sketch of life in beautiful Altruria. But the reader reacts to this speech with a sense that Howells has presented a parody of all past utopias, and that the Altrurian is our national conscience and not a real person—that Altruria is, literally, no place. Such a cerebral utopia, perhaps understandably, never had half the influence of Bellamy's more naive and more fervent account.

These three writers agreed on one thing: The existing American society was moving rapidly toward a great crisis made inevitable by its inherent contradictions. The only options involved the transition period and what happened beyond it. Each writer, in a near ambivalent perspective, condemned the selfish, competitive ethic still affirmed in America but agreed that the economy moved toward concentration and even complete monopoly.

The problem was not in the direction—they applauded collectivism—but in the private, selfish, exploitative nature of the existing system. Only Gronlund analyzed, in statistical detail, the nature of the American economy, its long-term trends, and the fate of the working classes in a system in which competitive wage rates allowed workers to collect less than half of the value their labor created. As Gronlund perceived our economy, the fleecing owners of capital competed against small producers in order to gain control of the market, but they favored collusion among themselves. To Gronlund the existing capitalist system was a necessary link with an inevitable socialist future, although he saw that the steps toward that future rested on human choice, as did earlier movements out of slavery and feudalism. He wrote his book to enlist a small cadre of people willing to assume leadership and who, with minimal suffering and cost, could guide American society through its final climactic crisis and into a new era of cooperation.

Neither Howells nor Bellamy attempted any systematic economic analysis of the old society. Mr. Homos referred to an Altrurian past remarkably similar to the America of 1894, or to an epoch remembered in his country as the Accumulation, which preceded the glorious Evolution (pleasant euphemisms for corporate capitalism and the revolution). Bellamy characteristically used a vivid simile to describe the old America of 1887. It was like a great coach, drawn by a harnessed working class. The road was rough, with hills and ruts. The privileged passengers never got down, although some fell off in the rough places and then had to help pull. The best seats, on top of the coach, were inherited in most cases. The competition was keen for any vacant upper seats, and thus all passengers were a bit nervous and insecure. They also pitied the poor wretches pulling the coach, the workers lashed by hunger and who therefore often fainted at their ropes and in hard places could go on only with agonized lurching and plunging. Then all the coach riders called out encouragement, begged patience, and talked of the rewards that awaited good workers in a life beyond the grave. Some even tossed down salves and liniments for the crippled and injured. Their pity was sincere, but mixed with fear. In a rough spot (and these came more often in the latter days) the coach might tip over. Already many were shaken off at the worst spots, leaving fewer and fewer at the top. But such fears only made the passengers cling all the more tightly to their seats. No one sensed a better way for a society to move along. It had always been so. It always would be so.

Neither Gronlund, Bellamy, nor Howells showed any sympathy for an older individualism or for the traditional American reverence for the free artisan. They accepted the corporate world abuilding and simply wanted to push its evolution to completion. The critical problem, as Gronlund realized, was how to move from a privately owned, highly centralized economy to a cooperative commonwealth, completely centralized but publicly owned. The men at the top had to be shoved off, for it was naive to expect them to surrender their position. Gronlund believed the ultimate crisis of American capitalism lay ten to fifty years in the future. By then wage workers in factories would be the norm, with all capital controlled by a few men, real wages declining, and business cycles more severe and more frequent. In the final great depression the laboring masses would rise and take control of all productive property, possibly after a massive general strike. Gronlund hoped the transition could be nonviolent; by the magnitude of change it would be revolutionary. Anything short of the overthrow of capitalism—such as voluntary cooperatives, trade union bargaining, welfare legislation, monetary tricks, or the single tax—could only impede or postpone the scientifically necessary revolution. But if the owners should submit to the loss of their ill-gotten gains, Gronlund was willing to consider a modified form of compensation. If they resisted, if they forced bloodshed on the country, they would lose all.

Had Gronlund enjoyed the retrospective vision of Bellamy and the Altrurian, he could only have rejoiced at how easily the transition actually occurred. In Altruria, when the Accumulation reached its ultimate limits, the working classes finally awakened to their plight. Because they enjoyed both the franchise and a numerical majority, almost as one they decided to vote out the old system and nationalize the economy. Their unions led them in the takeover. The capitalists vainly tried to regain power but did not have the votes. Soon, beguiled by the peaceful and fulfilling new order, they thanked God for the change and their own deliverance from the hectic, mad old order, for they had been desperately unhappy despite all their wealth and power. As Bellamy explained the post-1887 history of the United States, a few capitalists rather soon gained a complete monopoly over everything. When this happened, a people's syndicate formed a new political party, voted for public control over the monopoly, rededicating it to the good of all. As in Altruria, many American capitalists saw the necessary logic of events and joined in the peaceful transition.

Gronlund gave the most detailed analysis of the coming new economy but actually foresaw a less radical transformation than did Bellamy and Howells. Like them, he stressed duty and discipline. In a cooperative commonwealth, instead of working for a private monopoly, one would work as a public employee and thus for oneself. The new state-owned economy could eliminate competition, get rid of duplication and waste, and, above all, turn back to labor all that labor created. The reorganization would mean increased demand, which, joined with the efficiency (a great value for all three men) and new technology, would insure very high living standards and abundant leisure. Although Gronlund stressed the honor that would attach to work, and the opportunity for each person to develop his own skills, he joined Bellamy and Howells in an almost un-American emphasis upon leisure, as if each man still saw odious aspects to work even under ideal circumstances. Gronlund foresaw vast, state-owned industries or departments, and, at least for a time, a variable wage scale. Only after two generations, when everyone had his training from the state, did he contemplate equal wages for all.

Gronlund specifically repudiated communalism or forced equality. The citizens of his cooperative commonwealth would still own consumer property and retain the right to bequeath it to their children. Small farmers might even retain ownership of their farms during a transition period. But there would be no profits, no rents, and no interest. Thus, Gronlund was most daring in his plans for distribution. He wanted to replace money by labor credits, based on some average unit of labor. The state would assign production quotas to the productive departments, store goods in huge, regional depots, and sell to consumers at the natural price (based on the labor actually expended).

Bellamy expanded on the more radical aspects of Gronlund. By 2000 all Americans had to serve for twenty-four years in a vast, efficient industrial army, under military discipline. Obviously there was no longer a labor problem; everyone accepted such service as a patriotic duty. One entered the service at twenty-one, spent three years in unskilled, assigned labor (a type of basic training), and then chose a field of work based on aptitude and interest. Hours varied according to the perceived difficulty of the task, with zealous volunteers performing all hazardous tasks on behalf of national recognition. Retirement, at age forty-five, led to years of creative leisure. The industrial soldiers received no wages and needed none, for everyone in the society received an equal annual credit card, good for enough purchases to provide a near-luxurious lifestyle. The incentive for work included prizes, patriotism, a chance to move up in rank, and more attractive jobs for the best achievers. Professionals had their own guilds, with rigorous training and licensing requirements.

Like Gronlund, Bellamy described industrial sections and guilds, all grouped in ten large industrial departments. Each had annual production quotas and distributed its production to regional warehouses. From samples in regional commissaries or shopping malls, shoppers selected items, paid by credit card, and received delivery within an hour or so. Although in 2000 Americans lived in comfortable, detached houses, much of their life had a communal flavor. Central laundries and kitchens practically eliminated housework, while most families chose to take their meals in luxurious, artful dining halls.

Howells revealed few economic details. In Altruria an army of laborers worked short hours and enjoyed an equal distribution of goods. Altrurians had common dining facilities. All shared in the more onerous tasks, as in Communist China during the Great Leap Forward. All were artisans; all enjoyed much leisure and a relaxed atmosphere. No one hurried. Altruria had no foreign commerce, used no money, and allowed no foolish changes of fashion.

Only Gronlund and Bellamy had detailed political recommendations. Gronlund glorified society as an organism and used Hobbesian, Hegelian, Marxist, and Spencerian ideas in his eclectic political recommendations. The state would be supreme in the cooperative commonwealth, but "state" referred to more than government: It was the whole, united people, the commonwealth. The state owned all, created all rights, made all rules, sustained all civilization. Duty was the motif. All must work for state goals. Fickle individual aspiration counted for little. All men had worth as equal participants in the state, just as much as if they were necessary but subordinate parts of a body. Gronlund thus endorsed the virtue of solidarity and defined freedom as the freedom to do the right thing, to fulfill one's role in the social organism, to choose what was in the interest of all. He acclaimed a new democracy, meaning not voting rights (he carefully restricted those) but a classless society without a ruling class.

From this perspective Gronlund found little to applaud in traditional American institutions. He wanted to abolish the states, the federal constitution, the monarchlike presidency, the houses of Congress, all checks and balances, all political parties—in other words, government as most people understand it. He wanted to replace all this with a system of administration, with everyone administering something. But some would have to administer not just a task, but other men. He proposed a presbyterian or Soviet hierarchy, with tiered elections up to each higher level, but all power down from the top. Workers in each industrial department would elect their own chief. These first-order administrators would elect to higher councils, and so on. All administrators would serve on good behavior and could be removed only by superiors, not by electors. The people beneath did not properly meddle in the details of higher administration. A top-level directorate passed the few rules required by the society but submitted them to the people in a referendum—the only mass voting. These heads also elected a chief administrator. Gronlund wanted no lawyers, few laws, no judicial review, and no precedent law. Trained judges would decide all cases on merit, but in the absence of property Gronlund foresaw almost no crime. He did want harsh penalties for anti-social behavior even as he expected all to work hard and to identify their interests completely with the commonwealth.

Bellamy described a slightly different mode for selecting a natural aristocracy in 2000. His industrial army was, in reality, the only political order that existed. Like any army, it was ruled by ranked officers, headed by a commander in chief or president. Lower officers commanded local departments. Two orders of generals commanded national guilds and the ten great departments. A congress met only once in five years to approve or disapprove the work of the departments. The officers at each level attained their position by a unique election process—the retired members of each guild and department elected them. All retired people jointly elected a president from among retired departmental generals. Because an ordered, disciplined life prevailed, crime had almost disappeared. But for the few needed trials, a few honored men over forty-five served as judges, without lawyers or juries. Bellamy reported no state department, as diplomats were useless in a world without war—most countries of Europe and Latin America had emulated America and now made up a friendly trading bloc.

When talking of the new social order in a cooperative commonwealth, each of our three utopian writers indulged in superlatives that, on close analysis, often seem little more than appealing but vague generalities. All citizens of a cooperative commonwealth were public spirited, all pursued an occupation of choice, all seemed creative, all were fulfilled and happy. Bellamy even portrayed an unbelievably healthy society, with physical education and robustness all around. None of the three men talked of death, of sickness, or even of any irritating differences in taste. All emphasized the new equality and freedom of women, even as each stressed the radically different nature of women. Gronlund said they differed in temperament, intellect, muscles, and in a monthly incapacity of three or four days. Bellamy celebrated femininity. Each advocated equal pay, equal franchise, and equal legal status. They believed economic independence would end prostitution, make marriage a truly equal partnership, free women from forced marriages, and, as Gronlund suggested, make divorce an open choice for women trapped by economic dependence in cruel marriages (a form of legalized prostitution). Bellamy even suggested that free women, who could choose husbands without economic compulsion, would happily refuse to marry boors and vulgarians and ignoramuses, forcing such men to remain celibate (apparently he did not dream of ignorant or vulgar women). Thus, a type of natural selection, a desired form of eugenics, helped account for the superb physical specimens in 2000.

All three men acclaimed free public education, and particularly the type of training that permits a wise choice of vocation. Both Gronlund and Bellamy saw teaching as one of the major industrial sectors. All three men celebrated the quantum improvement of morals in a cooperative commonwealth that stood for communal concern and responsibility. The universal affluence removed the principal motives for antisocial behavior, the cause of most private vice. Instead of venting frustration against others, the dutiful citizen of the cooperative commonwealth could direct it toward civic improvement. Gronlund particularly stressed the ascendancy of sympathy, the prime social virtue. It would replace such capitalist virtues as benevolence and pity, for it springs from fellow feeling or comradeship or felt brotherhood. Finally, all three men gave a vague, nontheological, social gospel veneer to their accounts. Mr. Homos seemed to identify everything in Altruria with the spirit of Christ. Gronlund, in Spencerian language, stressed the continued sense of one's relationship to the unknown, the continued relevance of awe and a sense of mystery, and thus recommended a new religion of humanity. With heaven realized, he anticipated few lingering concerns with immorality. Bellamy climaxed his *Looking Backward* with a sermon, delivered over the community's music intercom system (one of the few technological gimmicks in either utopia). I find it sentimental social gospel modernism at its worst, a stream of moralistic clichés that he might have picked up from some fashionable pulpit. But at the time the eschewal of doctrine, of dogma, of serious theology on behalf of an ecumenical brotherhood and moral concern surely had tremendous appeal.

The publication of these three utopian books coincided with a renewed interest in colonization. In 1894 a Unitarian minister in California formed a short-lived Altruria colony at Santa Rosa. The colony, in its seven-month existence, tried several commercial ventures, constructed some houses and tents, and established a school and a newspaper. Yet it was always more of a weekend retreat for idealistic urbanites than a going colony, although it did spawn several Altruria clubs in California. A group of Christian socialists, centered in New York City, tried a very similar venture in North Carolina. When this failed, they opened a large, much-publicized colony in Georgia in 1896. Called the Christian Commonwealth, it attracted support even from Tolstoy but barely survived for four years. Neither of these efforts led to any national movement.

Bellamy's *Looking Backward*, however, led to over 150 Nationalist clubs, each working toward his goals, but few interested in demonstration colonies. An exception was the Boston Club, and most particularly one member—Cyrus F. Williams. We will meet him again. Meanwhile, Julius A. Wayland took the lead in colonization. A former Indiana businessman who converted to socialism after reading Gronlund, Wayland founded the most popular socialist journal in America—the *Coming Nation*. Impatient to demonstrate his ideals, he and a group of disciples founded the first cooperative commonwealth at Tennessee City, Tennessee, in 1894. Appropriately called Ruskin, it seemed to have had an auspicious beginning. Wayland deeded his newspaper to the colony but left after a year, angry over local policies, and later formed another successful newspaper. Plagued by poor land and declining subscriptions, the colonists at Ruskin first moved to new land, then completely disbanded in 1899. But despite early failure, Ruskin became one of the stimulants of a major national effort to found cooperative commonwealths.

Additional support came from two other groups—a three-chapter Brotherhood of the Cooperative Commonwealth, and Eugene Debs's American Railroad Union. The small brotherhood, with all its chapters in Maine, wanted to colonize a western state and eventually gain control of its government. Debs, after serving his jail sentence for defying an injunction in the Pullman strike, converted to socialism and welcomed both political action and colonization, strategies that he publicized in his *Railway Times*. In 1896 he called for a union of socialist, nationalist, and cooperative groups but failed to achieve much support or interest at a St. Louis convention, which had to compete with the nearby Populist convention. Still interested in a refuge for unemployed rail workers, Debs called a second national convention in Chicago in 1897. Here the Maine brotherhood, Ruskin colonists, railroad radicals, and a number of urban socialist politicians united in a new combined political party and colonization society, the Social Democracy of America. Both the political action groups and the colonization boosters committed themselves to an American cooperative commonwealth but could never really agree on means. Some of the politicians, such as Victor Berger of Milwaukee, had near contempt for the colonizers.

But for a year a three-member Colonizing Committee gained the most enthusiastic member support and received almost all the public attention. The committee included Cyrus Williams of the old Boston Nationalist Club; Richard Hinton, a former friend and biographer of John Brown and an exile from the dogmatically Marxist Socialist Labor party; and W. P. Borland, a Kropotkin disciple from the railroad union. The committee tried several money-gathering schemes with small success and contemplated either Idaho or Washington as target states for massive colonizing. They envisioned hundreds of colonies of about five hundred people each, with fifty such colonies making up a county in their new cooperative commonwealth. For almost a year the committee negotiated for a four-thousand-acre tract of land in the Cumberland Mountains of Tennessee and even planned a railroad connection to it, only to give up because of unacceptable financing arrangements. They also looked at land in Georgia and actually contracted for some gold-mining land in Colorado. I cannot begin to tell you how hard the committee worked, how many frustrations it suffered, or how much the members wanted to live up to all the hopes centered in its activities. Yet by the annual convention of 1898 it had almost nothing to report for its year's efforts. Meanwhile, the one existing cooperative commonwealth at Ruskin was already in a shambles.

The 1898 convention of the Social Democracy, meeting again in Chicago, developed into a no-compromise fight between the political and colonizing wings, with poor Debs trying to placate each group. The colonizers claimed to be more American in their tactics, had a slight majority, and organized the convention after a crucial 52–37 vote. The minority, led by Berger, met separately and formed a new Social Democratic party. Because this party coalesced with a schismatic faction of the Socialist Labor party in 1900 to sponsor a joint ticket, headed by Debs, and then in 1901 became the influential and enduring American Socialist party, few historians have bothered to find out what happened to the winning group within the Social Democracy. It was on them that the colonizing strategy depended. Because Debs slowly moved to the growing political faction, the Social Democracy lacked political leadership. Within a month it disbanded as a political entity, with most members supporting Debs in 1900. But the colonizers replaced it with a new fraternal and insurance order called the Cooperative Brotherhood. It was to continue the work of the former colonizing committee and was headed by Willard and Hinton.

In 1898 the two men purchased or leased one thousand acres of land on the western shores of Puget Sound, across from Tacoma. Here they incorporated a new colony, called Burley, which was to be the successor of Ruskin and the prototype of a whole series of cooperative commonwealths in America. For almost ten years a fluctuating group of colonists kept the near-bankrupt colony going, sustained largely by gifts and by nonresident membership dues, which, after ten years, earned one full retirement rights in the colony. The colony never developed a viable economy and always received most of its income from the sale of timber and sawed lumber. Somehow the colonists never succeeded in agriculture, and most small industries lasted only a year or so. At first the colony had to turn away applicants for resident membership (it lacked even minimal facilities), but later it could not retain enough members to keep its lumber mill going and thus had to resort to wage employees from the outside.

Burley was never strong enough to implement its most idealistic goals. It welcomed any applicant able to pay membership dues and soon muted its ideology into a generalized emphasis upon cooperation. Grandiose plans for expansion led only to a few supportive discussion groups and a few scattered cooperative stores. Yet in their newspaper the colonists maintained a fairly consistent Bellamy-type idealism, which sounded good for distant readers but which concealed the harsh realities of the colony. For a short time the colony did use a labor check or credit card, with coupons redeemable in the colony stores. But unlike *Looking Backward*, there was precious little to buy with the credit. Life was always frontier ruggedness at its best or worst. Some formerly urban members took extended leaves back into "civilization." Ten directors, elected by members, made up the colony government, and, as conditions worsened, they had to act in a dictatorial way. Although the entire brotherhood had over one thousand members in 1900, the colony population remained in the 100-125 level and, after an internal split in 1901, never again grew to that number. In fact, from 1901 on, after the first three years of enthusiasm, the colony steadily declined. In 1906 its major newspaper ceased publication. Only the liquidation of assets occupied the next two years, although the Brotherhood may have lived on for many years.*

With the decline of Burley the organized attempt to establish a cooperative commonwealth seemed at an end. The fervor had peaked from 1894 to about 1901. But in 1913 Job Harriman—a Los Angeles lawyer, a former guest at Altruria, a former member of a Bellamy Nationalist club, a past member of the Socialist Labor party, a vice presidential candidate with Debs in 1900, and a Socialist candidate for mayor of Los Angeles in 1911—launched the Llano colony in a valley north of Los Angeles. I have told the story of Llano, the last cooperative commonwealth, in a book and will not repeat it here. It endured longer than any other socialist colony in American history. From early, ephemeral successes in California, the Llano colony moved near Leesville, Louisiana, in 1918 and there maintained a troubled existence until the mid-thirties. I visited the last director of the colony on the old colony site in 1959, a year before he died. At that time a wide circle of Llano alumni still kept up the movement. They published a news sheet in California well into the 1960s. Survivors of the Llano colony even inspired some of the youthful colonizers of the last decade. Thus, the cooperative commonwealth has some faint continuity with the present.

I have not mentioned three or four other tiny, ephemeral colonies inspired by the cooperative commonwealth idea. They all shared the difficulties of Ruskin, Burley, and Llano. Despite their utopian background, none of the colonies ever had, or maintained, a coherent, internalized ideology. Clichés and vague hopes had to suffice. Except for a few leaders, the colonies attracted people with low skills: desperate, confused, beaten men and women, or pitiful, aged, or terribly eccentric people seeking more of a refuge than a challenge. No colony ever developed an adequate economic base, and cooperators seemed peculiarly inept in agricultural areas. Thus, the repeated story: Colonies survived through appeals to outside benefactors and found their prime asset to be carefully compiled mailing lists of softhearted radicals in America and abroad. Each colony suffered from contentious leaders, and all floundered in intense, passionate dissent, which, given the heterogeneity of colonists, was all but inevitable. Instead of consensus the colonies typically boasted as exciting a spectrum of cultists as one could find anywhere short of Greenwich Village.

In spite of these depressing realities, I hesitate to talk of the failure of Ruskin or Burley or Llano. The colonies could not endure. They never came close to their loftiest hopes. But in talking with people who were at Llano, I gain the same impression another author gained from ex–Brook Farmers. To be in such a colony, to experience the dreams, even to suffer the hardships, were somehow exhilarating. Thus, many looked back to a tattered Llano, in the scrawny cutover pines of northern Louisiana, as providing the golden years of their life. It solaced for a lifetime. For some a year or two was quite enough, yet not regretted. Given qualitative criteria, I think most such colonies, in a sense, succeeded, even when we take into account the nostalgia present in lingering memories. Maybe even that—the warm afterglow, heightened by passing years and other frustrated dreams—is also a human good.

I end with a confession. I do not easily or gladly move back into the subject of utopias, a topic of earlier scholarship and of continuing fascination. The very subject is a bit disturbing. It uncovers a bit of guilt, even as it provokes envy. We all, in reflective moments, relish our own utopian fancies, our reverse commentaries on the inadequacies of our present life. We envision our golden city, or village, or garden retreat. We all dream of simplicity, creative work, fulfilling personal relationships, brilliant conversation, or rewarding games and festivals. But for most of us our dreams are enough—almost. We have made at least a marginally successful accommodation with existing institutions, or, like Howells, we have learned how to suffuse our institutions with irony or detached understanding and thus tolerate them or even, in a perverse sort of way, enjoy their worst inanities. This is quite an achievement. It may be a consolation. But just here enters the nagging guilt. The ragged and motley and contentious men and women of Burley or Llano did not accommodate so well. They had the courage to do something about their dreams, unrealistic though they were. Their colonies failed, but I keep wondering if the many ways I fail my own vision is not more damning. And maybe we document our failure when, as at this conference, we can indulge our distant and cerebral fascination with such colonies by scavenging among their ruins for sociological souvenirs.

*I gained most of my knowledge of Burley from an honors thesis by Richard Winterbottom, "The Co-operative Brotherhood and Its Colony at Burley, Washington, 1898–1906" (University of Wisconsin, 1972).

Arthurdale Revisited

This has been a nostalgia trip for me. It takes me back forty years, to when I was a graduate student just beginning a dissertation on the New Deal community program. So long ago. So much has happened since then—to me, to the world around me. For me in the mid-fifties the New Deal seemed close, tied to the personal memories of my boyhood on a small, no longer profitable farm in the mountains of east Tennessee. My family lived in a former sharecropper's cabin, without electricity, without running water or even any nearby spring, with chickens visible through the holes in the floor. In so many ways I was a child of that greatest and last depression.

Arthurdale helped initiate a fascinating government initiative—community building. This effort began in May 1933 with congressional authorization of a small subsistence homesteads program. When the first emergency session of Congress in 1933 failed to act on several independent bills providing for some type of homesteads, Senator John H. Bankhead of Alabama was able to insert one paragraph (section 208 of Title II) into the polyglot National Industrial Recovery Act of 1933. This section, part of a large public works scheme, authorized $25 million to aid in the redistribution of population away from industrial centers by providing loans or other aid to enable families to purchase subsistence homesteads. The president had free reign in designing the means to gain this goal. Bankhead's addendum reflected a great deal of momentum on behalf of subsistence homesteads, but far from any consensus on exactly what type. Support for some such program came from agricultural economists committed to the retirement of submarginal land, from back-to-land romantics and faddists, from city planners infatuated with the possibilities of garden cities, and from southern congressmen appalled by rural tenancy and committed to some program to help farmers gain ownership of land.

Roosevelt established a small Division of Subsistence Homesteads in the Department of the Interior. It survived for two years, initiated thirty-four diverse communities, spent only about $8 million of its original authorization, and in 1935 turned its uncompleted communities over to a new and more centralized Resettlement Administration (RA). Most of the division's projects, roughly twenty-four in all, were close to cities or towns. Called "industrial" homesteads, these best fulfilled the expressed intent in the legislation—to redistribute unemployed people from industrial centers. These projects often involved relatively small subsistence plots, some of no more than an acre or two. The expectation was that settlers would be able to gain at least part-time employment in the nearby cities, a realistic hope. In time almost all these small communities were swallowed up by the expansion of nearby cities.

In addition to these near suburban projects, the division began three fully rural communities, with large enough plots, or enough outlying fields, to make possible what local sponsors hoped, unrealistically, would be self-supporting farms. One scattered project involved resettled residents pushed out of the new Shenandoah National Parkway. Two other projects were garden cities, with almost no agricultural enterprises. But the four communities that gained the most publicity, and suffered the most criticism, were in isolated rural areas. Of these Arthurdale would be the most famous or notorious. All four, which were to meet the special needs of stranded workers, were supposed to combine subsistence agriculture with employment in mines or new factories. The problem was that, in the thirties, it proved almost impossible to entice employers to these remote villages.

Even as Congress approved subsistence homesteads legislation in May 1933, it also authorized an expanded relief program, under a new Federal Emergency Relief Administration (FERA). This agency, under certain guidelines, provided relief funds to the states for local distribution. State relief administrators had considerable leeway in how they used these funds. In Texas the relief administrator—Lawrence Westbrook—and an architectural crony—David Williams—decided to move several unemployed workers, who had formerly been farmers, into the pine woods of east Texas, there to construct their own new community and gain subsistence and income from farming. In 1934 the FERA created a Division of Rural Rehabilitation and Stranded Populations and began coordination of various rural relief efforts in each state, with the actual spending by chartered state rural rehabilitation corporations. Several of these state corporations, under some guidance from Washington, followed the Texas precedent and collectively built approximately twenty-eight rural communities. Most relied entirely upon agriculture as an economic base, either in individual farmsteads or on large cooperative farms surrounding clustered villages.

With an almost $5 billion relief appropriation in 1935, the Roosevelt administration revamped its whole approach to relief. A more centralized

Works Progress Administration (WPA) spent most of this appropriation for a massive jobs program. It absorbed and reorganized the former programs of the state-based FERA. The new WPA kept until 1939 five of the largest and most controversial rural rehabilitation communities but transferred the rest to a brand new agency, the Resettlement Administration (RA), headed by a controversial former brain truster, Rexford G. Tugwell. The RA absorbed all rural relief and rehabilitation programs, took over the uncompleted subsistence homesteads projects, and began its own communities. Tugwell was most concerned with urban resettlement, a commitment that led to three greenbelt cities that have had a very significant impact on modern city planning. In rural areas he concentrated on farm-based communities, some with dispersed farmsteads, some with subsistence plots surrounded by cooperative farm enterprises, and a few fully communal or corporate type farms. Of these projects, enough involved compact settlement to bring the total number of planned New Deal communities to approximately one hundred, although the definitions have to be arbitrary.

In 1937 the RA merged into a new Farm Security Administration (FSA) in the Department of Agriculture. The FSA would complete the various homestead, rehabilitation, and resettlement communities, initiate a few new ones, and in World War II begin the complex process of liquidating and selling each community. As a whole, the community program turned out to be very costly on a unit basis, continuously controversial, but enduringly fascinating because of its ambitious goals and the openly experimental or innovative nature of several community programs—from architecture, to new tenure patterns, to cooperative enterprises.

Back to subsistence homesteads and Arthurdale. The key term in 1933 was "subsistence." This emphasis remained central only for about three years. Even by 1935 RA bureaucrats responsible for community building no longer stressed subsistence agriculture, an idea that had seemed so beguiling in the dark days of 1932 and 1933. Thus, to understand Arthurdale, we need to recapture the unique outlook of 1933, one that made subsistence farming so appealing. To do this, we have to revisit a strange interlude in American history. Arthurdale is a perfect focus for such a return. It was the first subsistence homesteads community (in incorporation, public dedication, and early construction). Clarence Pickett and the American Friends Service Committee had already plotted subsistence or self-help strategies for local coal miners before Roosevelt's inauguration. Pickett gained local support, received needed backing from agriculturalists at West Virginia University, helped gain the early attention of Eleanor Roosevelt and soon her zealous commitment to subsistence homesteads, helped create the political will needed to gain legislative funding, and then became assistant director of the new Division of

Subsistence Homesteads. Others have told this local story. Some of you lived it. I will not retell it but ,rather, try to make clear why the idea of subsistence homesteads gained, for a very few years, such broad support.

The years from 1932 to 1935 make up a fascinating interlude in American history. The anomalous quality of this interlude was a necessary condition for a subsistence homesteads program. These years were exceptional, first of all, because of the severity of the Great Depression. This had a profound impact on both agriculture and manufacturing. Farm incomes fell by half from 1930 to 1933. Surpluses, lack of demand, and rampant farm foreclosures suggested that agriculture in America had peaked, that demand would never again justify such productivity. Some farmers would have to leave commercial agriculture. Other farm operators would have to convert some of their marginal lands to nonagricultural uses. Thus, the demand for already redundant farm laborers would further decline, displacing thousands. What could these people do? Where could they go? Not to the cities, where there were no jobs. In fact, briefly, a stream of unemployed city workers were actually moving back to the country. In the early thirties, for the only time in our history, the flow of people to cities reversed; the number of people who listed their occupation as farmer increased.

Farmworkers were increasingly underemployed. In the cities up to one-fourth of former workers had no jobs and no incomes. Up to another fourth suffered reduced hours. Unlike in agriculture, everyone expected that most such jobs would revive with economic recovery, but it seemed unlikely that we would ever need as large a workforce as was employed in 1929. Demand would not be sufficient because of three factors that seemed very important in 1933: First was a virtual collapse of world trade and, with nationalistic regimes ascendant in Europe, no likely early revival of our former export markets. Second was the end of immigration, based in part on exclusionary policies that went into effect in the mid-twenties, but also on the diminished appeal of a depressed United States. Briefly, in the early thirties, more people left the United States than arrived, the only time in our history when we had such a reverse flow. Finally, birthrates were moving to a historic low. It seemed that no couples wanted children or believed they could afford to rear them. Thus, throughout Europe as well as America, intellectuals worried about population decline, about too few people in the immediate future. Without export markets, and without a growing domestic population, we seemed to have arrived at a mature economy, one that would not have the increased demand needed to continue the modest patterns of annual growth that prevailed before 1929. The problem of the future would be how to distribute a stable product, a theme that Roosevelt introduced into his campaign speeches in 1932.

What is so clear to us was not clear to people in 1933—that the early years of the thirties were unique. Almost every development from 1940 on reversed the concerns of the early thirties. The low birthrates of the thirties gave way to our baby boom, while world populations soared. Commerce with both western Europe and eastern Asia moved close to a free market after 1945 and boomed. Consumer demands helped fuel an unprecedented growth rate of around 3 percent annually in the three postwar decades. Agricultural demand revived with the baby boom and joined with a revolution in agricultural productivity from 1950 to 1970 (a doubling of product along with a 50 percent reduction in the agricultural workforce). Immigration resumed and boomed by the eighties. The population flow, even by 1935, was clearly back toward cities. Above all, an expected postwar depression never materialized.

The anomalous early thirties provided one explanation for often fervent support for subsistence homesteads. Another necessary condition for such an emphasis on "subsistence" involved historic continuities. Such homesteads seemed to fit the capacities and needs of millions of needy Americans—unemployed urban workers, workers permanently stranded in such declining industries as coal, and unneeded tenants or small farm operators whose inefficient labors could no longer provide them a living. By a good estimate, this was approximately one-third of the workforce in 1933.

Subsistence homesteads seemed a perfect answer. Homesteaders, because of purely subsistence production, would add nothing to the glutted agricultural market, although home subsistence would slightly reduce the demand for bought foodstuffs. Part-time employment in manufacturing or service industries promised to so expand the workforce as to reduce unemployment, although admittedly even part-time work added a bit to the total national product. But if a large enough portion of laborers worked only twenty hours a week, we would have no unemployment, and if subsistence farmers enjoyed a monetary income, they would be able to spend it almost entirely on nonagricultural goods. In theory their purchasing power for durable goods would be greater than urban workers', who had to spend over half their wages for food and rent. The often unnoted assumption behind this solution was the ability, and the willingness, of a large share of unemployed Americans to move back to a subsistence form of agriculture. Was this a justified assumption? Not today, but possibly so in 1933.

To an extent, the often nostalgic references in 1933 to a former subsistence form of agriculture involved a myth. In America we never had much purely subsistence agriculture. From the colonial period on, our farmers grew products for the market, including a large export market. Farmers wanted to sell a surplus in order to buy needed tools, luxury consumer goods, exotic foods such as tea, coffee, and sugar, labor-intensive products such as woven cloth and shoes, and even domestic foods or tobacco products that did not suit their own climate. This meant that even back-country farmers tried to grow some marketable product, if nothing more than distilled spirits, and to become part of the complex network of exchange stretching to Europe.

Yet until the 1920s almost all farm families gained a type of economic security through subsistence production and types of local exchange. In lean years, in times of flood or drought or depression, they could usually survive—not happily, but without extreme hardship. Either as families, or as a community, they provided for most of their necessities by growing vegetable gardens, planting orchards, milking cows, butchering their own fattened hogs, keeping chickens, cutting their own wood for heat and cooking. They pickled, dried, and later canned fruit from orchards, or scavenged the woods for raspberries, blackberries, and chestnuts. They had beehives, pressed sorghum cane and boiled the juice into syrup, used ashes and spare fat to make soap, often had their own looms for weaving and lasts for shoe repair, and they sewed and darned their own clothing. They repaired harnesses, shoed their own horses, and used draft horses for local transportation. After 1920 this changed, slowly at first, then pre-cipitously after 1950, leading to present day specialized farmers who buy all their food from Kroger, and dairy farmers who buy pasteurized milk. Subsistence was a communal, not just an individual or family, achievement. Most tasks involved neighbors in groups, exchanges of labor, or reliance on skilled local artisans. Subsistence for each family involved local networks of exchange. Local mill owners turned wheat and corn into flour and meal. Local blacksmiths repaired tools. Only a few women oper-ated looms or had frames for quilting. Perhaps only one man was profi-cient at meat cutting and thus was in great demand at butchering time. The point is that by such self-help and local exchange individual neigh-borhoods were able to be relatively self-sufficient in foods, fuel, and, to a large extent, services.

In 1933 at least a majority of urban workers were still close to this sub-sistence tradition. Manufacturing jobs, even as late as the twenties, were often irregular or seasonal. The movement from farm to city and back again was continuous. In the twenties, to use one example, Detroit auto-mobile companies routinely dismissed most assembly workers in the summer while they retooled for new models. Many single workers, like my father, moved from farms to Detroit annually but meantime did some farming in the summer. And except in a few huge cities, most factory workers retained the skills of childhood and, as conditions allowed, used them even when they lived in cities. That is, they grew backyard gardens, kept a chicken coop or—when laws allowed or they could defy the rules—

kept two hogs for meat. As many as could, either in a large lot or in nearby country areas, kept a milk cow. Even if the need for such tasks no longer existed in the city, they nevertheless retained the skills necessary to resume them, and in the wake of massive unemployment in the thirties, millions either moved back to farms or tried to grow their own food.

Gradually, the opportunity for such self-providence was declining. City codes curtailed in-city hogs and chickens, new generations were losing the needed skills, and patterns of employment were becoming more permanent. By the thirties, much more so than in earlier depressions, millions of people were completely dependent on wages or on public welfare for survival. It was this fact that overwhelmed earlier and more informal welfare services. This new vulnerability, on an ever larger scale, made it imperative that politicians find means of avoiding or ameliorating future economic cycles and led, fitfully and gradually, to our present regulatory and welfare state—one that now provides assurance that the Great Depression was also the last.

Today subsistence homesteads make little sense. How many young people, even the few on our remaining 1.5 million farms, learn subsistence skills? I doubt if a majority of young people even know how to grow a successful vegetable garden, although gardening remains a very popular hobby. But who knows how to raise chickens for eggs or broilers, to care for or even milk a cow, to raise and fatten even two shoats, to turn apples into cider or the vinegar needed to pickle cucumbers or hog's feet, to mature successful fruit crops or to dry the fruit, to identify cress or polk greens in the springtime, or to find and preserve berries in the summer? Some people may love to hunt or fish, but how many would like to do it as a necessity for having good protein on the table? That is, how many people, if they owned the five-acre homesteads prevalent at Arthurdale and had access to communal pastures and woodlots, could so use them as to provide most basic necessities? And even if they could learn the skills, how many would be willing to do all the laborious, unending work required? Milking even one cow, slopping two hogs, and cracking corn for twenty chickens twice a day, seven days a week, are not inviting activities for our indulgent generation. How many people are up to cutting wood for a kitchen range and, during the hot summer, firing it up every day not only to cook but to can and preserve an unending stream of fruits and vegetables? How many even have the stomach to wring a fryer's neck, or to cut the throat of a hog so as to drain its blood, or to castrate a young bull?

For Americans who lived in rural areas (a majority until 1920), or even in rural areas and small towns and cities (a majority in 1933), these forms of self-sufficiency were still familiar. This was true also for most stranded miners in West Virginia. Of course, people often needed to improve such skills. It is a myth that all farm families were expert at these tasks. They needed instruction, and the Extension Service, with its farm and home demonstration agents, stood ready to offer such help, as it did to home-steaders at Arthurdale.

To reinforce my point about the familiarity of most workers with such subsistence skills, I want to cite some easily forgotten facts about our economy. In 1933 something like 35 percent of our workforce was still on farms. Our farm population peaked at around 32 million in 1916 and remained near this level (over 30 million) until 1930, or one-fourth of the total. The farm population may briefly have surpassed the 1916 level in 1933, as city people moved back to deserted tenant cabins. The number of farmworkers peaked around 1910 but again remained rather stable to 1930, when they numbered over 9 million, or still considerably more than in the manufacturing sector. The precipitous drop came only after 1940. The actual number of farms peaked in the mid-thirties, at near 7 million, and since then has dropped to about 1.5 million. I cite such figures to show how recent, and how dramatic, has been the shift from agricultural to service industries, and how much closer people in the Great Depression were to a rural, agricultural, and subsistence mode of life. In a sense the idea of subsistence homesteads, as Marxists liked to point out, was atavis-tic. It involved efforts to regain lost skills, recapture or restore a declining way of living. But it was not as unrealistic as it might seem from today's perspective.

Was subsistence agriculture and part-time wage employment an eco-nomically feasible answer to the problems of 1933? Arthurdale and other homesteads provided no clear answer. As it turned out, nowhere in Amer-ica could self-help remedies lead to anything like the living standards enjoyed by the carefully selected homesteaders at Arthurdale. Both the housing and the bountiful community services reflected major outside subsidies to the homesteaders, most from the federal government, some from private benefactors recruited by Eleanor Roosevelt. In a sense this was concealed New Deal welfare, or even good old-fashioned pork bar-rel. Conceived as welfare for a particularly unfortunate minority of stranded miners, it might seem almost just. But note that only a minute number of miners, in three such communities, could become homestead-ers and live in such nice homes, with modern conveniences. For them this might have seemed a special type of undeserved New Deal grace.

The lack of jobs was not the whole problem. Even if—and this turned out to be the tragic "if" of Arthurdale—the Post Office Department, or pri-vate firms, could have provided the contemplated part-time jobs, even then competitive wages would never have allowed part-time, possibly even full-time, workers to have paid back the costs of their homesteads and the village infrastructure. In the conditions of the thirties, with pre-

vailing wage rates, economically feasible villages would have had to utilize cheap cabins and to dispense with most village amenities. Thus, even
a somewhat less luxurious Arthurdale would have required major government subsidies. If the government had generalized such subsidies,
offered them to all unemployed people, this would have required per
capita welfare expenditures several times over those offered WPA workers, and a total cost unimaginable and unaffordable in the thirties. The
effective income of Arthurdale residents was double that of ordinary
laborers in the competitive economy.

Was such a solution, begging its cost, an attractive alternative for
stranded workers? This is a very difficult question. Of course, families
eagerly applied to move to Arthurdale. They would have been fools not
to, although the move raised insecurities about their seemingly mounting
indebtedness. But if subsidies had not been involved, would this have
seemed an attractive alternative? Would unemployed miners, if given the
chance and provided access to land, have gladly accepted half-time
employment in the mines and turned to subsistence agriculture in order
to survive? Some would have. Most would not. The experience on most
subsistence homesteads was that, with World War II, residents gladly
moved back to full employment and tended to neglect their small farmsteads, at least as an important source of income.

Yet an often overlooked trend in the larger society did have some simi-
larities to subsistence homesteads, a trend still too little studied. Millions
of rural Americans lost their former means of livelihood in the depression
thirties. They had no Arthurdale to move to. Yet they grew and preserved
more foods than before, cut their own fuel, and scrounged for any possible work. That is, they voluntarily, and out of necessity, adopted subsistence strategies. Some picked up dollar-a-day seasonal jobs on surviving
farms. Some were able to gain WPA jobs. Some migrated, as the famous
Okies. What was soon clear was that a large percentage of small farmers,
or tenant farmers, would never again be able to make a full living on the
farm. The agricultural changes of the thirties, mandated by surpluses,
influenced by such new machines as cotton pickers, and above all encouraged by new government programs, insured that the number of farm
workers would decline precipitously, a process that began as early as
1940.

What happened in much of the upper South, particularly in the Piedmont industrial belt, was something that closely resembled what bureaucrats planned for Arthurdale. Former full-time farmers sought wage
work, or what they often called public work, and at least in World War II
easily gained such jobs. My father even found a factory job in 1936. His
wages saved our farm from foreclosure, and he planned in time to move
back to full-time farming but, of course, never was able to do this. In the

war years all the local farmers, almost without exception, took factory jobs. But they did not sell their farms or move to cities. In fact, in much of the upper South factories clustered in basically rural areas—the factories in the fields that planners dreamed of at Arthurdale. What such newly employed, and incompletely acculturated, factory workers did was continue to farm—to grow small tobacco patches, to keep cows and even continue selling B-grade milk, and above all to hold on to their gardens, milk cows, fatting hogs, and woodstoves. Low wages often seemed munificent, simply because they had no rent to pay, bought little food, and even grew enough for the market to pay local taxes.

This pattern still prevails in much of the country, to some extent in almost all of it. Today most rural people do not make a living in agriculture; only a few do. Except in the corn belt, usually fewer than 10 percent of workers in rural counties gain their sole income from agriculture. In the Piedmont the boundaries between city and country are blurred, with sprawling strip development along almost all roads, and the most concentrated manufacturing employment in any part of America. North Carolina is the state that best epitomizes this pattern. Here workers still reveal a preference for small farmsteads, for acreage, despite all the esthetic horrors that have resulted from sprawling patterns of development. And, superficially, these "rurban" people, to coin a new word, seem to have realized something close to the Arthurdale dream, or what they might call, with a bit of desperation at times, the best of city and country. Fly over eastern America at night, and the ubiquitous yard lights document the population density. Fly over by day and marvel at the remaining stretches of pasture and forest land. People live in some of the forests, but cows graze the fields, and behind most houses one can see, even from the air, the obligatory vegetable garden or potato patch. Given all this, one might say that Arthurdale was prophetic.

Not so. The view from above falsely suggests a profitable form of subsistence agriculture. This is a mirage. Almost no real income accrues to those who own what seem like updated subsistence farmsteads. In fact, most people pay a penalty, at least in transportation costs, for living out on their ever smaller and misnamed farms. The gardens are worthy as hobbies, or sources of exercise or better-flavored foods. Except for exceptionally talented gardeners, with access to inexpensive land and water, home vegetable production saves little if at all in food costs. Most would-be ranchers lose money on their grazing steers. The reasons for this are the postwar productivity gains in commercial agriculture tied to both technology and scale, the resulting efficiency of modern farms, and the effect of such agriculture on the costs of maintaining home gardens, orchards, and pastures.

Today it is not profitable, even if one discounts the value of labor, to grow most of the items we consume. As a fanatic home gardener, I do not want to diminish the value of esthetic or gastronomical returns. But with the cost of pesticides, or the even higher cost of organic alternatives, plus the high cost of seeds, fertilizers, tools, and water, most home vegetables come at a high unit price, higher than when purchased at a store or local farmer's market. Such has been the effect of commercial use or misuse of pesticides upon insect ecologies that insect and fungal problems are ten times greater than when I was a boy. A regular, expensive, and dangerous regime of spraying is now necessary for useful crops of peaches or apples. And even if zoning laws, or indulgent neighbors, permitted, one cannot justify backyard chickens, hogs, or milk cows. The unit prices are simply too low in stores, again because of an agricultural miracle that provides Americans with food at the lowest cost, proportionate to overall incomes, of any people in history. If you do not believe me, try growing chickens for broilers or for eggs in your backyard, and see if you can keep the unit cost anywhere near as low as what you buy in a grocery store. It was the relative inefficiency of American agriculture in 1933 that made home providence seem economically plausible, the unbelievable efficiency of a highly specialized agriculture today that now makes it so implausible. In 1933 the average farmer was closer to the seventeenth century, in both technology and productivity, than to the agriculture of today.

By so stressing economic sufficiency, by attending to the meaning of the word "subsistence," I have ignored one compelling goal of those who planned subsistence homesteads—an improved quality of life based on an enriched communal experience. This is to implicate the romantic expectations of planners and possibly even homesteaders. The key word was "cooperation," the great panacea of idealistic dreamers of the thirties. Individual clients would gain economic security through part-time wage work and by subsistence agriculture, but this was only half the story. The other half involved the prospects of a regained communal life, rich and rewarding in itself. As many of the economic activities as possible were to be organized cooperatively, which is to say democratically. In stranded communities like Arthurdale, at times the only wage employment was in one or more cooperative. This emphasis upon neighborly trust and sup-port paralleled all manner of clubs and interest groups, attempts to design progressive schools and, in most communities, to create a fully involving form of local government, usually town meetings, with all the nostalgic images these suggested.

In such projects as Arthurdale, the community building goals often seemed as unachievable as did new sources of income. The idealistic goals of planners and patrons often did not match the expectations of homesteaders. Few cooperatives were enduringly successful. Friction almost invariably developed between officials and clients, leading in some projects to virtual warfare. Perhaps uniquely at Arthurdale the residents both enjoyed, and at times suffered from, the patronage of the president of the United States, of Eleanor Roosevelt, of Louis Howe, of Elsie Clapp, of Bernard Baruch, and any number of other famous people. Journalists and visitors so often came to visit that some people felt as if they lived in a fishbowl. And as the expenses mounted, they worried how they would ever be able to pay the costs and gain what they so often most wanted—ownership of their little farm. They were soon just like other Americans who saved World War II wages to buy a few acres and to build a small home, or, if this proved economically unfeasible, to buy a mobile home—that esthetic disaster that mars so much of rural America today.

In almost every New Deal community a moment of truth arrived when the construction phase ended, and with it jobs for homesteaders. They then worried about finding a job, and about how they would ever be able to earn and save enough to purchase their home. When the government made this easy, they leaped at the opportunity and gained the most compelling of American ideals—ownership of home and land, although the land soon had largely a symbolic and esthetic rather than an economic value. Insofar as they were able to buy their home, most homesteaders remained grateful for the community programs of the New Deal and to varying degrees retained (a few survivors still retain) a special self-consciousness, a type of solidarity, a public spirit. In this sense they embody some of the communal rewards so esteemed by those patrons who tried to do good for stranded miners, displaced sharecroppers, or unemployed factory workers.

By all the evidence of this conference, Arthurdale was a glorious success as a community. A warm glow now suffuses memories of its early years. I do not think these memories are necessarily deceptive. But present celebrations may conceal the reasons for such a sense of communal solidarity. A strong sense of community is most often the product of shared adversity. The comradeship of battle is the most enduring of all. The early Arthurdale had more than its share of tensions, fears, and frustrations. Patronage, however generous, may lead to gratitude, but it always produces a more bitter harvest—resentment. It is easy for later generations at Arthurdale to celebrate beginnings. They do not remember. And for the old-timers, it is easier to remember the times of fulfillment than the periods of frustration.

Memory need not deceive, but it is mercifully selective. It screens out the anxieties that accompany even times of great achievement. I do not deplore the nostalgic glow that has made this conference so inspirational. For youth, nostalgia is an unbecoming indulgence. It offers a sentimental and easy bypass around the hard and rocky road of engagement and responsibility. Not so for those who are very old. The battles, for them, are all over, the illusions of youth long since dissipated. For them nostalgia is a consolation and a blessing, often one of the few left. And whatever the early problems, no doubt for the families who moved to Arthurdale from 1933 to 1937, it at first seemed like something close to heaven. Nor is it surprising that these busy, challenging years marked the most memorable adventure of their lives.

3

✢

The Road to a Regulatory and Welfare State

At several times in my career I have returned to the subject of my dissertation and first book—the depression and New Deal and, with it, the maturation of a regulatory and welfare state. Yet in my teaching, and in my primary scholarship, I moved into intellectual history and the history of philosophy after I moved to the University of Maryland in 1959. But outside my university most historians continued to identify me with my first book. They presumed, at the very least, that I was a twentieth-century historian. In either 1963 or 1964 someone from Thomas Y. Crowell wrote to ask if I would be interested in doing a small, interpretive book on the New Deal, as part of a new American history series edited by John Hope Franklin and Abraham S. Eisenstadt. Franklin, who had taught in our summer school at Maryland, had identified me as a possible author in what Crowell hoped would be a large series, one that featured young historians. I agreed to write a thirty-five-thousand-word book, with the completion date of September 1, 1965, when Crowell hoped to publish the first books of the series. The company signed at least fifteen contracts at this beginning effort.

At this time I was hard at work on a very large and difficult project on American philosophy, a project that eventuated in 1968 in *Puritans and Pragmatists: Eight Eminent American Thinkers* (Dodd, Mead). In the summer of 1965, near the end of my Guggenheim Fellowship, I took time off from my attempt to complete a chapter on George Santayana and in a

51

month had written the draft of this little book. I submitted it to Crowell in August, or a few weeks before the deadline written into my contract. For reasons unclear, none of the other authors met their deadline, and thus Crowell held my book for nearly two years, until it could launch the series with three books rather than one. Despite one very harsh outside reader's report, the editors believed that the book almost perfectly fulfilled the intent of the series—a new, brash, and controversial perspective on the New Deal. It appeared in 1967 as a hardback entitled *FDR and the Origins of the Welfare State;* the paperback was simply called *The New Deal.* Subsequently, I have twice written new editions of the paperback. This little book continues to sell well thirty years later. In total it has sold more than all my other books combined and is probably better known than any article or book I have published.

In other contexts I continued, on occasion, to write about the depression and New Deal or about the continued development of a welfare state. This was most true when, in the eighties, I completed a biography of Lyndon Johnson (*Big Daddy from the Pedernales*).

The first of the following two essays provides the setting for a rapid growth of federal responsibilities—the Great Depression. This is the first half of a prepared speech I was unable to deliver, as promised, at Southwestern Louisiana. Just as I prepared to leave Madison, Wisconsin, I received a phone call with the almost unbelievable news—south Louisiana was immobilized by an ice storm, the first that anyone could remember that far south. The airport was closed. I sent along the speech by mail, and the organizers of the canceled conference used it as part of an introduction to a collection of Farm Security Administration photographs on Louisiana, *Louisiana Gothic: Recollections of the 1930s,* edited by Glenn R. Conrad and Vaughan B. Baker (Lafayette: University of Southwestern Louisiana, 1984).

The second essay, never published, is one of three lectures that I delivered in India in 1986 while on a lecture tour supported by the United States Information Agency. In it I tried to introduce to an Indian audience the American version of a welfare and regulatory state, with special emphasis on Lyndon Johnson's Great Society. To do this, I had to provide a background on economic policy in the United States and to delineate some of the distinctively American features of such policy. The audience, largely Indian university professors, included many Marxists. In this context I wanted to explain the United States yet not seem overly apologetic. The approach seemed to work and led to some lively discussions.

These two essays, from the perspective of the central theme of this book, reflect the economic side of ever-increasing federal power and diminishing autonomy at the local level. In most economic areas the people of local villages have to cope with a large array of federal regulations and contribute to numerous welfare programs. Such a limit on private choice, on entrepreneurial freedom, does not mean that the people of a village are worse off than in the past. In most cases the opposite is true. But they are clearly less free.

The Last
and Greatest Depression

Only those over fifty can remember the Great Depression. I am over fifty. But anyone over fifty, my children remind me, cannot extend their memory so far back without having it colored by nostalgia. The protective screen of personal memory suffuses too many past images with a soft glow. Thus, the memories of even the worst of times have become, for some of us, also memories of the best of times—the times of childhood and youth, familiar, haunting, inescapable. But to know ourselves, we have to reach back to those depression memories and risk all the nostalgia. Of course, our personal memories are selective. In a few cases we could not bear them otherwise. But they need not be dishonest. I hope mine are not.

In a very special sense I am a child of that far-off depression. My parents, newly married, decided to give up ill-paying factory jobs in a small mountain town in east Tennessee in early 1929. They moved to a small, fifty-acre farm inherited ten years earlier by my father. He had mortgaged it for five hundred dollars, to build a barn and a sharecropper's cabin. The cabin gave shelter to my parents as they cleared away bushes and briars to plant their first tobacco crop. It seemed to them, in what turned out to be an illusion, that they could pay off the mortgage with one or two successful crops, then build themselves a decent house. During the summer of 1929 they worked feverishly, even as they awaited the birth of their first child. On Thursday, October 24, my anxious father rushed off to get a country physician. In the cabin, early the next morning, I was born. That Thursday became enduringly famous—Black Thursday—the first day of complete panic on Wall Street, the beginning of the great crash. Our mortgage remained unpaid. And I lived my first ten years in that sharecropper's cabin. Only the generosity of a neighbor, who held the mortgage, kept my family from losing the farm.

It was in light of this personal history that I included the following preface in a talk I gave at the University of Southwestern Louisiana well over a decade ago:

> The depression of the thirties had a more enduring impact on Americans than any war of this century. By good fortune America escaped bombing and internal destruction in either of its wars. Those who fought abroad often had life-shattering experiences. Most stayed home and knew war only at an insulated distance. But almost no one could escape the depression, although a minority profited from it. The adults who lived through it, the children who grew up in its midst, became very different people because of it. Their very self-image, their identity, would forever carry with it an indelible brand—depression made. They knew by immediate experience, and would remember for a lifetime, what it was like when the American economy mocked all its widely acclaimed possibilities of unending growth and great affluence. Those who suffered the most still have their nightmares, still carry the marks of extreme insecurity, still participate with mixed guilt and exultation in present prosperity, still nourish the pecuniary caution and almost apocalyptic forebodings so typical of a scarce and meager economy.

The Great Depression was well named. It lasted longer and bit deeper than any before. It was both the last and the greatest depression. Why such severity? The full answer involves complex problems in international finance and trade, which were critical to developments in our domestic economy up through 1931. After that year, with the United States increasingly isolated economically, the continuing depression became primarily a domestic problem. Government policies were not sufficient to avert the international collapse before 1931 or to gain full recovery between 1932 and 1940.

The depression lasted a full decade, an unprecedented time for such an economic collapse. In a sense we had not one but four successive depressions. First, we suffered a mild downturn in the summer of 1929, which became an acute recession after the stock market crash of 1929. Farm prices, particularly those dependent upon exports, collapsed in 1930. At the same time, the market for durable goods, such as automobiles, dropped sharply; nevertheless, an upturn seemed under way by the spring of 1931.

Then came a second disaster, or what might be called a second depression. The near collapse of the European banking and credit systems, particularly those in Austria and Germany in the summer of 1931, led to disastrous effects on debt payments, reparations, and trade. The depression became an international debacle. President Hoover vainly tried to shore up the crumbling international payments system. He failed. This meant a severe, extended international depression, with great suffering in both the United States and Europe during the winter of 1931–32. The European collapse had immense significance: It contributed directly to the rise of Adolf Hitler and to the coming of World War II. Yet in the United States major new recovery measures adopted by Congress and the Hoover administration seemed to have some effect in the summer of 1932. At least people justifiably thought that the worst might be over.

Despite the hopes, the economy began to unravel in new ways in the autumn of 1932, this time led by a near collapse of the American banking system. New fears had fed on the insecurities of the presidential election, then ballooned during the long wait from November to March for Roosevelt's inauguration. For four months the United States suffered a complete dearth of political leadership because Hoover and president-elect Roosevelt were unable to agree on any cooperative action. The Great Depression reached its lowest depths in the spring and summer of 1933, making 1933 the most depressed year in American history. Once again either time or new policies had a significant impact by 1934. Recovery seemed under way. Stimulated by large work-relief expenditures in 1935, a few economic indexes regained their 1929 levels by the election of 1936, although unemployment remained at depression levels.

Once again the hopes of complete recovery proved illusory. Slowed government expenditures in 1937 and the lack of any compensatory private demand produced a fourth and final collapse. This new, 1937 depression confirmed growing beliefs that such periodic collapses were now normal and inevitable. This last depression peaked early in 1938, but we gained no full recovery until the beginnings of World War II.

Instead of trying to locate the necessary conditions for the Great Depression—even economists cannot agree on these—I want to look at some of the dynamics of such a depression. One problem is why it proved such a cruel blow to so many American people. Another is how much it affected popular expectations and, thus, patterns of economic behavior.

Acute suffering during business declines goes back to the American Revolution. By the 1830s such business cycles were already capable of devastating city craftsmen, those cut off from rural retreats or even backyard gardens. Private charity had to take care of the worst suffering. But relatively few people were so cut off from immediate subsistence—from firewood and foodstuffs. Thus, as much as early depressions hurt, they often accelerated capital growth, as for example in new farm improvements. People simply worked harder during depressions to try to make ends meet.

Our economy changed slowly from one made up of proprietary units to one typically made up of large firms, or from diversified individual production to greater and greater specialization. This meant much greater economic interdependence for most people. It meant a larger and larger proportion of wage workers, those with no easy path back to a farm or shop. Yet the old habits of self-providence, plus local pathways of exchange or barter, survived surprisingly well into the twentieth century. Older, complex neighborhood networks still revived in times of need. Even in the mid-twenties a shrinking proportion of factory workers still gained only seasonal employment and habitually returned to villages or farms during the off season.

Of equal importance, native-born Americans remained quite reluctant to accept a collectivized economy, or at least to accept all of its implications. They continued to fear, or resent, large firms and never embraced permanent wage labor as an American norm. So strong was the proprietary ideal that workers continued to dream of their own shop, of someday being their own boss. Class consciousness among wage workers proved, at best, ephemeral. Unlike European countries, with a tradition of dependent workers, the United States did not build any supports under our interdependent economy—no unemployment insurance, no old-age insurance or healthcare programs, no planned or expandable public works programs, no system of transfer payments to those most vulnerable. In short, we had no welfare state in 1930 or 1931.

Many people recognized and stressed the developing levels of vulnerability. The experience of a short depression in 1921–22 revealed the possible breadth of suffering as well as the new potential for violence or even revolution. What had happened in Russia scared people. Herbert Hoover, when still secretary of commerce in the mid-twenties, tried to get a large economic stabilization fund—several billion dollars for planned public works, to be plugged in, to arrest any beginning downturn. And in limited ways he tried stabilization measures in 1930–31, even using $300 million to shore up cotton and wheat prices, but these subsidies proved only a drop in the bucket.

In 1932 the federal government had precious little economic leverage. Its small budget—approximately 3 percent of the gross national product—had minimal impact. And almost nothing served to cushion the impact of massive unemployment, underemployment, or, for farmers, disastrously low prices and incomes. Private charity was quickly exhausted. It worked reasonably well for a time—for depression number one, but not for number two. The cumulative wave of successive downturns was calamitous. The old remedies worked only to a limited extent. As many as could returned home to the farm, not to eat well but to eat. Deserted tenant cabins were at least briefly reoccupied. For two years the flow of population was away from cities. And in thousands of cases neighborhoods formed self-help cooperatives or resumed old, almost forgotten patterns of barter. To a much greater extent than today, people still retained some of the old skills—how to use an ax, to milk a cow or a goat, to raise chickens, to butcher hogs, to grow a backyard garden, to can fruits and vegetables. But only a few city folk could take this escape route— thus, the degree, and extent, of the shock and incomprehension. One almost thought again of Thomas Jefferson's old warning about the vulnerability of a nation of hirelings. By 1930 approximately half the American workforce was made up of hirelings—that is, hourly wage workers living in cities on their weekly paychecks.

The depression inevitably changed existing patterns of expectation and behavior. In an earlier, more meager or primitive, economy, when everyone lived closer to a subsistence level, the great economic imperative had been more production. Surpluses, or a lack of demand, were then almost inconceivable. If I produce for myself, I obviously wait eagerly for the consumption. If my neighbor and I specialize—I grow beans and he milks cows— then as many surplus beans as I grow stand as just so much demand for my neighbor's milk. I am not going to starve as I count my hoarded beans, nor will my neighbor drown in milk while he weakens for the want of protein. In such a simple economy, what one produces is, ipso facto, just so much demand. Demand and production are all but equivalent.

This all changes as subsistence gives way to a more affluent economy, to one that furnishes most people comforts and even luxuries. Then, to an ever greater extent, people have discretionary incomes. They can make choices about spending or not spending. In a stable society few people will choose to hoard wages. That would be foolish. If they save, they really indirectly spend. That is, they put their savings in a bank, and then the bank lends the money to someone to buy either capital or consumer goods. Thus, demand would seem to keep right up with production. Not necessarily so. The elastic or variable element is credit or demand money.

Consumers in the twenties discovered in a big way how to live off their future, through consumer credit, the glory of the installment plan. Such a use of credit helped account for the generally high level of consumer demand in the twenties. Of course, one can court disaster if one gambles away too much of one's future. Credit for consumer goods does not lead to productive assets. One has to pay out of future earnings. Credit for capital goods may pay for itself, if the capital produces plentifully in the future. But even here one can get into trouble if one drastically overestimates the future earning potential of capital goods. Many individuals did just this in the stock market boom of 1928 and 1929; for corporations to have grown rapidly enough to justify stock prices at the peak of the boom would have required, quite literally, a miracle. Thus, the high values were speculative and not realistic. But in many areas people pushed their effective demand to new levels in the twenties. They lived off future earnings, enjoying a strategy that is absolutely essential in our present economy.

The stock market crash taught a lesson—one, as usual, learned too well. People became more cautious even in 1930. A few affluent people increased their savings, ordinarily no problem, as savings go into banks and then into capital spending (new plants, new tools), something that did not usually happen after 1931 because of slackening demand. Existing plants were underutilized. Banks saw their paper assets so depreciate that they could not cover their liabilities. People took out deposits, but almost no one negotiated new loans under the now more stringent requirements. Thus, even if one wanted to borrow—and few did—it was harder to get approval. We had moved into a credit collapse, which by 1933 had moved many people back toward a cash or even barter economy. Our money supply plummeted. The now unused credit potential of people helped account for the lack of demand. The vicious cycle went on and on. Lowered incomes meant lowered prices, which meant lowered demand and, in turn, lowered production.

The expectations of people had to accommodate slowly to the new reality. Many people believed we had finally attained a stable, no-growth economy. President Roosevelt even suggested that we would have no more booms like that of the twenties. Caution and prudence became bywords. Anxious workers, called back to a job, saved pennies for the next layoff and never thought about an installment purchase. At the top, corporate managers held on to precautionary pools of earnings and never thought of launching a new factory. We developed the psychology that goes with depression, an outlook dramatically reinforced in 1937 and 1938. This belated downturn proved the cautious to be the wise. My parents lived on in our sharecropper's cabin until 1939, until they had saved enough money to build a terribly skimpy new house.

In this context the limited expenditures of the federal government made up the critical margin of demand in the American economy. Large relief expenditures in 1935 and 1936 pushed the economy back toward its 1929 levels. The drastic relief cuts that followed the illusion of recovery helped produce the new panic. Private demand by 1937 was simply not sufficient to take up the slack of lowered government expenditures. Resumed relief in late 1938 started the old but slow climb back toward recovery. Then, in 1940, and even more in 1941, defense expenditures finally did the job. We gained full recovery by mid-1942. The unused plants, the idle workers, now responded to the huge infusion of federal funds as the Great Depression gave way to the great war.

The depression had a tremendous impact on American political behavior and, through New Deal legislation, upon our economic institutions. The primacy of economic issues eclipsed the earlier and deep cultural rifts in the Democratic party—between a rural, Protestant, solidly Democratic South, and the ethnic, largely Catholic and Jewish, working-class Democrats of northern cities. Both groups joined in their support of Roosevelt, even as New Deal measures helped solidify Democratic support among wage workers, among a majority of blacks who could vote, and at least temporarily among a large proportion of farmers. Within four years a minority party became the majority party, and so it would remain for the next four decades. But as early as 1937 internal tensions within the Democratic majority (soon to be called the New Deal coalition) had already subverted any broad congressional consensus on policies. Roosevelt alone retained the support of all these groups, and behind his opaque personality lurked deep ideological and cultural cleavages. Only briefly in the mid-1960s, under Lyndon B. Johnson, and in a very special but short-lived political climate, did a similar coalition gain legislative victories comparable to those in Roosevelt's first term.

As a response to both the stock market crash and to the depression, Congress during Roosevelt's first term extended, in almost a quantum leap, federal economic regulation. In part this action entailed the more rigorous enforcement of earlier laws, such as those that established the Interstate Commerce Commission and the Federal Trade Commission, or a strengthening of older agencies through new amendments, as in the case of the revised Federal Reserve System. In other cases economic regulation meant new regulatory authority. An ambitious effort to coordinate all industrial production in the National Recovery Administration proved temporary, but several types of coordination in agriculture have continued to the present. New laws gave the federal government the power to control corporate issues and the stock market, to supervise labor negotiations, and to monitor utility companies. These set precedents for the future, or for the later expansion in the sixties of federal regulation into practically every area of American life, from voting registration to environmental standards to occupational safety to consumer protection.

Perhaps of greater significance, the depression made possible the beginnings of federal controls over individual incomes. In a series of measures, some temporary, some permanent, the Roosevelt administration accepted at least some degree of federal responsibility for emergency relief, became an employer of last resort, began subsidies for public housing and slum clearance, began the social security retirement fund, supervised a state-administered system of unemployment insurance, and began grants to local governments for categorical welfare, with aid to dependent children becoming the most important. These relief programs were often temporary, predicated on the depression emergency, but even the work projects presaged later employment and job training efforts. The housing and various social security programs not only remained but also quickly expanded so as to dwarf their depression origins. One can easily exaggerate the welfare commitment of the Roosevelt administration. At best the early expenditures reflected a minute redistribution of the national income, and by any fair measure the value of new federal subsidies or tax concessions to various producers far outweighed the value of funds directed to those at the bottom. These early welfare benefits helped treat the symptoms of depression, but they were never sufficient to cure it, let alone prevent a future one. In the thirties welfare expenditures beyond emergency relief represented less than 1 percent of the gross national product. Only a weak tool of economic management in the thirties, social transfers today constitute an economic stabilization fund of a magnitude never dreamed of, or desired, by Herbert Hoover back in the twenties.

These transfers were not yet of such a magnitude as to do much to avert a depression immediately after World War II. The wartime expenditures created an excessive demand and extreme pressures for inflation. But everyone recognized these expenditures as exceptional and temporary. The war, it seems, did not remove the limited expectations, the cautious habits that Americans acquired during the depression thirties. Most Americans waited apprehensively for a postwar depression. By any sound guess, such a depression should have followed demobilization and the saturation of pent-up wartime demand for goods. A new depression, in other words, was due in the early fifties, or, if a bit off schedule, at least by the middle or late fifties. It never arrived, although a series of recessions in the fifties kept alive the now deeply rooted apprehensions of all persons old enough to remember the thirties.

The reasons the American economy overcame these recessions, and continued to expand, are many and complex. The growing demand for goods and services fed on low energy costs, on the continued postponement of social overhead costs such as those for air and water pollution, on a baby boom and rapid population growth, on artificially low interest rates and an extended boom in private housing, and on almost revolutionary increases in agricultural productivity. The federal government helped sustain the demand, not yet by significant welfare transfers, not by deficit spending (the federal debt as a percentage of gross national product declined rapidly after the war), but by policies insuring monetary growth, by investment-oriented fiscal policies, by extensive foreign aid (this amounted to major export subsidies for American producers), and by a near wartime level of military expenditures. In a sense the cold war contributed to American prosperity, not only because of military costs but because of the incentives it gave the United States to invest in European and Japanese recovery.

In the 1960s the United States moved over a psychological threshold. Rapidly expanding social services and a sustained high level of military spending added to effective demand. Even older Americans slowly adapted to a near boom economy, to modest but predictable inflation, and to a now normative use of credit in almost every area of American life. Younger Americans could not remember a depression and never reflected the pecuniary caution of their parents. By the end of the decade inflation already loomed as a greater concern than deflation. The economic strains of the seventies—higher energy costs, slowing productivity, a leveling off of the agricultural revolution, new environmental costs, decreasing foreign aid and defense spending, and higher interest rates—caused all types of economic difficulties and all but stopped the earlier growth in real incomes. But by the end of the decade the pressing economic problem was stagflation, or excessive demand, rapidly increasing prices, declining productivity, and low capital growth, or problems that almost exactly reversed those of 1932.

Such changes do not mean that another depression is impossible. They do mean that any depression in the near future will have quite different causes, and effects, than the one in the thirties. Ironically, it is increasingly difficult to specify what the word "depression" would mean today. What level of unemployment, or how major and how long a decline in the gross national product, would constitute a depression? No one knows, for unlike recession we have no formalized conventions governing the use of the word "depression." It is as if the very word is out of date, a relic of the distant past. What is clear is that any future depression, as much as the severe recession of 1981–83, will be to some extent a product of deliberate policy, not at all like the unavoidable, surprising, unwanted cataclysm of the thirties. Today the federal government has too much access to economic information and sophisticated advice, too much economic leverage, both in monetary management and in fiscal matters (it consumes or redistributes over 20 percent of the gross national product), to stand by and watch the economy collapse as it did in 1932–33. The government has a hundred weapons to use to stimulate demand. Thus, any upcoming depression, should we ever agree upon the defining characteristics of such, will involve calculated risks in certain areas, such as employment, on behalf of other long-term economic goals, such as stable prices. Another Great Depression is simply not in the offing.

The Great Society: The Climax
of Policy Reform in America

In the 1960s, under Lyndon Johnson, a distinctively American response to a highly collectivized, interdependent, and dependency-creating economic system reached its apex. We then went as far as we are likely to go in a socialization of management through regulation, and a socialization of product through transfer payments. Beyond such economic legislation the Johnson administration did more than all previous administrations combined to move the United States to full citizenship rights for blacks and women. It also passed the most significant legislation so far in our history affecting the arts and humanities. In five years Congress passed over four hundred major bills, more than in any former or subsequent administration. Insofar as reform relates to legislation, this was the greatest reform decade of our history.

The word "reform" is often loaded—we use it for proposed changes that we find desirable, not for others. But here I use it for any desired changes whatsoever, which means that it is too broad and general to have much discriminate meaning. By choice I will emphasize reforms effected through public policy. That is only part of the story of reform in America, for it excludes all manner of private proposals, pushed by persuasion and not legislation, and ranging from nudism and vegetarianism to the moral preachments in religious revivals to fascinating communal colonies. But sooner or later most American reformers have turned to governments, local or federal, for support, as occurred with such important and at first private reforms as antislavery and temperance, which soon became abolition and prohibition.

What has been surprisingly weak in America have been proposals for basic structural changes in our system of government. Most reforms have found a lodging place within our Constitution or, at most, have involved minor amendments to it. The only major constitutional change came with the Fourteenth Amendment (it created national citizenship and fully consolidated the states into one larger nation), but at the time few appreciated

63

its implications even as few sought the changes it eventually effected. Such is the breath of enabling powers in our Constitution as presently interpreted that almost any program, however radical, might be constitutional, or require only a few enabling amendments.

In the nineteenth century the deeper divisions, and the object of various reforms, were not structural, but matters of policy, particularly economic policy. One primary role of the early federal government was facilitating private development. But by the 1830s deep divisions developed over federal economic policy, and these in turn informed the platforms of a developing two-party system.

In brief, the Whigs wanted a more positive federal role in economic development. They denied any basis of sectoral conflict, stressed a harmony of interests, and tried to avoid even any mention of class conflict. They worked for intensive, coordinated, balanced development within regions or the nation as a whole. They stressed new markets for agricultural industries but wanted to subsidize the development of new and heavy manufacturing, through internal improvements, protective tariffs, and centralized banking and credit facilities. The Whigs, occasionally influenced by Fourier and other utopian socialists, had a vision of a cooperative national community.

The Jacksonians embraced class politics. They sharpened class antagonisms, talked endlessly of the dangers of special privilege and of large wealth, and in conspiratorial language condemned a new financial and commercial elite. They believed an expanded economic role for the federal government would only help the rich and exploit the poor. They talked often of wage slavery and were deeply suspicious of our few early factories. They stressed the benefits of a free market, tried to reduce the costs of public lands, and valued cheap and unobtrusive government. They kept alive a vision of a simple, decentralized country of independent proprietors, of farmers and small household manufacturers.

The radicals in pre–Civil War America were the agrarians, with Thomas Skidmore of New York the most vehement. Made up largely of urban artisans, united in workingmen's parties, the agrarians wanted to realize what had been promised in the American Revolution—a right to property. They wanted to set limits on the size of land holding, to provide free, nonalienable homesteads to unpropertied families, and, in Skidmore's case, to give every child a claim to an equal share of all property in the society and a free education in special boarding schools. Skidmore condemned the cowardice of Jefferson because he left the only important right out of the Declaration of Independence. The euphemism "pursuit of happiness" allowed politicians to escape the hard task—giving everyone his share of what God gave to all people. In fact, the agrarians argued that no one took the right of property seriously. Instead, even the Jacksonians bribed workers with the vote, a pale substitute for their birthright—equal access to nature. The Jacksonian appeals to equal opportunity were empty if every American did not have a right to property and a fully equal education. Otherwise, some had a head start, an unfair advantage in the game of life.

Cheap land helped keep open entrepreneurial opportunities well beyond the Civil War. Until after 1900 few native-born white males had to work for wages. Most remained proprietors, with over half in rural areas and engaged in agriculture, small manufacturing, or retail trade. But large cities, ugly factories, and an underclass, largely immigrant, revealed a new America, one more productive overall, but one with increased class cleavages and more obvious dependence and poverty. Fewer and fewer laborers had the skills or the means to go onto the land, and improved farming techniques meant that few were needed. Besides, land prices went up steadily. Rents rose, and for the first time Americans began to face the early costs of resource scarcity. In this context two brilliant reformers offered diametrically opposed solutions.

Henry George followed the agrarians. He wanted to keep nature open to all, and to take from people the unearned increments represented in high rents. Thus he adopted the old agrarian idea, originated in Britain by Thomas Spence at the time of the American Revolution—a single tax on land, an easy way of fully socializing land. The state would take all the value added by relative scarcity or better location, leaving the so-called owner only with the values added by improvements, by work. In cities this meant that almost all land values would go to the public in taxes. And the opening of land to those who would use it, the end of all speculation, would create new entrepreneurial opportunities, moving America back toward universal proprietorship. Everyone could have access. And access rights are the key to the single tax movement, the last major reform movement in America to take property rights seriously. I do not believe agrarian and distributist movements in the 1930s attracted enough support to be deemed major.

Edward Bellamy had an opposite vision. He saw collectivism as the wave of the future. He did not value an older individualism or celebrate the free artisan or farmer. Just the opposite. In the most influential utopian novel ever written by an American—*Looking Backward*—he leaped ahead one hundred years and described a socialist paradise. A mild Marxist, he glowingly described a fully collectivized and centralized society, ruled by a type of managerial elite, but one abundant in its consumptive returns as well as in leisure and art. Unlike Marx, he spent little time on the means of achieving such a heaven. It seems that, as private corporations grew in size, Americans came to realize that there was no way back to private property and simply decided to complete the process and set up one big collectivity. They thus got rid of all competition and class conflict. The people soon lost all selfish or competitive values and gladly gave their years of service to the nation. Apparently, they soon also lost the values that go with the ownership and management of individual property, and came to give much less importance to the rights of self-expression and to the franchise.

After 1900 economic development in America moved toward the collectivism valued by Bellamy. Very gradually production and services moved out of the household or personalized shop into large and more impersonal firms. Slowly, the number of owner-workers declined, from approximately 50 percent in 1900 to less than 10 percent today. Local networks of exchange, even the skills required for subsistence, atrophied. Given the efficiency of, and thus the small number employed in, its agriculture, then America arguably gained the most collectivized economy in the world. Of course, the productive units are still primarily private, in a strictly legal sense, but in effect our largest corporations are major public agencies. Those who, in legal terms, own do not manage, and those who manage do not own. Thus, private property in the traditional sense has disappeared. But in our policy choices we have followed neither George nor Bellamy. We have not tried to restore property, to open up entrepreneurial opportunities for everyone. Nor have we nationalized even key industries. Instead, in a series of political efforts, we have tried to preserve or gain social justice without sacrificing the productive efficiency of large centralized units and without risking the high degree of discipline or repression suggested by a socialized plant. As I mentioned earlier, we have tried the elusive middle way, with a limited socialization of management through regulation and a limited socialization of the final product through welfare transfers.

At present, the majority view seems to be that we have gone quite far enough, perhaps too far, in these directions. At least in economic policy we are no longer expanding regulations, are even moving toward deregulation in critical areas, and in welfare we have at least stopped a half-century expansion of benefits. That is why I believe that Lyndon Johnson's Great Society reflected a climax of the regulatory-welfare approach, or what had become the orthodox American way. In a sense Ronald Reagan was the most radical president of this century, for he rejected much of this orthodoxy.

What is not often grasped is the long opposition of Americans to collectivism. The old proprietary ideal lived on. People resisted, and suffered a great loss of self-esteem, when they had to give up entrepreneurship for employment. In some sense employment is un-American, the most basic problem of our society, for the ideals of our origins made America the land without employment, the land of universal ownership and self-direction. The main legal agency of collectivism, the limited dividend corporation, long appeared to a majority of Americans as subversive and was much hated, as were the captains of industry. Large firms did not begin to win public acceptance until World War I, and the fear of monopoly and of excessive market power still exerts an impact on American politics. One can get votes for attacking General Motors or General Electric. Similarly, Americans tried, by various guises, to deny employee status. In the long run, high wages, glorious consumptive returns, and better working conditions have sweetened the medicine, but even today opinion surveys find large numbers of employees still nourishing the illusion that wage labor is a temporary expedient, a pathway to going into business for themselves. Thus, not only have Americans feared corporations, they have also resisted class consciousness or solidarity, have been reluctant to join unions or in other ways certify a resented status—permanent wage workers. In Europe formerly dependent rural peasants accepted the discipline, and the dependent status, of factory work much more readily than did Americans.

Public policy has reflected these fears and resentments. Late in the nineteenth century federal legislation at least halfheartedly restricted trusts and monopolies and began to regulate the worst abuses of interstate firms. In the early twentieth century various reform groups tried to get more effective regulations over competitive and marketing practices, set up the first weak consumer protection laws, and at the state level began the first, tentative efforts to control working conditions (safety laws, child labor laws, workmen's compensation, and minimum wages for a few categories of workers). In this sense the government began to intrude into private management, but not in very basic ways. In the depression thirties we dramatically expanded the scope of regulation in banking, financial markets, labor-management relations, and agricultural production and pricing. Equally important, we much more strenuously enforced existing laws. In reaction to the depression, we virtually began our welfare state, with vast relief programs, the first forms of social security, categorical aid programs for the aged and for dependent children, a considerable public housing program, and all manner of lending and tax relief programs for other perceived public ends. The benefits of these New Deal programs largely extended downward to unemployed workers and financially beleaguered farmers, and up to numerous business and middle-income interests, but did not relate as closely to the problems of blacks or the very poorest groups, those who in the thirties had almost no political leverage.

After World War II, Democratic congressmen and President Harry Truman tried to extend both regulation and welfare benefits. They were successful in efforts to increase public housing and social security benefits and to raise minimum wages. They failed to gain public health insurance, equal employment opportunities for blacks, and federal aid for public schools. Generally, they ignored growing environmental problems, the worst problems of large cities, and deeply entrenched pockets of poverty. Any systematic extension of regulation and welfare ran aground on deep class and racial divisions. Labor legislation was hazardous because of divided sentiments about organized labor. Federal aid to education floundered on church-state issues. Even modest civil rights bills faced successful southern vetoes. And any open engagement of poverty touched sensitive nerves, not the least among those who met the criteria of poverty. Thus, by 1960, in the wake of an undaring Eisenhower administration, all these issues became agenda items for the new Kennedy-Johnson administration. But the roadblocks were high, seemingly insurmountable in the Kennedy years. Before his assassination he failed to get a major civil rights act, federal aid to education, and a large share of proposed environmental legislation through a reluctant Congress. This provides the background for the Great Society.

In five years the Johnson administration gained major legislation in all these areas. In such a brief time it at least doubled the scope of federal legislation, particularly in civil rights, environmental protection, and consumer protection. It more than doubled the number of welfare programs and by 1968, before the more costly programs were well under way, had already increased welfare payments by 45 percent. It gained a vast program of federal aid to education, along with over twenty education bills. It gained socialized health care for the aged and for low-income Americans. It passed, by far, the most daring housing and urban programs ever dreamed of in America. It secured three almost revolutionary civil rights acts, including virtually ironclad protection of voting rights for blacks, and fair employment opportunities for both blacks and women. It enacted a vast range of antipoverty programs, from food stamps to job corps to community action, with the latter daring in its direct involvement of the poor. It established the first major governmental support for the arts and humanities, secured several beautification bills, and made unprecedentedly rapid increases in the land devoted to parks, wildlife, and wilderness. Never before had the Congress passed so much critical legislation in such a short time. The pace of legislative action was three times that of the mid-thirties, the only other likely comparison.

By such a list of legislative initiatives I hope to make my point. This was the climax of the stream of corrective legislation that began in the late nineteenth century. Some use such loaded words as "progressive" and "liberal" to describe it, but such words obscure more than they clarify. I do not think this is the occasion to go into the details of the bills. They were complex but well drafted, resulted from the most extensive series of task force investigations ever attempted in America, and most of them turned out to do about what the supporters expected. In fact, over 90 percent of the legislation is still in effect and is at the heart of our domestic policy today. That is, much of the environmental, consumer, and occupational regulations of today came from the Great Society. The main props of federal welfare—food stamps, Medicare and Medicaid, categorical aids, particularly to families with dependent children, and dozens of targeted grant programs all date from, or received major increases during, the sixties. The three civil rights bills have revolutionized race relations in the South and jointly provide as sweeping a vindication of legal equality as any government can provide. The federal aid to education programs continue. Only some of the more daring urban and antipoverty programs have lapsed or been repealed. The Great Society lives on.

Why did it happen? I have four major answers. First, the death of Kennedy gave a martyr's veneer to many of the bills and did more than anything else to lessen effective opposition. Second, the dramatic expansion of federal programs came in a decade of unceasing economic growth. The costs seemed manageable, payable from annual increases of tax revenue without higher rates. We now know the prosperity was ephemeral, tied to several adventitious factors present in the sixties. But such legislation was inconceivable without prosperity, for so much of it was conscience legislation, directed at minority groups with little political power. Third, the legislative harvest reflected the superb political skills of our ablest president-legislator—Johnson. From the choice of academic task forces to skillful congressional liaison, he played the game perfectly. He courted and manipulated the needed congressmen, building majority coalitions on every major bill he proposed in 1964 and 1965. Soon the bills came so rapidly that not even congressmen understood more than a few. Finally, the legislation represented a belated harvest. Most of it had been brewing for years, and by now the regulatory-welfare approach had finally been accepted by Americans. It had become the orthodox way to deal with perceived problems. It was, in other words, not strange, new, or daring. Johnson was a master at defusing any ideological dynamite in bills. He never had a coherent program. He had no goal except to solve all the problems that people complained about. And who is against solving problems? Such a nonideological but generous program of needed repairs seemed conventional, and it was, except in the rapidity of change and the often unnoted long-term costs of many new programs, such as Medicare.

This American middle way stopped just a bit short of the social democratic policies adopted in western Europe and in Australia and New Zealand. That is, we have not intruded as much upon private management, and we have not adopted as many social welfare measures. We have tried to leave as many choices as possible open to private initiative, to avoid as much dependency as possible, and to maximize the leeway for private expression and pluralistic accommodation. We have tried to maintain a libertarian society and have compromised to an extent on an egalitarian one. We value individual freedom more than fraternity or solidarity. Our operative values are more individualistic than communal. A proprietary past, the absence of feudal deference or a state church, has carried over and shaped our accommodation with an independent economy, but not without tensions and strains.

In the sixties the most vocal dissent from a regulatory-welfare state came from the left. In the eighties the most vocal criticism has come from the right. Only one issue joins the two critical perspectives—a fear of dependence and powerlessness. The more radical critics of the sixties echoed Bellamy. Regulation and welfare only papered over the inequities of our economic system, even as our foreign policy forced the resource- and commodity-supplying third world to bear the burden for our consumptive cornucopia. Oligarchy and competition at home paralleled selfish consumer values, and an absence of communal values and rewards. Some youth repudiated libertarian freedoms, embraced solidarity, wanted to achieve an equality in returns, and quite frankly admired Cuba or Maoist China. But one can doubt that these critics, in the actual showdown, would be willing to sacrifice the living standards, the personal freedom, or the meritocratic rewards demanded by such communal systems. When tested, most Americans are addicted to all three.

All along right-wing critics have protested the dependency produced by welfare, and the loss of freedom occasioned by market-distorting regulation. A few latter-day disciples of Henry George still talk wistfully of restored property and free enterprise, a nice nostalgia trip but so utterly unrealistic as to seem more quaint than dangerous. Can one really imagine breaking up large concentrations of wealth and moving back toward individual or local cooperative ownership?

A majority of right-wing critics want much less—a return to less regulated competition among large firms, and fewer imposed priorities by government. They are relatively sanguine about major environmental problems, and argue that, in the long term, equity goals are better achieved by leaving people alone than by doling out welfare payments. Guiding much such criticism is older market or monetarist economic theory. Like the nineteenth-century Jacksonians, these people argue that controls and subsidies distort production, lower efficiency, and in the long term impoverish a society. Welfare destroys pride and self-confidence, creates permanent dependent classes, and is an ever-growing drain on the incomes of the productive classes. A welfare state faces proliferating claims for benefits, until soon everyone is a recipient of some privilege, and every aspect of life becomes politicized. To this there is no end.

Finally, such an intrusive state leads to a large, engorged, ultimately insensitive and inefficient bureaucracy.

What about the future? I see no early change in the direction of public policy. It is hard to imagine practical alternatives. Thus, in periodic shifts of political fashion, I suspect the right and left will, alternatively, force minor amendments in the scope of regulation and the extent of transfers. What seems most unlikely is any strong support for a socialization of plant. Few have such elevated opinions of our government, or of the possibilities of the political process, to see in nationalization any solution to problems even of equity, let alone as a means of realizing economic growth. Ironically, the government may, nonetheless, have to take over private firms, at least temporarily. If we move toward classic socialism, it will probably be because the government cannot, in times of recession, allow major corporations to cease production or major banks or other financial institutions to fail. If the United States moves toward increased government ownership, it will be because of rescue operations, or socialism by the back door.

4

✢

First Principles
of American Government

I now turn to a subject that has been at the center of my teaching and scholarship for over thirty years—the foundational principles that provide a moral sanction for American political and economic institutions. This kind of scholarship requires an engagement with normative political and economic theory and with the whole history of Western moral philosophy. These are not easy subjects. Yet I have lectured more often in these areas than any other, struggling to render very complex ideas in such clear and simple language that almost any American can understand the ideals that helped shape our most basic institutions. Here one confronts the most important commonality in our otherwise increasingly diverse society. At times I have been almost desperate to communicate effectively in this area. It has not been easy. The two speeches I include in this section involve some careful and subtle analysis. They will demand a more careful reading than any other in this book, in part because I tried to compress, in a brief space, some of the key insights from two of my books.

After years of work, in 1974 I published a relatively brief book with a very long title: *Self-Evident Truths, Being a Discourse on the Origins & Development of the First Principles of American Government—Popular Sovereignty, Natural Rights, and Balance & Separation of Powers* (Bloomington: University of Indiana Press). I had not written it with the bicentennial of our Declaration of Independence in mind, but of course readers quickly identified it as one of many books written to celebrate the bicentennial. In 1976 I was overwhelmed with invitations to lecture and gave at least one such lecture each month. Thus, I kept rethinking the themes in *Self-Evident Truths*. To complement the political analysis, I published a rather long book in 1980 on economic theory: *Prophets of Prosperity: America's First Political Economists* (Bloomington: Indiana University Press). Needless to say, this book led to few lecture invitations, but much of the content complemented *Self-Evident Truths*. Because both these books were largely accessible only to scholars, I wanted to make their content more accessible to student audiences. Thus, in 1994, I published a short, tightly focused book: *The Four Foundations of American Government* (Arlington Heights, Ill.: Harlan Davidson). I consider it, by far, the best book I ever wrote. Just as I completed this book, I used its chapters as the format of a week-long seminar at the University of Oklahoma. On one evening during that week, I presented a formal lecture at the law school on liberty, property, and expressive freedoms. This reflected what I thought were some of the most original and challenging themes in my forthcoming book.

In 1995 I accepted an invitation to give the keynote address at the annual conference of college history teachers in Indiana, in this case at the old communal site at New Harmony. Because the conference theme involved something called "democracy," I tried to open up most of the semantic traps created by this loaded word and in so doing drew heavily from a chapter in *Four Foundations*. Thus, this lecture complements the Oklahoma emphasis upon various forms of liberty or freedom.

Liberty, Property, and Expressive Freedoms

As many of you know, I am here to conduct a week-long seminar on the first principles of American government. The four themes are (1) popular or constitutional government, (2) limits on government or the problem of rights, (3) balanced government, or issues relating to form, and (4) democratic government, or the aspects of American government responsive to voters. For this paper I have chosen to speak not on a fully symmetrical topic, such as on the natural-rights trinity of life, liberty, and property. Instead, I want to focus on only two of these rights—liberty and property.

By the understanding of our founders, liberty and property were inherent, or natural, rights. They rested upon objective moral standards, standards rooted in nature or nature's god, and thus universally applicable. Anyone who thinks about what is right or wrong will concede that respect for life, for liberty, and for the products of one's labor is morally obligatory. Conversely, to deprive others of life, to enslave others, or to steal their hard-earned property, is to do wrong. A right, in this context, is the opposite of a wrong, and such rights are, by definition, inseparable from personhood and thus inalienable. I am not ignoring the right to life because its status is obvious or its meaning always clear (the abortion debate is witness to contested meanings), but because I want to incorporate into my lecture what, to many Americans, now seem the most important rights of all—those expressive rights listed in the First Amendment. I hope to demonstrate that such expressive rights are not parallel to, or in many senses even comparable to, natural rights.

The word "liberty" is so ambiguous today that it invites confusion. The meaning, in natural rights theory, comes closest to "being at liberty": autonomous, independent, free from any involuntary subordination to other people or to governments. The opposite of being at liberty is being a slave or being in prison, or in any situation in which one's person is under the control of others. The emphasis upon liberty, particularly by aggrieved minorities, makes up a modern and continuing project—to escape from disabilities tied to birth or family, not to merit or achievement.

The eighteenth-century defense of liberty did not mean a repudiation of all types of hierarchy and subordination. Certain forms of dependency seemed rooted in nature—the abject dependency of children, and the semidependency of women based on the assumed weaknesses of gender. Nor did a right to liberty preclude various types of voluntary, contractual dependence, as in indentures, apprenticeships, and wage employment. The claim to liberty was directed at ascriptive and inherited disabilities, those recognized and honored by the state, such as black slavery in America, remnants of feudalism in Europe, or other inherited and legally based privileges, such as special land-owning or hunting prerogatives. If liberty is a natural right, then all forms of arbitrary and involuntary or birth-determined dependence represent natural wrongs, examples of injustice. Implicit in the claim to liberty is that God did not so make humans as to create some as dependents, some as masters. When people live in a state of nature—that is, without a government—no one has jurisdiction over another. Each is equally responsible for obeying, and enforcing, the only law there is—the moral law. Thus Jefferson's eloquent wording: "All men are created equal."

Such liberty clearly implicates property. Without access to productive property, one is necessarily dependent on others. In American history the appeal to liberty has remained very important. Excluded classes of people—particularly women, blacks, and homosexuals—those that have suffered disabilities because of their status, because of birth or group characteristics, have continually appealed to their right to liberty. They have begged and appealed and occasionally fought to get official recognition that they, too, were born equal. This is an ongoing struggle, at least for homosexuals.

Property, as a natural right, is the most contested and complex of all the trinity of rights. It became one of the trinity when early-modern Europeans tried to deduce the implications of justice, or what had traditionally been the standard moral justification for government. As the sixteenth-century disciples of John Calvin, the Huguenots, tried to win acceptance in France, their more radical spokesmen condemned French monarchs for monopolizing salt mines or other natural resources that God had given to all the people. They claimed a right of free access to such resources, or one of the earliest specific claims to a right to property. Yet it was John Locke, more than anyone before him, who recognized the perplexing problems of equity posed by property. In a confusing, exceedingly elliptical way, he tried to introduce a new level of clarity to discussions of property rights in his *Second Treatise of Government*. His chapter "On Property" is one of the classic texts of Western civilization.

Implicit in Locke's chapter was his appreciation that the most compelling reason for a people to join together in a commonwealth involves property. In primitive hunting and gathering societies, where natural resources easily supply all human needs, government might rightly seem more of a danger than a necessity. Locke mistakenly thought native Americans lived outside any commonwealth, in a state of nature. Because of its economic privations, he did not glorify such a simple life. As population increases, nature cannot supply human needs without cultivation. This complicates social relationships, for cultivation at least requires the enclosure of fields and protected access to them. This raised dramatically the potential for jealousy and competition, and thus the likelihood of insecurity, conflict, and overt warfare.

It was the next step in human progress that made political organization all but inevitable—commercial exchange based on the use of money. In a sense Locke made money the serpent in the garden of innocence, for it permits accumulations of great wealth by a few, in some cases legitimately, but with the danger of monopoly and privilege on one hand, jealousies and resentments on the other. Such complex exchange also raises enormously the problem of determining what distributive justice requires. In a commercial economy, it is no longer convenient for each individual to be responsible for enforcing the moral law. Problems of equity now invite continuous friction. A commercial society simply cries out for government and a growing body of statutory law to regulate all complex property relationships. It is in this sense that property is the root cause of government, and laws governing property relationships the major responsibility of any government. Locke easily collapsed life and liberty into property and thus, at times, sounded as if the only critical issue in political theory was property.

He was correct in his logic if not in the implied historical progression of human societies. Thus, Locke emphasized the need for government (the terrible insecurities of a commercial society without government), the proper ends a legitimate government must serve (primarily the protection of legitimate property), the ways a government comes into existence (by the consent of people increasingly insecure in their estates and possessions), and the principal abuses by government (failure to protect the just property of citizens or, even worse, the arbitrary confiscation of private property).

To sustain his argument not only for government, but for limits upon government, Locke had to demonstrate that property is a natural or universal right. This meant that, in a state of nature, with no government and no statutory laws regulating possessions, individuals have a moral claim to certain types of possessions, and that other people have a moral obligation to respect these possessions. If this were not the case in a state of nature, then no one in a civil society could claim an inherent or morally inalienable right to any type of property. All property claims would then rest upon positive law, justified by utility rather than by objective right.

What forms of property are natural? Locke set very strict limits. In a hunting and gathering society, one assimilates any harvested nuts or berries to oneself by labor, by harvesting them. One has a moral claim to them, so long as one does not gather more than one can consume, and so long as one's gathering does not preclude others from access to such foods. The principle here is that God gave the fruit of the earth to humans in common. Originally the earth was one great commons, as it still is for primitive people.

Locke also believed God gave land and mineral resources to all people. When cultivation becomes necessary to support a growing population, or to raise living standards, then access to and enclosure of prepared fields becomes a form of natural property, made so by the labor involved in improvements and limited by what is needed for the consumption of the possessing families. Locke even stipulated that enclosure was not a natural right if it excluded others from land of equal quality, or a restriction so severe that it left begging what people were to do when land scarcity became the rule. These two types of property—labor-assimilated products directly from nature, and secure access to enclosed and improved parts of nature—exhausted the forms of natural property. One can claim a moral right only to such property. Even in a civil society, one in which positive laws regulate all forms of ownership, a person still has a claim to these two forms of property. In this sense the right to property is a positive claim upon a society, a right through labor to acquire and hold certain possessions and to have a protected access to the bounty of nature. Such property is necessary for being at liberty and also for sustaining life.

For Locke money was not a natural form of property, and in origin not a statutory form either. By "money" he meant a conventional medium of exchange, usually precious metals. These are not consumable. This means one has no moral claim of access to them. In an argument full of implications, but one of the most challengeable in all of his writings, Locke asserted that all humankind, or at least all who lived in developed societies, had consented to the use of money. Thus, money rested not on nature, not on positive law, but on universal consent. Until money, great accumulations of property were inherently wrong, contrary to the law of nature, for they involved waste or monopoly control over what others had to have for a livelihood. With a money economy one could exchange an excess of consumable items for money, without depriving anyone of food. Some people might, through time, accumulate great wealth in the form of money, which gave them enormous power to buy labor, tools, or consumer goods.

In a state of nature, accumulation was wrong only when it led to waste or excluded other people from nature. Such accumulation could easily become monopolistic and exclusive and thus invited, even necessitated, governmental regulation to protect the threatened rights of poor citizens or, in rare cases, the just claims of the affluent against aggression by the jealous poor. Locke did not address the multiple implications present in his theories about property. From one perspective the likelihood of early scarcity seemed to preclude individual property and require some form of communal ownership and fair rules of distribution—or what would become, reared on Locke's own labor theory of value, various single-tax or socialist programs. Yet Locke's openness to money, commercial transactions, and large accumulations of wealth easily suggested a free-market economy, and indeed some of Locke's work in political economy pointed toward Adam Smith. What was unambiguous in Locke was the natural status of certain types of possession, and thus the obligation of any government that claims legitimacy to protect property along with liberty and life. What was most radical in Locke was his claim that a legitimate, limited government, whatever the forms of statutory property it creates, cannot by right prevent people from gaining access to their share of nature, to what God gave to the whole human family.

When Americans declared their independence in 1776, it was on the basis that Britain had threatened their liberty and their property. As the various former colonies formed new governments, they each tried to make clear the rights for which they avowedly fought. They did this either in the preamble to their constitutions or in declarations of right. The Virginia Declaration included the most influential statement of natural rights and thus of the right to property. George Mason, its author, stressed that people have certain inherent rights when they enter society. Even in creating constitutions, a people cannot "deprive or divest their posterity" of these rights, "namely the enjoyment of life and liberty, with the means of acquiring and possessing property, and pursuing and obtaining happiness and safety." A month later, when Jefferson composed the preamble to the Declaration of Independence, he abbreviated Mason's more precise wording. At the time, his elliptical phrasing could not confuse anyone, for the listing of natural rights had become formulaic. "That all men are created equal. That they are endowed by their creator with certain unalienable rights: that among these are life, liberty, and the pursuit of happiness."

In time Americans seemed to lose any understanding of property as a natural right. In particular they failed to appreciate its positive and radical meaning. Today such has been the vulgarization of the meaning of property rights that some miss the whole point, or even view property rights as the reverse of human rights. They do not equate property rights with economic opportunity. The right to property is first of all a right to have something, and only then, under careful qualifications, a right to retain possessions. The right of access to nature, to the means of our subsistence, is not the same as a right to a job. In fact, employment may entail so much dependence as to threaten liberty, and a society that sets major barriers to either individual or cooperative ownership of the means of production jeopardizes property. Natural property is the type that assures independence and autonomy, that frees one from dependence upon a master, that allows responsible individual or collective decision making about its use, that bestows pride and self-respect.

By the American Revolution the understanding of "rights" was in flux. Out of this flux came some of the confusions that still reduce "rights talk" to a shouting match. The word "right," in natural rights reasoning, had an exclusively moral content. It was not leeway to do something, a permitted sphere of action. If a right is permissive, a matter of uninhibited expression, then clearly it is not unalienable or inherent. A government can grant such permissions or withdraw them. To talk this way is to leave completely behind the ancient tradition of natural rights. Yet even by the American Revolution such uses of the word "right" had already begun to confuse political discourse.

Involved in natural rights is an appeal to authority. In a sense the preamble to the Declaration of Independence, and the more extended rights claims in state declarations, reflected an American update of the ancient idea of divine rights. The appeal to nature, to the order of things, to what God created or intended, to objective and universal moral standards, is an appeal beyond any human institution. As Mason put it in Virginia, the sovereign people, even in forming their sacred covenants of government, cannot deprive their posterity of these rights. It is because these are divine rights that they are beyond the power of government. They define the limits on any government worthy of human allegiance. Moral principles, or natural law, is thus a type of unwritten constitution that is one step above any human-created charter of government. Bills of rights may call attention to such rights but are in no sense the source of or justification of them.

In colonial America most white males, when not indentured, enjoyed their natural rights and were proud of it. They proudly claimed the status of free men. Insofar as governments involved elections, they could aspire to votes, at least when they met certain requirements, such as property ownership. Above all, they could own property, usually meaning a farm. And in their dealings with government they enjoyed traditional English procedural rights, or what seemed to be critical to the rights of life, liberty, and property. In all these ways they had escaped the last remnants of feudal dependency, and a Europe in which only a minority of people had any chance to own unencumbered land or capital. It was the liberating economic reality of America that gave new meaning to both liberty and property. It is ironic that, today, when Americans speak of freedom, they rarely refer to economic opportunity, or to ownership, but rather they usually refer to First Amendment freedoms—press, speech, petition, assembly, and worship. By any measurement we today enjoy much greater freedom in these expressive areas—so much so that most colonial Americans would be horrified. It is not as clear that we have a comparable access to property, or that we have as much autonomy or independence, as did our colonial forebears.

What has changed? Colonial Americans usually lived in cohesive and homogeneous communities, very similar to traditional European villages. In their tight communities they were exclusive and repressive, particularly in New England, among the very Americans who earliest and loudest proclaimed popular sovereignty and natural rights. Puritans generally wanted more government, more discipline, not less. After all, governments exist to enforce rules. By definition governments restrict what citizens may do. In a sense all laws restrict some form of self-expression. Laws force people to be righteous. The goal of government is morality. That is what legislation is about, to assure a minimal level of responsibility on the part of citizens. The full demands of morality may extend far beyond what governments try to control, but the most basic demands of morality are exactly what governments attend to, beginning with such obvious crimes as murder, rape, and theft. Governments tell people that they will receive punishment if they so express themselves as to kill or maim or leave destitute other people. In puritan New England the people demanded tough laws and generally supported rigorous enforcement, and over a much wider area of personal expression than today. They did not want their villages defiled by blasphemous or heterodox speech, by heretical religious sects, by an irresponsible or slanderous press. Thus, they enacted laws that severely regulated or restricted such forms of expression, even as they also strictly regulated economic activity.

What changed, in time, was the social context. Even the colonies soon became more diverse, particularly in the cities. However exclusive and repressive the local villages throughout America, the colonies as a whole had to accommodate at least some diversity. At the same time, political institutions became more mature, fears of disorder and anarchy lessened, and political factions or parties competed for office. This meant a more pluralistic social order. In states like Rhode Island and Pennsylvania, with numerous sects or ethnic groups, tolerance became a means of public order, not the opposite. By the Revolution, and the political divisions and struggles within each colony, Americans were increasingly demanding more leeway in speech and press. At the federal level, if not in all the states, religious diversity mandated not just tolerance but state neutrality and protection of freedom in worship. By the Alien and Sedition acts of 1798, the Jeffersonian Republicans, the main target of rather severe federal repression, fought for enlarged conceptions of free speech and press, although not nearly the leeway taken for granted today.

Expressive rights are very different from natural rights. They are not inherent and do not involve an appeal to universal moral standards. In principle all expressive rights are context determined and relative, and necessarily defined by constitutional or statutory law. It may be good policy to allow a wide leeway for private speech, but such leeway is never absolute. Even in the most libertarian society, such as contemporary America, governments have to enforce limits upon speech and press, as reflected in laws against malicious slander. The leeway allowed can shift according to circumstances, as reflected in wartime censorship. What a citizen can claim in the way of expressive leeway is only what the commonwealth establishes. In this sense governments grant and define such rights. In America the justification of expanded leeway for private expression has more often been utility than moral right. The virtual exemption of public officials from the protection of slander laws is now justified by the need to keep our political process open. One of the most effective arguments against the 1798 Sedition Act was the need, in republican America, for well-informed citizens.

The transition in the understanding of rights was well under way by the ratification of the federal Constitution of 1787. It contained no bill of rights. The delegates considered such but, aware of the pitfalls in gaining an acceptable document, ultimately included in the preamble only a phrase—"secure the blessings of liberty to ourselves and our posterity." Because the Constitution granted only specific powers to the new federal government, no detailed list of rights seemed necessary. The eloquent statements of such at the state level seemed sufficient, and Alexander Hamilton, in *The Federalist*, so defended the omission, and in addition pointed out the pitfalls of any detailed list (by implication, the federal government might claim authority in areas not mentioned).

Despite the cogency of Hamilton's arguments, opponents of the Constitution leaped on the omission of guaranteed rights and persuaded large numbers of Americans that this was a fatal flaw. Even Jefferson, who had been in France during the convention, was alarmed at such an omission. Thus, in several states the proponents of the Constitution assured delegates to state ratifying conventions that they would work, in the first Congress, for a series of rights amendments. The first Congress considered many such amendments, approved twelve, and the required number of states ratified ten, or what we now somewhat confusingly call our Bill of Rights.

These ten amendments involved a great deal more than either natural rights or expressive freedoms. One involved state-federal relations, another expressed state solicitude for a local militia and thus a protected local privilege to bear arms. One symbolic but soon anachronistic amendment denied to the federal government the right to quarter troops in private homes. The only direct reaffirmation of natural rights was in a section of Amendment Five (no person can "be deprived of life, liberty, or property, without due process of law"). Five complex amendments added to the three procedural safeguards already in the Constitution (the right of habeas corpus, no bills of attainder, and no ex post facto laws). These five amendments placed severe restrictions on search and seizure, required grand jury indictments, protected citizens from double jeopardy and self-incrimination, guaranteed a speedy trial before a local jury of peers, extended the right of jury trial to major civil cases, required a clear bill of indictment, gave the accused the right to confront witnesses and to subpoena witnesses, provided for assistance of counsel, and prohibited excessive bail or cruel and unusual punishments. Although in no sense natural rights, or universally applicable, these constraints seemed well-calculated means to protect life, liberty, and property. In total these dozen procedural mandates represent the most sweeping and inclusive limitations upon police and prosecutorial authority ever devised.

The newly valued expressive freedoms were all listed in the First Amendment. This amendment denied the federal Congress any power to make laws abridging freedom of speech or the press, or limiting the right of the people peaceably to assemble or to petition their government for a redress of grievances. Because the Constitution did not grant to Congress any law-making power in these areas, this part of the amendment seemed redundant or, possibly, dangerous. Did it now mean Congress could enact laws concerning speech, press, assembly, or petition so long as such laws did not abridge the existing level of freedom? The First Amendment also clarified the relationship of the new federal government to religion. The government could not enact laws "respecting an establishment of religion," a provision at the time that removed fears that the federal government might interfere with state establishments (as in three New England states) or with religious disabilities for minorities in almost every state constitution. It is doubtful that Congress, when it submitted this amendment, envisioned any attempt at a federal establishment. Finally, this amendment provided that Congress could not prohibit the free exercise of religion, a limitation upon federal power that did not always coexist easily with the establishment clause.

These constitutional amendments placed restrictions only on the federal government. The states continued to violate many of these guarantees well into the twentieth century. Because of a lack of uniformity, and local violations of procedures well established at the national level, the most important rights amendment of all would be the fourteenth, one ratified just after the Civil War. Already the Thirteenth Amendment had abolished slavery and thus brought blacks into the arena of freedom and, in theory, of guaranteed rights. Later the nineteenth would almost do this for women. Ostensibly to add further force to emancipation, Congress approved the Fourteenth Amendment and required ratification by southern states as a condition of restored representation in Congress (this added a coercive aspect to its ratification).

Only the first two sections of the Fourteenth Amendment expanded rights. Section 2, by tying representation in Congress to the number of permissible voters, was a lame attempt to give the vote to blacks, but this section was quickly superseded by the Fifteenth Amendment. Section 1 is the most important single part of our present Constitution. It made all persons born and naturalized in the United States citizens of the United States and the state in which they resided. This was the first recognition of national citizenship. It then set up a series of limitations on state governments: They could not abridge the privileges or immunities of any citizen, deprive any person of life, liberty, or property without due process of law, nor deny to any person in their jurisdiction the equal protection of the laws. These provisions created one national community and one citizenry. The sweeping limitations upon the states had one clear goal—protection of the rights of freedmen. The courts would first extend the reach of these limitations to protect corporations (legal persons) against state regulation. In the twentieth century the courts would, in a series of cases, use the due process and equal protection clauses to force the states to live up to the standard of the federal Bill of Rights (often called incorporation). In this sense the Fourteenth Amendment universalized the Bill of Rights.

At the time the states ratified the First Amendment, their intent was to endorse a level of expressive freedom just about midway between the exclusive and quite repressive puritan towns of the seventeenth century, and the wide-open libertarian society of today. The Puritans so valued communal order and rigorous and uniform moral standards that they, at least in their towns, approached a type of totalitarianism—a shared truth, no room for dissent, and the ostracism, exclusion, or punishment of those who would not accept the local orthodoxy. Literally, the village was a society in which everyone scrutinized everyone else, and in which everyone was a policeman in behalf of conformity. Such a tight communal order was completely consistent with liberty and property, but not with any leeway for deviance. But the town was a small local community, voluntary in origin. In the larger context of British empire, the Puritans desired a much greater tolerance for diversity. After all, they were religious dissenters themselves. Even as they refused admittance of Quakers, they defended their right to settle in Pennsylvania.

Here we have a type of distributive pluralism. In 1791 the First Amendment endorsed such a pluralism. The amendment prohibited federal suppression of speech or press or federal regulation of religion. In the union as a whole diversity could prevail, and did. At the state and local level repression remained the norm, although from the seventeenth century on local governments had gradually permitted more self-expression or imposed milder sentences for irresponsible speech or publishing. Religious toleration was all but universal in the United States, but not yet equality for all religious groups.

Since 1791 the United States has moved from a distributive pluralism—wide leeway for expression within the nation, varied and more limited leeway in local communities—to an inclusive pluralism. The Fourteenth Amendment marked the formal side of such a transition. The actual transition in attitudes and practice is largely a twentieth-century phenomenon, and the transition is far from complete even yet. By "inclusive pluralism" I mean a social order in which widely diverse people, with varying beliefs and values, enjoy the right to affirm and live such beliefs anywhere in America. They do not have to retreat to their local, isolated communities to do their own thing. They can do it anywhere—affirm what a majority may view as the most eccentric or dangerous beliefs, live out the most esoteric preferences or fantasies. Today the Bill of Rights, which originally protected local and often repressive communities from federal intervention, now forces local governments to grant freedom of speech, press, and worship to any minority that asks for protection. The irony is most visible in religion. The same provision of the First Amendment that originally prevented federal laws controlling local establishments of religion now precludes local establishments.

The enduring problem with expressive freedoms is one of policy: What is the proper mix of communal solidarity and enforced responsibility on one side, and of tolerance and individual self-expression on the other? Almost no one wants to go back to the puritan model of local solidarity, but many now yearn for the sense of community, the soothing commonalities of belief and values, the strong sense of almost sacrificial communal responsibility, the clear sense of identity and standards, that marked formerly homogeneous towns and villages. As the new communal movement testifies, many Americans want to return to the village, not revolt against it.

Today almost no one wants to go to the other extreme—to a libertarian social order with almost no limits on self-expression. We moved closest to that in the sixties for forms of cultural expression; closest to it in the eighties in entrepreneurial self-expression. A few still affirm a libertarian society in all areas of self-expression. They want no limits, not just on the most expansive meanings of speech, press, or religion, but on drug use, on economic enterprise, on commercial transactions, on environmental exploitation. The haunting problem of a libertarian society is that of identity and ultimately even sanity. Indeed, if a wide array of beliefs and values are shared and internalized, we may need few laws. But in the midst of our present diversity, in a society that has essayed, more than any before it in history, to create a social order that encompasses all races, all religions, and at least a great range of cultural differences, we clearly do not have enough shared and internalized beliefs or values to hold us all together. Thus, the contemporary confusions, the loneliness, and the craving for a renewed sense of communal responsibility, for solidarity and unity.

In the past, dominant local majorities in America denied a voice, and power, to minorities. Officially, we have reversed ourselves. We both affirm the equality, and thus the inherent or natural rights, of all people, even as we grant everyone a wide leeway for self-expression. We have finally given every minority a voice, although in the babble of shouted claims we may not be able to hear them. In my estimation expressive freedoms reflect the easy national achievement—our political institutions are still so stable, our often unnoticed commonalities of basic belief so well internalized, that it is not a great risk to allow everyone to say or write almost anything he or she wants, or to affirm and practice whatever religion one finds appealing. The more difficult national commitment is what it was in 1776—to juristic equality and natural rights. These rights involve the great, enduring issues of equity and of justice.

Democracy

"Democracy" has become a rich word. It suggests many different images. Accordingly, it is so ambiguous today as to be almost useless. I never use the word in polite company. But today my assigned topic involves the word, even as it is the key term for this conference. Thus, I will join most of the previous speakers at this conference and try to address the announced theme: democracy in historical perspective.

Until the late eighteenth century, in both Europe and America, the word "democracy" generally had a pejorative meaning. Today, in spite of all the ambiguities, the word usually has a positive meaning. Around the world diverse governments and a wide spectrum of political parties claim the label. This dramatic shift in the popularity of the word reflects not so much a change in moral and political theory as a shift in the specific images intended by the label. One can trace the shift from a pejorative use in colonial America, to the harsh condemnation by John Adams, to a more positive image by the early nineteenth century, to a celebratory use by Andrew Jackson and George Bancroft in the 1830s, or to a somewhat different and much more anxious use by Alexis de Tocqueville.

In its literal, etymological sense, "democracy" means rule by the people. This is not very helpful. It begs criteria for defining a people and for determining what it means to rule. In fact, beginning with Greek city-states, democracy has almost always entailed majority rule by a quite restricted class of citizens. In this use a democracy is a political system in which citizens, however admitted to this privilege, either meet in assemblies to pass laws and to appoint those who enforce them, or, in larger commonwealths, gather on regular occasions to elect, and instruct, delegates to a governing assembly.

So defined, a democracy had a bad press from Aristotle on, and for good reason. It meant unlimited rule by a majority. It meant a simple and absolute form of government. No moral constraints and no traditional covenants or constitutions defined and limited its powers. No aristocracy had a veto on popular enactments. No chief magistrate mediated between the few and many or provided a symbol of unity for the whole community.

Already my language has implicated the two major concerns about a democratic form of government: One is class based, the other rooted in moral philosophy or religious beliefs. The class concern has been expressed in all theories of mixed government, beginning with those of Aristotle and Polybius. A democracy, in which power resides completely in the broad mass of people, fails to protect and to utilize the talents of an aristocracy, whether such an aristocracy rests upon birth, talent, virtue, wealth, or charisma. Without such an aristocratic balance, it seemed to almost everyone that a democracy would be vulnerable to momentary passions, to factionalism, and to the allure of demagogues. It would yield to the majority in all cases and thus not be able to reflect the interest of the whole community. It also would lack a principle of unity at the top. Thus, a democracy was likely to be very unstable, and out of such instability would come a demand, by the people, for a tyrant or dictator to restore order. Of all simple, unbalanced, and absolute forms of government—monarchy, aristocracy, and democracy—a democracy seemed most dangerous.

In addition to suffering from a lack of class balance, a democracy lacked any principle of authority above that of sheer, massed numbers. A majority in a popular assembly can do as it wishes, even to the point of enslaving or killing unpopular minorities. It faces no limits, not that of a higher or god-given moral law or even the constraints of tradition and custom. Thus, a democracy was an illegitimate form of government, for any legitimate government is limited, a government of laws rather than of people, of right rather than of sheer massed power.

Americans have never chosen a democratic form of government. They perhaps came closest in puritan New England. In small towns, as in later villages and towns throughout most of America, local majorities often assumed near absolute power, freely repressed unwanted minorities, and ignored whatever constraints existed in charters or constitutions. Such local majorities, in homogeneous communities, often moved very close to a totalitarian form of democracy. That is, they demanded adherence to a local orthodoxy in belief, enforced strict conformity to local moral standards, and often brutally suppressed or ostracized minorities who rejected communal values. Yet in the degree and depth of citizen involvement, such totalitarian democracies came closer than any others to the ideal typical democracy that almost everyone condemned until the eighteenth century. Note that such defenders of the New England way as Governor John Winthrop always denied that the Puritans had fallen into democracy. He argued that the people accepted constraints upon their power, such as the laws of God and the provisions of charters.

I have just published a small book on the four foundations of American government. In the book I try to show how democratic participation relates to the other three foundations. Americans at the time of indpendence, or soon thereafter, committed themselves to governments that were based upon the consent of a sovereign people, limited by objective moral criteria, balanced in form, and only then open to continuing participation by citizens.

A belief that governments, to be legitimate, have to rest on the consent of those governed was an early gospel in colonial America. This belief led in America to a unique constitutional process, one that transcends the ordinary work of government. The people are sovereign. They have a moral right to determine the form and powers of their governments. The governments they establish are never sovereign, but dependent. In America these principles led to a distinctive constitutional process—elected constitutional conventions, popular ratification, provisions for amendment, and a special form of constitutional review by courts. Nothing in the doctrine of consent, or popular sovereignty, mandates that a people choose a government directly responsive to popular majorities, and no American governments would be democratic in this sense. But even if an unwise people should choose a single assembly democracy, that assembly is still as much a creature of their sovereignty, as subject to the terms of their constitution, as is a constitutional monarch.

Perhaps even more important in America were moral limits on government. Americans made clear that even the people in drafting constitutions had no moral right to violate certain constraints that relate closely to the reasons that people choose to have government. In the eighteenth century a belief in such constraints rested on a conviction that all people are subject to an objective moral order, a higher law, and thus aware of conduct that is universally wrong, contrary to right reason, to conscience, or to God's will. Those who govern have a moral duty to uphold such universal principles of right. In particular, a government should promote justice and provide the possibilities of happiness for all citizens by respecting and protecting their inalienable or natural right to life, to liberty, and, most important because most vulnerable, to property, in the sense of secure access to one's share of nature and the right to retain the hard-won products of one's own labor. These moral limits on any legitimate government, one worthy of respect and obedience, created the tradition of reserved rights, often reflected in bills or declarations of right.

How can a people keep governments from violating natural rights or exceeding the powers delegated to them? This is a question of means. The American answer involved a particular type of republican government that incorporated aspects of traditional mixed government, with its internal checks and balances, and aspects of the modern idea of a separation of branches and functions. From the ancient concept of mixture Americans chose bicameral assemblies and a strong monarchlike executive.

Drawing upon the more modern idea of separation, Americans rejected a parliamentary system, with its overlap of executive and legislative branches. But Americans did not move to complete separation. Instead, they designed governments with only partially separate branches and gave each branch enough functional overlap with others to assure its own independence. They hoped these complex internal checks and balances would impede the direct implementation of popular or oligarchical opinion.

Only within the context of constitutional delegation, reserved rights, and internal balances did Americans choose a form of government that provided for broad popular participation. Voting is only part of this story. But elections are at least one means to keep governments honest and righteous. This is the democratic principle in our governments, and one often misunderstood. The actual role of citizens would depend, in ways not anticipated by those who designed early constitutions, upon the role of a two-party system. Within all the constraints, citizens have always had a powerful influence upon the choice of leaders and the choice of policies, but note that the constraints—the submission to a higher moral law and to constitutional covenants, plus the formal balancing mechanisms—have generally but not always (remember 1861) prevented deep divisions over the most basic issues. They have protected politics in America from the historical dangers of mass politics or the tyranny of majorities.

When Americans, after 1776, had the opportunity to create new governments, they severely constrained what citizens or their representatives could do. The moral constraints, still tied to Semitic theism and a belief in inherent natural rights, set what John Rawls has called side constraints on government. It is out of bounds for the federal government, and today state governments, arbitrarily to take a life, to enslave a person, to deny access to economic opportunities, in the same sense that torture is not a legitimate tool in interrogating criminal suspects. Not only have we constrained governments by a conception of inviolate human rights, by what we perceive as broad and general but still universally applicable ethical mandates, but we further constrained our federal government by procedural guarantees that rest not on nature or a higher law, but on English precedents.

Given all these limits upon the popular will, one may conclude that very little in America was democratic. Not so. Constitutional and moral limits on government, plus the impediments to hasty action lodged in various balancing mechanisms, made broad popular participation relatively safe and thus widely applauded. Even in the colonial period our governments had been unusually open to citizen input and to office holding. The accessibility of land or other tools of production created a proprietary society. Most white male heads of households could aspire to ownership of land or the tools of an artisan, and thus to freemanship. Voting did not mean then what it does today, and always in any polity the most critical issues are best resolved by some type of consensus, not by majority votes. But in various informal ways propertied citizens had access to policy making, at times a great deal more effective access than today. By the Revolution few religious disabilities remained in any state, and property or taxable qualifications were minimal. In this sense we began with a responsive polity, or a limited and constitutional form of democracy. On the most basic issues we had a rule of law. On more proximate issues of policy, the people or their representatives decided.

The first independent state governments were more directly responsive to citizens than today. Of course, they more severely limited access to citizenship, but for citizens the leeway for effecting majority opinion was increased by state constitutions that severely curtailed the power of governors, made some upper houses appointive, and thus gave a preponderance of power to elected lower houses. In time all the states pulled back from such dominant assemblies, with new constitutions providing for strong governors with modified veto powers, elected senates, and increased prestige and power for appointive judges. In other words, the states eventually modeled their state governments on the federal Constitution of 1787 and in this sense backed away from a more direct, populistic type of democracy. They heeded the widespread call for more internal checks and balances.

No doubt the vulnerability of early state governments to popular majorities had something to do with the call for a convention in the summer of 1787. It seemed to many influential Americans, including those struggling with the budgetary and diplomatic weaknesses of the federal government under the articles, that democratic politics at the state level had been irresponsible. The states, often under popular pressures, had failed to pay their federal assessments, had so reneged on foreign debts as to jeopardize the faith and credit of the union, had experimented with reckless and inflationary paper currencies, and had in some cases lacked the capacity to control local factionalism or, in Massachusetts, an open rebellion.

The new federal Constitution did not reverse a trend toward a broader franchise at the local level. It accelerated it. What it did was remove from state jurisdiction several powers that the states had allegedly abused. In a sense the federal Constitution severely diminished the dangers that popular factions posed to an effective diplomacy, to a unified and well-funded military, to prosperous foreign trade, and perhaps above all to a protected internal common market. By federalizing these issues the Constitution made it safe to permit a large degree of popular democracy at the state level. Because the subsequent amendments that we now call the Bill of Rights applied only to the federal government, this meant, among other things, that local majorities could continue to repress and abuse minorities as they saw fit. Majority rule is usually antithetical to liberty, but the concerns that led to a new federal Constitution reflected fears about a prosperous commercial order much more than any solicitude for local minorities.

What the federal Constitution did was specifically exclude from state jurisdiction the very powers that had, from a national perspective, led to gross abuse. Thus, the federal Constitution not only enumerated the powers of the new federal Congress, but it also specifically denied to the states any control over foreign policy, money and currency, and tariffs, and forbade states from enacting bills of attainder, passing ex post facto laws, or impairing contracts. With great circumspection because of intense local loyalties to state militia, the Constitution provided for federalizing local militia in times of emergency and set the rules and regulations for such state armies. In the guaranty clause it also secured the power to intervene to protect republicanism at the state level and, on request of governors, to use force to quell popular insurgencies. These extensions of federal power, and critical new limitations on state governments, alleviated the gravest concerns over irresponsible democracy at the state level.

Note one often overlooked effect of the new federal Constitution: Because it isolated common national issues from the control of local majorities or local factions, it offered a continuing license for state governments to do what they wanted in accommodating a populistic form of politics. For example, it made it reasonably safe for states to grant the franchise to wage-dependent workers, a nice sop to those who had fewer and fewer opportunities to own land or tools.

This federal license for unchecked local democracy would erode after the Civil War, and in two major respects. One would be the enlargement of federal economic and environmental regulation, on behalf of a better functioning internal market and at times on behalf of greater fairness. The other, and today most obvious, check, was the shift from a distributive pluralism, one in which state governments or local majorities could do what they wanted, to the inclusive pluralism of today. Formally anchored in twentieth-century interpretations of the due process and equal rights clauses of the Fourteenth Amendment, the federal government now protects minority rights at the local level, often against the intense hostility of local majorities. In these two areas—economic regulation and protection of minority rights—the federal government has placed major new limitations upon local democracy. It has even invaded the formerly most sacrosanct spheres of local democratic control, such as enforcement of criminal law, control over public schools, and the embodiment in law of sectarian religious beliefs and values. In this sense local majorities are less powerful in America than ever before, and a rule of law more determinative.

Objective authority, not votes, controls the most critical issues. I would therefore argue that in America the power of local majorities has steadily eroded from around 1900 to the present.

At the federal level the trend has been somewhat different. In the immediate aftermath of the ratification of the federal Constitution, the development of a two-party system eroded the effort at Philadelphia to balance the popularly elected House with carefully screened and indirectly elected presidents and senators. Much more than anyone at Philadelphia expected or desired, both the presidency and the Senate quickly became political and partisan offices, directly responsive to majorities. The two-party system, anchored and supported by the unit rule that came to prevail under the electoral college, focused issues, gave added power to popular presidents, effectively neutralized many of the intended checking devices during times of one-party dominance, contaminated local elections by the pull of party platforms or the appeal of candidates for national office, and at rare intervals such as in the 1930s created great pressures against even the prestige and independence of federal courts. Thus, in the perspective of 1787, local majorities have lost power, national majorities gained power, but in both cases one has to emphasize the continued constraints of constitutions, reserved rights, and internal checks.

I now want to consider other images that many people associate with the word "democracy." First is a form of equality, to broach another hopelessly loaded word. Jefferson placed this concept in the Declaration of Independence in one eloquent phrase: "All men are created equal." At the time the meaning was crystal clear. In nature, without government, no adult is rightfully subject to another. All forms of dependence and subordination are artificial, products of human institutions. Thus, as God created humans, they were all equally free and independent. Voluntary forms of subordination may be just; involuntary forms of dependence are unjust. This concept of equality was a powerful weapon in European efforts to overturn the last vestiges of feudalism. It made clear that any form of birthright privilege or disability was immoral. In the new United States the principle led to the abolition of entail and primogeniture laws, to the outlawing of all titles of nobility, and to efforts, successful only in the North, to abolish the clearest possible violation of the principle of human equality, black slavery.

For Alexis de Tocqueville the largely successful American efforts to be rid of all legal supports for an aristocracy seemed the most radical product of our Revolution. The absence of such an aristocracy, and of the forms of deference that went with it, documented the birth of what he called democracy, a democracy sure to spread to Europe. In his view this form of social equality carried very high risks. He was usually mistaken in his analysis, overly gloomy in anticipating a type of totalitarian and thus nonlibertarian democracy as the future for America. He used the term "democracy" not primarily for a political system, but for the type of human personality (isolated, ambitious, lonely, and individualistic), and the type of social interaction, that went along with this type of equality. These personality traits, in Tocqueville's perspective, would impact politics and would in time produce an ugly type of mass politics. But this time had not yet arrived in America. In 1831 Tocqueville applauded the surviving elements of authority—in the courts, in popular respect for law and lawyers, and in the almost universal religiosity of Americans. These might not survive even in America and, in any case, were not present in France. He wrote his precautionary warnings for a French audience, not an American one.

One prevalent use of the word "democracy" is almost the opposite of the one adopted by Tocqueville. This is the association of the word with a wide array of expressive freedoms—for speech, press, petition, assembly, religion, entrepreneurship. I find this a paradoxical and confusing use of the word. Instead of Tocqueville's image of a democracy as a homogeneous mass of people, with a single dominant and coercive opinion, without room for basic dissent or exceptional achievement, this image of a democracy is libertarian. Protection of such expressive freedoms may offer an antidote to the oppressive democracy feared by Tocqueville. From the battles over the Sedition Act of 1798 on, advocates of greater leeway for private expression have portrayed such as an indispensable tool for cultivating informed and responsible citizens.

Note that the ever-enlarging leeway for private expression that has marked American history since 1798 has been a matter of constitutional and statutory determination. We have granted such leeway as a matter of policy. The degree of leeway afforded speech or print or worship is always to some extent contextual and relative, as exemplified by censorship in time of war or by continuing laws against slander. Expressive freedoms are very different from inherent or natural rights, as they originate not in nature, not in ethical absolutes, but in public policy. Yet today such expressive freedoms are so deeply embodied in our self-concept, so rooted in struggles stretching back over two centuries, so anchored in the First Amendment of our Constitution, that they have taken on much of the moral authority of natural rights.

Once again a paradox. At the local level, in homogeneous villages and towns, democratic majorities have consistently fought against such a libertarian order in behalf of exclusive communal values. It has been cosmopolitan elites, often in alliance with aggrieved minorities, who have most often supported a broader leeway for self-expression and asked for federal protection of such liberties. Thus, one could rightly ask if such liberties, and a broad tolerance for diversity, are not more nearly an example of aristocratic limits on democratic politics than a product of majority will. Just as natural rights reflect appeals to a higher law, to a form of authority outside the bounds of legislation, so the present support for cultural pluralism may reflect an appeal to moral values that rest not on the will of any majority, but on the effective advocacy of an educated minority. Liberties, rather than a product of democratic politics, are simply another check upon its excesses.

I end with another and much more elusive use of the word "democratic." In May of 1965 I attended the first national teach-in on the Vietnam war, in Washington, D.C. For some reason one powerful memory remains. It involved Isaac Deutscher, the former Communist and biographer of Lenin, Trotsky, and Stalin. An old man only two years short of death, he indulged in some nostalgia. He talked with great feeling about his youth, a time when he and other idealists had enlisted in what they believed to be great crusades. Then, he said, words like "democracy," "socialism," and "communism" carried intense meaning and symbolized great human hopes. No more. The battles were all over, and even the rare victories bittersweet or tarnished. Who could now in good faith utter these overused and vulgarized words? Tyrants have ruled in their name; demagogues prostituted them to raw ambition. Thus, the hopes and dreams of his youth had given way to the cynicism, the indulgent smiles, that appropriately accompany any present use of such words as "democracy." Deutscher's requiem for such symbolic words reduced the audience to tears.

Perhaps once upon a time, long ago, in a more innocent America, the word "democracy" carried the powerful meaning that Deutscher recalled from his youth. It is notable that the two words that Americans have most often used to express national ideals have been "republican" and "democratic." It is not surprising, therefore, although it may be very disillusioning, that our two main political parties have claimed these words. In such a symbolic use careful definitions are not only futile but may seem destructive. Democracy stands for what is good about America, whether expressive freedoms, equality of opportunity, the sovereignty of the people and thus the special role of constitutions, veneration for a rule of law and for due process, a profound respect for universal human rights, solicitude for free markets, and a political system very open to citizen participation. Every reform movement, every crusade, including the civil rights movement, has appealed to democratic icons. The context, momentary concerns and goals, has shaped the meanings that hid behind the appeal to democracy. Whatever the context, Americans are supposed to be democratic, or at least applaud it, whatever the "it" happens to be.

When people choose to use the word "democracy" as the chief totem of national self-identity, it may not matter to them that the images suggested by the word are often contradictory or at least in tension with each other. For those who continue to so use the word (I am much too cynical, too jaded, and too addicted to conceptual clarity to be one of those)—for those who so use the word, my lecture today will seem overly tedious, too abstract, and, most damning of all, "undemocratic."

5

The Dilemmas
of Cultural Pluralism

My work in intellectual history has usually skirted broad cultural themes. I have found, and still find, these elusive, hard to pin down or to write about with any degree of precision. Yet at various times I have agreed to address some rather vague cultural values, most notably the ever-present tension between a desire for a close and fulfilling community and a commitment to pluralism or cultural diversity. I include two essays on this theme. Perhaps appropriately they are suggestive but not nearly as coherent as those I normally write. Both involve references to themes addressed in my books, and introduced in more detail in earlier essays in this book.

I composed the first essay, on the revolt of the village, to fulfill an invitation to lecture at the University of Hartford. This was, as far as I can recall, my first lecture ever in New England. The lecture was one of a series, all tied to a theme adopted by the Humanities Center—high culture under siege. I do not recall the year, but it was around 1984. I gave versions of this lecture elsewhere. Then in 1986 I spent a month in India, on a lecture tour supported by the United States Information Agency. At Hyderabad, at the American Studies Research Center, I presented a revised version of the Hartford lecture and still called it "Revolt of the Village." For some reason the audience reacted very favorably to this particular topic (more so than to two other lectures), and the center director asked if I would allow him to publish the lecture in the *Indian Journal of American Studies*. I gladly left the lecture with him. At least five years later I received a stack of reprints of the essay, in an issue of the journal dated 1987, but I believe an issue delayed in publication for several years. I include the original Hartford speech in this section. In a sense it is a theme essay for this entire volume.

The second essay also has a complex history. It grew out of some extended remarks I prepared, as an invited guest, for a seminar in American Studies here at Vanderbilt. It matured into a lecture that I delivered in Madison, Wisconsin, in 1993 or 1994. Finally, I revised it extensively for a talk I gave as part of our lecture-seminar series in the history department here at Vanderbilt. This lecture followed a university lecture on cultural pluralism by Arthur Schlesinger. I include the final version in this book.

Revolt of the Village

A long time ago, in the decade of my birth, scattered writers and frustrated intellectuals tried to escape their provincial roots. They were a lost generation, exiles from Main Street, in revolt against the village. They condemned parochial orthodoxies, intolerance, conformity, repression, vulgarity, and acquisitive values. They hated what they called puritanism. In their alienation they flocked together. They often found their own exclusive communities. But they preached openness, tolerance, and cosmopolitan values.

Today it is difficult to revolt against any village. Few have survived. The provinces have all yielded to cultural invasion. Repression has given way to liberation. The most eccentric, or shocking, minorities all lay claim to tolerance if not acceptance. Pluralism has reached its limits. Bohemia is everywhere. Even a few surviving Main Streets are often cluttered with X-rated movies and adult bookstores.

Not surprisingly, the heart yearns for what is missing. Communal solidarity has never seemed as enticing. In a dozen ways, diverse Americans are trying to regain, or reclaim, a village. Intellectuals celebrate community. Ethnic Americans—almost everyone—seek their cultural roots. Thousands toil away at genealogies. Old-time evangelical Christianity is booming. Even our courts are backing away from cosmopolitan standards, from the zealous protection of certain minority rights. In this sense the village has reclaimed new loyalties. And in several areas the assault upon pluralistic accommodation, upon universalist standards, seems to justify my title for this paper—"Revolt of the Village."

My theme is an elusive one. It seems appropriate for this setting—a humanities center. I must do justice to the implied subject—humankind, and to the announced theme of this conference—"High Culture under Siege." If any commitment distinguishes humanities centers, it is a firm commitment to human uniqueness, to recognizing and nourishing what distinguishes humans from all other mammals. In the Christian West something called the soul or spirit long seemed to identify what was essential to being human. In the wake of Darwin any substantive conception of soul or spirit has largely given way to a functional meaning, one tied ultimately to a symbolic language, to complex meaning systems, to culture.

Thus, quite literally, in our beginnings was the word. Two humanlike animals in a crisis of survival, or possibly out of the sheer exuberance of play, turned a cry, heretofore a mere signal, into a symbol. Most likely mates, they were the parents of humankind. Adam and Eve. For with the word, Homo became Homo sapiens, an ape that knows. This was our beginning. Spirit in swaddling clothes.

And the Word was almost God. It made possible the many gods that now sprang from people's now luxuriant imaginations. With the word also originated godlike creatures, those who could take thought, invent meanings, name things, relate objects. Above all, they could reflect on words. Thus the word enabled consciousness to become self-consciousness. Humanity displayed a new form of identity—not the static identity of things, but a fluid identity tied to verbalized memories and hopes. With the word came self-conscious purpose.

With the word also came at least the illusion of enormous power, a power to direct events toward chosen goals. The heretofore purposeless universe thus gained purpose. But with the word came anxiety and guilt. The word was thus the serpent in the garden of innocence. Eden violated. It brought an awareness of good and evil. It introduced conscience into the world of things, and with it an often horrible insecurity. For in the words of Santayana, the spirit is in the world but not of it, born of it but never fully at ease within it. An alien, and thus parent of alienation. And of sin—sin inseparately tied to the presence of the word, there at the beginning, born with it, unique to it. Thus, it was in all ways original.

Unlike things—unlike even plants and animals—humans have no essential or defining nature. They have their being only in and by the word. They are masters of words—they coin them, utter them, think with them. But they are also dependent upon words, captive to them, informed and shaped by meanings. They are products of particular cultural traditions, of communities bound together by shared meanings. To become an active participant in a community—to move from the sounds and signals of infancy, to learn language—to recapitulate the original emergence of words—to join the quest of Adam and Eve—is what it means to be human. With no nature, no form, no essence, humankind is ephemeral, fragile, elusive. Like the candle flame, spirit flickers and easily dies.

In its freedom, its occasional exuberance, spirit always risks frustration. Its most lofty ideals are temporal, historically conditioned, and unrealizable. Every victory is, to some extent, empty. Each idea yields to new ones. No goals prove final. No preferences endure forever. No order is complete. Our ego rests on quicksand. Change—growth when we can applaud—is inescapable. In a strict sense, every day brings a new person. Old dreams haunt as often as they inspire.

At odd moments we all want to return to the innocent garden. To quit the project that is human life. To curse Adam—why did he taste the forbidden fruit? Why did he launch his arrogant courtship of meaning? Let us give up on the Word, go back before the beginning, find peace as humble apes, at home in Eden. Alas, it is too late. One cannot go back. Self-consciousness precludes it. Besides, if we do not take thought, even our apelike bodies will surely die. We have eaten the beautiful and horrible fruit, become human in the presence of the word. Humankind will endure only so long as the flickering flame of self-consciousness continues to burn. When it burns out, when the last word is spoken, then primitive existence will again be without purpose, as it was before our beginnings.

A corollary to such a radical conception of humankind is that no science of humanity is possible. The egotistic and misdirected search for such has been the great modern heresy. Humanities centers stand in mute testimony to those people who, all along, have been wise enough to know better. Thus, culture, tied to evolving human meanings, is always open, under way, in process. We cannot judge cultural achievements by any fixed standards. None exist. But we can judge by objective standards, at least in part.

Your term "high culture" is, of course, elusive. No clear semantic conventions govern its use. In some contexts "high" probably means "highbrow," fashionable, conventional. I stipulate a more positive meaning—high culture, in any society or age, designates the apex of distinctively human achievements—the word made manifest in the most rigorous forms of knowledge, the most skillful artistry, and the most inclusive and sensitive moral commitments. Note that what determines such levels of attainment is not specific content—that varies according to time and context. For knowledge the criteria involve method—the often elaborate tests and procedures by which the knowledge gains acceptance. For artistry it involves the happy marriage of talent and imagination and hard-won skills of execution. For moral commitment it involves taste at the level of experience, knowledge about the consequences of actions, and the skills—primarily political—needed to effect purposes and goals.

As the Greeks first taught us, these three benchmarks of human attainment are interrelated. Truth, beauty, and the good are complementary. The hard work of truth seeking involves elements of both taste and artistry. Inquiry itself is an art. The effort to bring some form of unity to disparate phenomena—artistry—requires knowledge. And the struggle for the good implicates knowledge and skills. In a sense the most embracing object of human art is a just and thus a beautiful community, a political goal. Plato was correct.

Each of these quests combines aspects of the parochial and the universal. The type of truth sought and valued is a cultural variable. But formal
tools of inquiry, such as mathematics, prove useful in any cultural context,
even as quite generalized methods of problem solving seem to underline
all the sciences. The subject matter and the style of artistic effort vary
immensely over time, and from one society to another. Yet some skills are
common. What is needed to master a potter's wheel does not, in essence,
differ from one society to the next. Taste, and moral standards, vary
immensely from age to age. Yet insofar as people affirm life, then consistency alone suggests a universal repugnance to murder or slavery. And
just as certain basic animal needs are universal, so are types of pain and
suffering. These universal elements make it possible to evaluate cultural
achievements even across cultural boundaries and to do this by objective
standards—that is, by standards tied to methods, to levels of skill, to
breadth of sympathy, and not to any merely subjective preference. But I
quickly note that, always and appropriately, criticism involves both the
universal and contextual, both objective and subjective criteria.

You probably anticipate my next argument—that the mentality of the
village stands opposed to high culture as I have defined it. And, if I am
correct about the present resurgence of the village, then this is almost synonymous with a besieged high culture. Of course, it cannot be that simple. It is too easy, and too pat, to characterize villagers as ignorant,
morally dense philistines, although such an image has had wise currency
among American intellectuals. Such labels as know-nothingism, fundamentalism, anti-intellectualism, the paranoid style, and McCarthyism
punctuate our history texts, and such labels seem most often to fit small-
town and rural America, or at least people shaped by such a background.
Here are our perennial populists. The identification is unfair, but it has a
certain logic to it. Why unfair? Because truth seeking often occurs in small
communities, among people with shared beliefs, shared jargon, and
shared preferences. And, historically, the most demanding arts have
developed in a local, artisanal context, often even in generations of the
same family. Most literary arts exploit native customs, themes, and local
settings and mores. And a confident sense of identity, of self-worth, often
generated by a tight community may be a prerequisite of moral sensitiv-
ity and concern. For these reasons the theme of the village—of restricted
areas and clustered populations, of local people bound together by distinctive beliefs and preferences—does not, in itself, tell us anything at all
about the level of cultural attainment. That all depends upon which village. Greenwich Village or Middletown?

But the implied antagonism of high culture and the village has a logic,
which I now want to explore. Today, perhaps more than ever before, the
rigorous quest for knowledge, the most fashionable forms of artistic

endeavor, and even the arbitration of moral opinion all occur in nongeographical, expert, specialized communities. These somewhat artificial communities are, almost by definition, elitist and exclusive. They set high training or admission standards, exclude amateurs as well as charlatans, and by various credentials certify a competent elect. Laypeople need not apply. The knowledge is much too technical, the arts too esoteric, the moral dialectic too abstract. In certain contexts everyone has to defer to such specialized competence. Most people, with a mixture of gratitude and confusion, submit to modern medical care. Most laypeople, with more mystification than comprehension, pay their expected obeisance to the modern arts. And most people give at least occasional lip service to the universalist motifs of contemporary moral theory, a moral theory quite often certified in social legislation or court decisions.

But the response in each case involves uncomprehending deference before our modern magicians and priests. Such deference is parent to a sense of alienation, to resentment and anger. Older, geographically specific, culturally distinctive communities now host and nourish such alienation. They breed the suspicious counterattacks that make up the perennial siege of villagers against both high culture and highbrow culture. It is often hard to distinguish the two—to isolate scientific integrity from scientistic arrogance, awesome talent and disciplined skills from merely avant-garde posturing, prophetic moral criticism from self-serving rationalizations. Thus, the ordinary citizen of Middletown, alienated, defensive, lays siege to both. Or at interludes in his life reverts to ancient superstition, celebrates the old gods, and treasures all the traditional icons. Even technocrats support so-called creation science. College students dabble in astrology. And able businessmen or accomplished politicians approach foreign policy issues with the same blinding partisanship that they appropriately display at a football game.

The problem is obvious. Generations of social critics and educators have tried to solve it, to bridge the gap of knowledge and taste. On one side we have tried, with small success, to develop courses that will at least demystify the more technical sciences, that will provide students with some degree of technological and artistic sophistication.

On the other side, in a strategy best explored by John Dewey, we have tried to stress the continuities between the most abstract physical sciences and ordinary problem solving, or acknowledged the practical intelligence present in any village. We have tried to spread the important message that the fashionable or so-called fine arts—musical composition, literature, the plastic arts—make up only a minuscule portion of all human arts. We have broadened our definitions, sought out local handicrafts and folkways, and tried to bring creativity and beauty to the objects of everyday consumption. We have recognized that the effete world of museums and white-tie concerts is only a cultural window dressing, even a cultural sideshow, if it is a counterpoint to servile jobs, ugly cities, and plastic consumer goods. I could go on—a sermon is brewing—but this is not my task here. I deal with these issues all the time in struggling with academic curricula. The bridging problems are overwhelming. But a problem is different from a dilemma. Here I want to deal with some dilemmas.

In America today the advocates of high culture—in both the sciences and the arts—are almost by definition subversive of village or communal values. They are part of a dispersed national network of competence and taste. They are usually mobile and flock to highly pluralistic universities or urban centers. They have not only left, but have repudiated, home loyalties or, in their perspective, what they usually call provincial prejudices. They value—in their work, require—a wide leeway for self-expression or for artistic experimentation. They work at frontiers. They value innovation. They view issues from a broadly inclusive or national perspective. Today, unlike in the more Christian past, unlike in some Marxist countries, no common philosophical or religious beliefs provide the basis of ideological cohesion or moral consensus. Our intellectuals do not enlist in any all-embracing causes. In all these ways they have escaped most local loyalties, except in the narrow sense of professional self-protection. They value freedom and thus a type of solitude above solidarity. They are not part of tight, totalitarian communities. And, without pejorative intent, I emphasize that any true village is at least mildly totalitarian. That is, it includes people united by shared beliefs and preferences that touch upon every major human concern. Brother James. Comrade Budinski. A village stands for some shared identity, for commonly accepted moral standards. It is, to some extent, always an exclusive club, not that villagers often formalize the rules or even recognize how discriminating, how exclusive, how repressive they really are. Only nonconformists or rebels come to appreciate this.

By and large, solitary intellectuals have carried on a long and seemingly successful siege against village totalitarianism. I am one of these solitary intellectuals. I am not part of any cohesive community or sect. Solidarity, even that of a labor union, frightens me. I join causes, but I do not surrender to them. Familial labels—brother, comrade—make me nervous. I do not want to surrender my autonomy, my independent voice. As an admitted, professed intellectual, I have joined in the long siege against the village. I have supported the legislation and the critical court decisions that have opened up villages, forced them to accommodate minorities and to follow national standards of due process.

Periodically, I go home—to my parent's village in east Tennessee. It could be a village anywhere in America, except some of the local beliefs and preferences would be different. In the last few years the homecoming has been difficult for me, and for my relatives and boyhood friends. The cultural clash has been intense, as if we were literally worlds apart. The locals are almost apocalyptic in charting the moral decay of contemporary America. The issues are cultural in the main. They completely misunderstand the prayer decision and lament the lack of public devotions in the local schools. Some are agitated about the abortion issue, until a few years ago a nonissue. They are justifiably frightened by an upsurge in local crime, and almost vengefully cruel in how they would like to control it.

Behind the fears and concerns I sense a recent convergence of opinion, an intensified local orthodoxy, and a greater willingness to do what is very uncongenial to the people of that village—to speak out, to become political. But, as an ironical commentary, I do note that these cultural issues have not mobilized the village as completely as has its opposition to a planned landfill at its back door. And in fighting that battle, these villagers have reached out to their nominal enemies—experts, environmentalists, even the Sierra Club. At other times they will still mobilize on behalf of the Tennessee Valley Authority and public power, on behalf of social security benefits, or for agricultural price supports. Thus, in a confusing pattern, the home folks have embraced certain modern norms and policies, compete for certain benefits, even as they reflect a deep alienation from the values reflected in much social policy.

I think I have now identified a basic conflict—between certain forms of freedom and loyalty to a community. Either formally, or informally, a community, if it has any identity at all, has to be exclusive and in some sense intolerant. The same is true for any individual who has any clear identity, any coherent personality. The communal norms, if unopposed, if well internalized by individuals, need not be expressed as formal creeds or ideologies. They rarely are. They lurk in habits, are concealed in the nuances of a sectarian language present in any community. The exclusiveness need not take a legal form; subtle forms of disapproval and ostracism keep people in line or push out dissidents. The most effective community, or club, needs no written law and no police. Every person is judge and policeman. Freedom to worship as one pleases, or to say or write what one wants, or to sell goods at the prices competition allows, are all inimical to the values of a community—too egotistic and antisocial, too irresponsible and dangerous. Within the bounds of propriety set by the village, one may indeed enjoy considerable leeway in areas of self-expression, but boundaries have to be in place, or a community is impossible. Americans often try to avoid this necessary fact. We often, almost in the same breath, applaud both community and liberation.

I remember, in the climactic years of the civil rights movement, how the struggle created deep bonds of mutual affection—brother, sister. The closeness of a Baptist revival seemed to envelope a large coalition of diverse people. Among certain feminists I find the same sense of sisterhood, of equality and oneness. So long as the focus remains on a common, external enemy, at least the veneer of solidarity blesses such causes. But external enemies are insufficient glue for any broader and enduring community. And the very goal of liberation leads toward autonomy, toward solitary, lonely, but free individuals. In all such coalitional liberation movements the time bomb of deep cultural differences has soon exploded, and brothers and sisters, in their diverse new sects, have soon been at each other's throats. If one wants to live in a community, then one must sacrifice any right to do one's own thing. A village, by definition, is confining and oppressive to any would-be rebel. It is comforting, supportive to those who fully and dutifully affirm its identity.

I want to illustrate this conflict by a brief reference to liberties in America. The most traditional meaning of the word "liberty" is simply "at liberty"—not servile, not a slave or a bond servant, not even directly dependent upon another for job or livelihood. A second meaning of liberty involved the English tradition of due process, of procedural protections for those threatened by a loss of liberty, particularly in the courts, in criminal and civil procedures. The third meaning of liberty was not focal, not deemed terribly important by our colonial forebears, but seems to be at the forefront of public concern today. I refer to the freedom for individual self-expression, as in worship, speech, press, or economic enterprise.

The Europeans who settled America often came in search of liberty. But almost always they intended the first two types of liberty—to gain independence and citizenship and possibly enjoy due process. These were focal concerns of Puritans in New England. Note that the early settlers came from European villages, often dissenting villages. They came to America to find a place to do their own thing, in peace. Here they reestablished their tight, close towns and villages. Exclusive and intolerant, not less so in Mennonite villages in Pennsylvania or Anglican ones in North Carolina than in ones in Connecticut. Liberty, in this context, did not mean any great leeway for divergent forms of worship or for unencumbered speech or press. It was, rather, the freedom to set up a tight communal order and to be able to exclude those of unlike mind. No commune could survive if it tolerated rank heresy or allowed youthful rebels to say or print any or all of their immature and erroneous speculations. A village had to stand for something, to enforce its standards, or face disorder, division, and decay, as so well illustrated in that cesspool of pluralistic tolerance—Rhode Island.

Liberty then entailed being left alone. The imperial authorities in England had to practice restraint, allow local differences. Or else the dissenting villages in America had no security. Note the subtle accommodation that soon became a distinctive American achievement. We call it federalism. At the town or village level people could be as exclusive as they wanted, or as holy or pure as piety demanded. But larger, common concerns (trade, foreign policy) required more tolerance by provincial governments and the British imperial government, replaced later in America by our federal government. These more overarching governments would be tyrannical if they imposed common standards upon local communities. Thus, even the Puritans, with their most restrictive local villages, fought for freedom within the empire.

This conception of a free America, I submit, may well remain a working assumption of contemporary villages, such as mine in east Tennessee. It involves an almost forgotten version of pluralism, a pluralism reflected in the amazingly divergent beliefs and values of the thousands of villages and small towns scattered across colonial and early national America. Let them thrive in peace. Let them set their own rules. So long as they do not invade my village. So long as they do not try to nationalize their beliefs and their preferences. So long as they do not impose their knowledge, their arts, their moral preferences—that is, their high culture—on the rest of us.

The hard-won lessons of a diverse state, Pennsylvania, guided our founding fathers in the creation of our federal government. At the Convention of 1787, delegates appreciated the diversity of beliefs and practices in the wide reaches of America. Three states still had tax-supported public worship. Thus, a federal government has no business legislating in the controversial field of religion, either to establish a national church or to set limits on the freedom of worship. Locally, formal or informal restraints upon free speech and press remained very restrictive (they still do when villages are able to control their own affairs). Thus, the new government would assume no power to legislate in these sensitive areas. Leave such decisions to local governments. Then, in the Bill of Rights, added by amendment to the original Constitution, which simply delegated no authority in these areas, the new Congress reversed the language and set stringent restrictions upon the new federal government. But note—the Bill of Rights applied only to the federal government. In no way did these amendments restrict local government. Thus, the great accommodation—all manner of local conformity, but some assurance that almost any sect or faction, however eccentric, however intolerant, could find a niche somewhere in America. Most did.

We have rejected this form of pluralistic accommodation. Under cover of the equal protection and due process clauses of the Fourteenth Amendment, we have extended national citizenship and equal protection of the laws to all Americans, wherever they live. The Bill of Rights now applies to state and local governments. The strong federal protections for expressive freedom now set severe limits upon the power of local governments to regulate religion, press, speech, assembly, entrepreneurial activities, sex roles, voting requirements, and on and on. The village has been emasculated. It is legally defenseless before national standards. Informally, villages still do what they always have done—discriminate, ostracize, exclude. But at some legal peril, and subject always to federal intervention in behalf of minority "victims."

I end with some very carefully nuanced assertions, or the basis, I hope, of a discussion. The demands for federal restrictions on local practices are not all new. I need not recall the antislavery crusade. Whenever local laws or practices have seemed grievously unjust, an outcry of public opinion has pressured the federal government to impose uniform rules. For example, as a condition of statehood, Congress forced the Mormons in Utah to repudiate the practice, not the doctrinal foundation, of polygamy. That is, in this unusual case, the federal government restricted the right of free religious expression. In the twentieth century a whole series of congressional actions and court decisions has eroded the power of local governments, and most of all their former power to control minorities and to deny equal citizenship to all inhabitants. Now, by and large, I have fought for all of this. I would be appalled, am appalled, at any present indication that we are moving back to the way it was—for example, back to an informal Protestant establishment as reflected in official prayers or village-funded creches. I could cite a hundred such concerns. But note what I am saying. We have imposed upon villages a uniform standard of fairness and justice, a standard almost always applauded by intellectuals such as myself. Behind older village restrictions and exclusions I see mainly arbitrary categories (race, sex), or ignorance (as in fantastic myths or stereotypes used to stigmatize racial, ethnic, or religious groups), or esthetic myopia, as reflected in efforts to limit artistic experimentation. Is it not great that we are rid of all that junk, that we have made village bigots behave themselves? Cheer. High culture has largely won. Or so it might seem.

But has it? It is, as your announced theme makes clear, under siege. The rednecks are on the march. Main Street is in rebellion. The village is reasserting its claim. I can even see some justice in this fact. I can recognize elements of arrogance and self-righteousness, a type of cultural imperialism, reflected in certain federal policies, and I can still respond to the old ideal of pluralism—restraint at the center in order to accommodate differences at the local level, even accommodation of those who, in my perspective, are ignorant and immoral—tolerance for the intolerant. Note that it is hard to maintain even this degree of restraint when compelling moral issues are at stake. Can we allow South Africa to solve its own problems? How much more are we morally implicated by what happens in Boston or Chicago or Mississippi?

Besides, I am not sure such restraint is the issue today. As I listen to the people of almost any village, as I try to fathom cultural or religious or political reaction, I believe that what I hear is not an appeal for local autonomy, although people talk endlessly about federal usurpation. What I hear is a body of beliefs and preferences, frequently in direct opposition to high culture as I have defined it, but recommended as a new or recovered national standard. The people I listen to are advocating greater uniformity, not less. If I am correct, they are advocating a national village. The debate concerns what is appropriate for such a large and, in my perspective, still diverse noncommunity. When the issues are so drawn, I become fearful, defensive, for I feel threatened. As a solitary intellectual, I see myself as an incipient rebel. If they win, I know I will be the alien. I remain fully committed to my more pluralistic vision of America. I believe it more fair and just than their more monolithic vision. I may lose. I sometimes feel paranoid, threatened. After all, I publicly confess to being a humanist.

I offer no resolution. Unresolved dilemmas remain. At moments, when I feel most alone, most solitary, I nourish nostalgic memories of my boyhood village. Often in cerebral ways I celebrate community. But then I face hard facts. I cannot have my cake and eat it too. I wish I could. I wish I could enjoy the closeness, the mutual support, the comradeship of a village. But this means that it would have to be a particular village, with its own restrictive and essential beliefs and standards. To be a dutiful citizen, I would have to give up a degree of personal autonomy and freedom. Then I recognize the truth: that the village is my innocent garden. And that, long since, I ate my fill of its forbidden fruit.

What Holds Us Together?

My announced title is "What Holds Us Together?" The question implies that Americans have achieved something like a national community, that some social cement holds us together. In 1862 anyone in a war-torn and divided union would have laughed at such nonsense. We fought one of the most cruel and bloody civil wars in history, and rebuilt the union on the basis of coercion, not consensus. Deep cultural and racial conflict preceded, and followed, the war. Today the pitiful example of the original Americans, isolated in reservations, mired in joblessness, alcoholism, and despair, with shameful suicide rates, does not testify to any fulfilling national community. Yet since 1865 the United States has enjoyed one of the most stable political regimes in the world. At least in this sense we have held together very well.

Since 1787 Americans have been haunted by the problem of diversity: first, regional, religious, and sectional; later, racial and ethnic. Is there enough glue, and glue sticky enough, to bind us together as a large and very diverse society? And if so, what is the glue? Is it a common language, a shared political and legal system, a common core of Semitic religious beliefs and values, or what? And are these commonalities eroding today, as so many fear?

Today, we are, in many respects, a very pluralistic nation. But we did not become so by choices aimed at this result. The British who colonized what is now the United States were distinctive, not in accommodating cultural differences but for the exact opposite—an enormous resistance to racial and cultural differences. Until well into the twentieth century, most white Americans continued to reflect such cultural pride and arrogance. Until recently we have tried to exclude those whose differences were most conspicuous—non-Caucasians, non-Christians, even non-Protestants. Or, if such came anyway, as enslaved blacks or the Chinese on the West Coast or Hispanics in the Southwest, Americans adopted policies to isolate, subordinate, and insulate them, thus trying to neutralize their cultural impact.

This antipathy to major differences fit equally well two somewhat distinct and now passé images of American culture, images that remained powerful until World War II. Both involved an assumption that the United States had, or should develop, a distinctive and reasonably homogeneous culture. The first image fit the early republic. White Americans believed they had created a society qualitatively distinct even from that of western Europe. In the great expanse of America, northern European migrants enjoyed unique political institutions, wide-open economic opportunities, and nonestablished Protestant churches—an America at once republican, proprietary, and Protestant. What most distinguished America was not what it retained from the European past (no one could deny continuities), but what it had rejected from that past, what injustices it had left behind, what entrenched hierarchies it had escaped, what ascriptive or birthright inequalities it had overturned.

Of course, this confident, even boastful, image of America often concealed deep anxieties and insecurities. Many contested it, even as intellectuals often felt a sense of inferiority in comparison to the cultural achievement of Europe. It was not even clear that the new republic would survive, as sectional tensions, related to slavery, increased in each decade.

Another image of America matured in the late nineteenth century, an image abetted by historians whom we now refer to as institutionalists. In their perspective the United States was the final outcome of institutional developments stretching back a thousand years. The theme was one of continuity, organic growth, maturation. In the United States one could view the promise of European civilization as finally realized, much as Hegel saw it realized in Germany. Thus, America represented not a new culture but the perfection of old ones. It began in the German forests, with the first glimmers of representative government. It began in the Anglo-Saxon legal tradition, with the first glimmers of constitutionalism and the rule of law or objective authority. It began in the work of Wycliff and Huss, and most of all in the reforms of Luther and Calvin, as northern Europeans threw off the hierarchical authority and the superstitions of Roman Catholicism. It began among English yeomen who resisted Norman infeudation on behalf of freehold farms and entrepreneurial freedom. But it only so began. Because of entrenched habits and rigid institutions in old Europe, such intimations of human enlightenment were to find their fulfillment only in a new land, in America.

Smile indulgently if you want, but echoes of this Whiggish image still have a powerful impact upon Americans. It implies a hierarchy of human personality types, with those who took the lead in the development of liberating institutions clearly at the top. Just as clearly these were all from northern Europe. Our grandparents easily expressed these beliefs in racial language, with the word "race" denoting both genes and culture. Only certain Aryan tribes had attained stable self-government, rapid economic growth, and a spiritual and enlightened form of religion. Other peoples of the world could aspire to such achievements but over and over again proved that they were incapable of attaining them.

If the disabilities were genetic, then one could not hope for miracles. Such people would either accept guidance from Europeans or flounder in political anarchy or dictatorships, in political corruption and instability, in superstitious religions. If the disabilities were largely cultural, then over the centuries such benighted people might convert to Protestant Christianity and slowly learn the forms of self-discipline and respect for objective authority that make possible both good government and economic prosperity. But whether racial and beyond remediation, or cultural and subject to very slow change, the world situation was such in 1900 that most of humankind had not yet assimilated the values and habits that made one a northern European or an American. Thus, the greater the racial and cultural distance of would-be immigrants, the more Americans tried to bar entry into our republican paradise. By the 1920s we had all but closed our boundaries to those with any significant differences at all.

One clue to a distinctive American identity was our political institutions. Our founding generation affirmed classical and early-modern traditions in moral theory. They used such a normative background to shape new yet largely familiar political institutions. The core values, including those that clarified the minimal moral ends of government, were in a broad sense Christian and thus reflected both Hebraic and Greek roots. But the diversity of Christian sects in America precluded any common, state-supported religion, or what in Europe had long seemed the minimal glue needed for a national community.

In the Declaration of Independence, Thomas Jefferson appealed to a very general theism, which he mistakenly believed to be a common belief among all religions. Such a theism seemed essential, for without a belief in a creative god and in some system of rewards and punishments, people would lack the self-discipline so badly needed in a free republic. Jefferson believed the salvation doctrines, the mysteries, the sacraments of sectarian Christianity to be not only superstitions but a perennial source of conflict. But his rejection of the divisive superstructure of sectarian Christianity should not conceal how much more readily he turned to a theistic foundation. This anchored his belief in an ordered universe, and thus in the possibility of objective knowledge. A creative god had also implanted a sense of beauty and harmony, of what is just and equitable, in every human mind, and with knowledge and self-discipline this provided the basis of objective moral judgments, and thus a moral order.

Everyone who would take thought would arrive at certain common ethical commitments.

In the nineteenth century an evangelical form of Protestantism gained a near hegemonic cultural role. Americans rarely followed Jefferson in anchoring our national values in a general theism but rather identified them with an idealized Protestantism. Today, even a very generalized theism seems as much a local and human-created belief as does a belief in any distinctively Christian doctrine. Thus, modern intellectuals have tried to find other, nontheistic or nonfoundational justifications for a continued commitment to certain core values, particularly those embodied in the language of human rights. I am one of those intellectuals.

Reflecting these core values were our new and in many respects unique political institutions. They alone remain intact today. Here I can only note the four foundations of such governments—consent, moral limits, balance, and participation. Only within the context of constitutional delegation, reserved rights, and internal balances did Americans chose a form of government that provided for popular participation. Within all the constraints, citizens have always had a powerful influence upon the choice of leaders and the choice of policies. But note that the constraints—deference to a higher moral law and to constitutional covenants, plus the formal balancing mechanisms—have generally but not always (remember 1861) prevented deep divisions over the most basic issues. They have usually protected Americans from the dangers of mass politics or the tyranny of majorities.

Within this context of core values and these common political forms, Americans in the nineteenth century did accommodate a type of pluralism. They excluded from the national covenant both blacks and Indians, subordinated women, and isolated immigrants who would not quickly assimilate. Yet despite the white male hegemony, the country was vast, with important regional differences, dozens of religious sects, and varied and often almost isolated immigrant enclaves. The very expanse of land attracted new religious sects or socialist dreamers. In this sense the United States was already a pluralistic country, and recognition of regional differences justified severe constraints upon federal power, which the Constitution of 1787 largely restricted to foreign policy, control over the military, and protection of an internal common market.

The effective communities then were local ones, and they had a great deal of autonomy. In 1791 the First Amendment endorsed such a pluralism. It prohibited federal suppression of speech or press or federal regulation of religion. In the union as a whole, diversity could prevail, and did. But the federal Bill of Rights did not apply to the states. At the state and local level repression often remained the norm. Local communities excluded those who did not affirm the local orthodoxy. Majorities rejected the due process protection that applied to the federal government and often in effect created totalitarian forms of democracy. But this was not terribly restrictive, so long as plenty of space allowed others with different beliefs or values to go elsewhere and found their own homogeneous and exclusive communities. Notably, slaves lacked even this opportunity.

The distributive pluralism of the nineteenth century has given way, not without strenuous and continuing local resistance, to the inclusive pluralism of today. The Fourteenth Amendment marked the formal side of such a transition. The actual transition in attitudes and practice is largely a twentieth-century phenomenon, and the transition is far from complete even yet. On some issues our courts still defer to local standards. But not on very many.

Federal solicitude for individual rights has subverted the most sacrosanct spheres of local democratic control, such as the way communities enforce criminal law, control public schools, or publicly affirm sectarian beliefs and values. Today the First Amendment, which originally protected local and often repressive communities from federal intervention, now forces local governments to grant freedom of speech, press, and worship to any minority that asks for protection. The irony is most visible in religion. The same provisions of the First Amendment that originally prevented the federal government from regulating local establishments of religion now preclude local establishments.

Accompanying this solicitude for expressive freedoms has been a serious effort to give more than lip service to the moral principle that all people are created equal. To the challenge of outside immigrants has been added the even greater challenge of including as citizens, and giving voice and power to, formerly excluded servants, slaves, wage laborers, women, and homosexuals. Today women are forcing the most important cultural revolution in all of American history. Whether avowed feminists or antifeminists, whether sure of their purposes or deeply ambivalent, American women, almost as a whole, have become self-conscious and in various ways decidedly unhappy about their former assigned spheres and roles in American society. Now they are demanding and shaping new social relationships, with momentous but as yet not fully clear implications for labor markets, marriage, child rearing, education, politics, and even sports. Thus, all formerly marginal and subordinated groups are now moving into the arena of liberty and citizenship. Never has the mixture in the pot been as rich and flavorful, but never has the successful blending been so problematic.

In this context of an unprecedented and inclusive pluralism, the older Whiggish and often racially oriented conceptions of an American community are out of fashion, stigmatized. At the level of public policy, and in our normative beliefs, we have embraced new conceptions of American nationhood. We have finally eliminated all the racial and cultural disabilities in our immigration policy. In the last two decades, the largest share of immigrants has been Hispanic and Asiatic, not European. Involved in this shift have been two different, emerging conceptions of American culture, neither very clear and neither very resistant to critical analysis.

One version of pluralism was very popular just after World War II, during the early cold war and in the civil rights struggle. It reflected the easy and hopeful assumption that certain essential or defining American beliefs and values are reasonably coherent and universally appealing, although not necessarily exclusive or exhaustive. Over time all immigrants to America should be able to assimilate these normative beliefs and values. Our pot will melt them down, like ice cubes thrown into a pot of warm water. What is critical here is the belief that immigrants, whatever their color or past culture, can become good Americans. The disabilities they bring with them are rooted not in genes or blood, but only in habits subject to modification through experience and education. By this malleable view of humans, anyone, from anywhere, can become an American. But note that the immigrant has to change, fit herself to American beliefs, values, and institutions, remake herself. Thus becoming an American is a choice, even as America is a cause.

I call this the easy, Arminian view of cultural conversion and grace; it is generous, inclusive, even if intellectually soft. It has its own share of smugness if not arrogance (we are already the best). But it is psychologically and morally coherent, in the sense that one still can affirm that our core beliefs are in some sense objectively true, that our core values are firmly grounded in the realities of human experience. In assuming and affirming this degree of cultural self-assurance, our progenitors were correct; they were mistaken in correlating these values with such arbitrary criteria as race and nationality. Many people cite the success of recent Asiatic immigrants to vindicate this view.

The other, and most thoroughly pluralistic, outlook is difficult to state, and perhaps so incoherent as to be ultimately indefensible. I begin with a widely affirmed belief, that America is what it is because of the contributions of people of various cultures, nationalities, and religions. We are a rich and changing blend. We are now assimilating the cultural contributions of Hispanics and Asiatics. The soup in the pot will have a somewhat different flavor as a result, but surely a richer flavor. In this view the process of assimilation is two-way, with the larger, existing culture reshuffled a bit through the influence of immigrants or such newly enfranchised minorities as African Americans, even as immigrants have to accommodate themselves to the more stable aspects of American society. But what is critical to this perspective is that no beliefs, no traditions or customs, are privileged. For practical reasons all Americans may have to learn to function within a developed political and legal system, not because it is intrinsically superior to others (upon what grounds could one assert that?), but because such is necessary to achieve any political order at all. Perhaps immigrants will also have to learn English in order to succeed in the American economy. On all other issues, including religious beliefs and moral preferences, they may retain and treasure their separate identities.

Such a relativistic ideal seems to fit present realities. We hope to form a stable and fulfilling society that includes as fully participating equals all the varied racial, ethnic, and religious groups that now live here. We have at least in theory rejected all past modes of subordination, marginalization, or exclusion. I doubt that any people in human history ever aspired to such a degree of inclusiveness. I think the chances of full success are very low. Much in the present suggests that we are so far failing, as evidenced by intense local or parochial resistance to such an inclusive pluralism, by an increase in bloc voting and the growing role of race in urban politics, by the continued high level of violence and crime, by evidence of a widespread breakdown of the family, and by the increasingly marginal role of organized religion among the most alienated groups. Even though everyone is now legally free, free to stake claims to certain rights and entitlements, the babel of conflicting claims is so deafening that no one can even hear the demands.

As I have intimated already, I find a completely relativistic or multicultural ideal incoherent. It subverts any secure sense of either individual or group identity. Begging all the problems of justification, I believe that any community has to rest upon some firm convictions about matters of fact and value. To be someone is to affirm certain values and goals. This raises the problem of the core values, the internalized cement, that is needed to hold any diverse society together.

In the past, the public schools served as the principal means of transmitting the official values of our society, and thus the prerequisites of citizenship, to each new generation. In the age of distributive pluralism, local schools reflected the beliefs and values of local elites or local majorities. In most of America, in the nineteenth century, this meant the culture was supported by a hegemonic form of evangelical Protestantism, as Roman Catholics soon recognized and deplored.

Today the public schools face very different challenges in an age of inclusive pluralism. Cosmopolitan values, those of an educated elite, are indeed reflected in federal laws and enforced by the courts. This has led to all manner of local conflict over school policy and curriculum, as best illustrated by controversies over sponsored prayers in schools, over bilingual instruction, and over canonical texts. Schools are still supposed to teach certain core values, but it is now very difficult to find out what these are, or to find ways of expressing them that will not be a red flag to some self-conscious constituency. In such a context, often the principal value seems to be a largely empty one and in some contexts a very dangerous one—tolerance of all differences. With increasing fragmentation in the culture, it may be impossible to resist some retreat to localism and parochialism in education. Given the pluralism, does it any longer make sense to send all the culturally varied children off to the same, mixed schools? This was no trouble as long as the Whiggish consensus prevailed at the top. The schools had a clear mission, to transmit the true and good to the often benighted masses. But such elites no longer own and govern America, and even those who still try have lost most of their earlier moral confidence. Thus, the present dilemma—either a retreat to culturally specific schools (blacks go to their own schools and learn to value African American culture), or public schools with such an eclectic curriculum, with so many needed gestures to the various minorities clamoring for recognition and certification, that the whole idea of any core or unity is lost.

Almost all the dilemmas occasioned by a society that tries to achieve an inclusive pluralism are raised by employment policies. The redundant phrase "affirmative action" masks both policy and moral confusions. Section 7 of the Civil Rights Act of 1964 prohibits discrimination (penalties or preferences) in employment based on sex or membership in certain minorities. The immediate purpose was to correct the injustice of former, often officially sanctioned, favoritism for white males. The phrase "affirmative action" became part of efforts to achieve the goal of equal employment opportunity in what was clearly a competitive or meritocratic economy. Employers were supposed to do all possible to identify competitive candidates for jobs who were in categories of people so often overlooked in the past, and who were underrepresented, or not represented at all, among those whom they recruited and employed.

But soon, abetted by noble intentions or pushed by mobilized minorities, the term "affirmative action" came to symbolize a second imperative—gaining equal representation of defined groups in various occupations. Such egalitarian outcomes are simply not consistent with nondiscrimination, unless one assumes that abilities and skills are equally distributed among all identifiable groups. If not, equal outcomes mean deliberate preferences for some candidates, and thus discrimination. Both goals—an equal opportunity to compete for jobs, and equal levels of achievement by defined status groups—may be desirable, but they so conflict that no one coherent employment policy can serve both. Long-term policies involving education, job training, and some degree of cultural indoctrination may help equalize outcomes. One may support such policies, as I do. But to blend such goals into employment policies leads only to confusion, or to double-talk, as in affirmative action plans that affirm both nondiscrimination and preferences for minorities.

Any preferential treatment runs counter to a newly clarified core value in our political tradition—that no one should enjoy privileges, or suffer disabilities, because of birth status, because of family, race, or gender, or because of participation in any group. It may be true that, so far, the occasions when affirmative action policies have indeed led to preferential treatment for women or blacks have not yet matched the number of situations in which the traditional preference for white males has continued, legal or not. I suspect this is true. The long history of past privileges for white males may make it seem only sweet justice for our society, at least briefly, to reverse the scales. But many wrongs do not make a right.

Such special preferences in hiring have already created some of the bitterness in those who see themselves, correctly or not, as penalized. This bitterness might seem just if present compensatory preferences rewarded the past victims of discrimination, or if they punished the past perpetrators of such injustice. Usually they do not.

Much more critical than a maladjustment of rewards and punishments is the erosive effect of favoritism on its seeming beneficiaries. Nothing is a greater insult to my integrity than for someone to let me win in a competitive game. Nothing is more erosive of a sense of self-worth than gaining a position because of a well-intended but necessarily patronizing relaxation of standards. No self-respecting person, no minority, wants special treatment. If in time those who gain jobs or money or power by such special treatment lose self-respect, and affirm a system that works to this end, then we will have moved far toward a very cynical and amoral society, one in which various interest groups struggle to get as many favors as possible, with no concern for matters of merit or equity.

I turn now to what comes easy to me—a sermon, one involving a brief excursion into moral philosophy. As our society has become ever more diverse, I believe that the most important glue that still holds Americans together is the political culture that I earlier characterized by the four foundations. Immigrants become Americans by assimilating this culture, by learning the beliefs and values that go with it, and by becoming reasonably adept at functioning within it.

I emphasize our political culture because I believe it embodies a beleaguered national covenant. The two devils we now face are narrow provincialism on one hand, complete relativism on the other. For diverse peoples to live together, they must engage in an ongoing ethical dialogue and keep renegotiating what I have just referred to as a covenant, by which I mean mutual pledges and commitments to each other. Such a covenant, and such a dialogue, can transcend major cultural differences but never secure any full consensus. People everywhere affirm life, but not all people.

Those who affirm life must, as a matter of consistency, commit themselves to certain universal ethical commitments, or those still eloquently but loosely expressed in the language of human or natural rights. Masochists may not affirm such values. Those of us in such a broad covenant have no alternative but to judge and punish such life-hating individuals.

Complete relativists despair of any such covenants, or deny the possibility of fruitful ethical dialogue across major cultural boundaries. They refuse to judge and punish. Provincial people may easily affirm such a covenant, but they quickly subvert it by their rigid adherence to parochial maxims and rules. Often, in innocence, they absolutize the rules of their group. When they do this, they necessarily, and again without recognition or malice, relativize ethical principles.

A diverse society, more than a homogeneous one, requires the glue of widely shared and unqualified ethical commitments. Yet in a diverse society those who share in a social covenant have to recognize that the ends they serve will require very different implementing rules in different contexts. The same rules, the same laws, will not enhance life and liberty in all contexts.

Thus, the model for a diverse yet unified and stable society is an absolute ethic and a contextual or situational morality. The ethical mandate in such a pluralistic society has to be "Within the limits set by your covenant, do unto others as they would have you do for them. But when ethical principles are at stake, do unto others as you would have them do to you." Such a formula is a very difficult one to achieve. It is not easy for diverse people to develop and clarify common goals. It takes enormous effort to gain the knowledge and the cultural insights to decipher what these demand from us in our dealings with people whose heritage, whose religion, whose language, are very different from our own.

I have so far talked about such an inclusive covenant as one based on a simple affirmation of life. Such a general level of ethical concern is important in providing boundaries for local community building. Such broad ends are critical in ethical discourse across major national and cultural boundaries, or in trying to give modern form to the old idea of international law or to the idea of human rights. But as centuries of experience have demonstrated, people are not moved by, cannot live by, such universal standards alone, any more than they can respond to such oxymoronic concepts as a global community. We all live in local and in some sense necessarily exclusive communities, beginning with the nation-state. When I refer to American political values and institutions, I refer to a particular heritage, and thus to ways of doing things, to privileged beliefs and traditions, that are peculiar to that heritage.

This leads to what I call our national covenant. I hope it is ever more closely constrained by what people from various cultures, out of continuing ethical dialogue, agree to affirm as universal norms. Nonetheless, it will remain a covenant that is distinctive to Americans. Our constitutional system, our allegiance to human rights, our support of a wide range of due process protections, our openness to several forms of expressive freedom, are rooted in a largely British tradition, but one with both classical and Judeo-Christian roots. Our institutions will always have a particularistic or parochial aspect, however broadly accepted. Clearly, trial by jury is not necessary for justice; other juristic practices may serve justice better in other parts of the world. Judicial review by courts, or reverence for a written constitution may not be necessary for a humane social order. These are our preferred means for achieving such a lofty ethical goal. So long as they indeed serve rather than subvert such an end, then I believe we rightly affirm these institutional means, and rightly require those who would be citizens of our country to learn to live within them.

Such national covenants are not static, but if they are stable, they will always have deep roots in the past and change very slowly. I emphasize the process of renegotiating such covenants. They are human creations and provide a departure point for the ways in which we, in groups, continually redefine ourselves. As experiences change, as our political culture struggles with enormous challenges, the content of our covenant will change, and immigrants and the newly enfranchised will have their say in either reworking the covenant or giving new meaning to it. The ethical dialogue must not end. But at any one time, we as participants in a national polity have no alternative but to uphold some standards of membership and participation, not only at the level of the most basic and general ethical commitments, but also at the more restricted level of our distinctive institutions. We have no alternative but to take responsibility for the communal norms that we affirm, and to hold all who want to live in our midst to these norms, condemning and punishing those who violate them.

A particular cultural heritage, or past victimization and exclusion, may indeed help explain why some people reject or violate our communal norms. Such factors may rightfully lead us to temper justice with mercy. But they cannot excuse such deviance, for if they do, we then hold others to a lesser standard than ourselves, and in so doing deny their full human worth. We patronize them, and in today's world the worst sin of all is a tendency, among affluent and successful and well-meaning people, to patronize those who seem, in one way or another, either handicapped or victims. The urge to excuse when only explanations are in order leads toward a nihilistic and fatal refusal to judge anyone, to uphold any firm standards whatsoever. Then, indeed, everyone is welcome. No one is guilty. And, by the hardest of logic, no one is responsible.

6

✛

American Religion

The history of Christianity has been one of my most important interests throughout my scholarly career. Beginning with the Hutterites, in *Two Paths to Utopia* in 1964, I have written about religion as much as, or more than, any other subject. In particular, my last four books have all involved aspects of Christianity in America, beginning in 1990 with *Cane Ridge: America's Pentecost*, and continuing with two books published at North Carolina, *The Uneasy Center: Reformed Christianity in Antebellum America* (1995) and *American Originals: Homemade Varieties of Christianity* (1997), and ending with my most recent book, *When All the Gods Trembled: Darwinism, Scopes, and American Intellectuals* (Rowman & Littlefield, 1998). Because of these interests, I have presented numerous lectures on religious themes, all the way down to invited presentations to Sunday school classes.

For the selections for this book I chose two speeches that relate religion to the political process and to the dilemmas of cultural pluralism. I thought not only that these better fulfilled the theme of this book, but that they would be accessible to more readers, and of perhaps more interest than doctrinal or theological subjects. The first essay, on the Scopes trial, is the text of an address that I gave at Azusa Pacific University in early 1999, at a session sponsored both by that university and by the American Association for the Advancement of Science. The second essay engages the complex issue of state-church relations. I presented this as a lecture, in the summer of 1998, to supplement a special exhibit on American religious history at the Library of Congress.

The Scopes Trial Revisited

I think the Scopes trial in Dayton, Tennessee, in 1925 was one of the most significant trials in American history. Until that time it was certainly the most publicized trial, and the first trial to be broadcast on radio. Very important issues joined at the trial; very colorful personalities clashed. Too often, I think, commentators picture the trial as a confrontation between two abstract, almost undefinable entities—religion and science. Actually, all the protagonists, both in the trial and in the subsequent hearing before the Tennessee Supreme Court, were professedly religious. Except for one Jewish rabbi, and one defense attorney, Clarence Darrow, who was a religious humanist, all the protagonists were professed Christians.

Unfortunately, no firm semantic conventions govern the use of the word "religion." Any definition, to be very useful, must encompass both theistic and nontheistic religions. For my purposes I use the word substantively to designate beliefs about ultimate reality, types of fulfilling experience, various rituals, and sanctioned moral codes. Distinctive goals are enlightenment or wisdom, ecstasy, worldly success, or the achievement of salvation, meaning some form of life after death. Institutionally, religions variously involve sacred texts, shamans or priests, temples and shrines, and educational or proselytizing agencies. Christianity, one of the four largest world religions, is distinctive by its strong emphasis on correct belief and on salvation. It is the prototypical doctrinal and salvationist religion. It subordinates, but does not exclude, characteristics and goals that are more prominent in other religions, such as enlightenment in Hinduism and Buddhism, rituals and moral codes in Judaism and Islam, and ecstasy in several African religions.

Only Jewish and Christian beliefs were at stake in the Scopes trial. The issues involved not religion, as a class, but particular religions. Most of the battles involved professed Christians warring with each other. Behind these debates was the still intimidating influence of the cosmology present in the opening sections of Genesis in the Jewish scriptures, a cosmology shared by the three Semitic religions. This cosmology involves the work of a creative and providential male deity, one who created the earth, sun, moon, and stars, as well as all types or forms of life. This deity, according to his purposes, guided all processes of history, and endowed humans with many of the attributes of gods, including self-consciousness. This cosmology has faced challenges from many directions in the last two hundred years, but, for very complex reasons, the most telling challenges have involved knowledge about the past, particularly knowledge about Jewish and Christian scriptures, and about natural history, with the problem of human origins at the heart of that history. The Scopes trial, above all, involved the authority of ancient scriptures and competing stories about human origins, or, in brief, clashing historical interpretations.

Did the Scopes trial involve science? That also depends on definitions. The word "science" defies any commonly accepted definition. It is fully as muddy a word as religion. The word "science" variously refers to people who conduct certain types of inquiry—that is, to scientists—or to techniques or methods of inquiry, to institutions that support such inquiry, or even to the form or structure of knowledge that derives from such inquiry. In 1925 various competing theories about human origins all involved not generalizable theories or laws, but hypotheses about natural history. It makes more sense to me to classify the complex debate about human origins as a historical debate rather than a scientific one, particularly since none of the competing theories involved any laws or true generalizations. But, of course, many people include nongeneralizable historical knowledge—particularly about the natural world, and often also about social phenomena—as scientific. Thus, the word "scientific," in ordinary use, is very broad and quite vague. But, in any case, I emphatically deny that any entity, any actor called science was involved in any conflict with another entity or actor called religion. Both religion and science, when used this way, are sheer mystifications.

Yet most people at Dayton believed that modern theories about human descent had derived from the work of scientists, however they defined the term. In the background was Charles Darwin. But he was not in the foreground at the trial. Almost no one mentioned Darwin. What the Tennessee legislature, in the Butler Act, tried to exclude from the schools was any theory of organic evolution that involved the hereditary descent of humans from lower animals. Even if one conceded that a god willed the hereditary processes that linked humans to other primates, one could not teach such a theory in Tennessee schools. What the opponents of the act wanted to prove was, first, that hereditary descent was a fact, one all but beyond question, however many theories still competed about exactly how it took place. Second, that organic evolution, as an established fact, was consistent with an informed or enlightened form of Christianity. Note the qualifications: informed and enlightened. Everyone at Dayton realized that organic evolution was inconsistent with any literal understanding of the Genesis cosmology.

As the defense lawyers and experts insisted, the fact of emergent new species through time was evident to geologists by 1800. Many naturalists and philosophical idealists advanced theories about how such organic change took place. None of the explanations was coherent or persuasive to hard-headed naturalists. This set the problem for Charles Darwin. Soon after 1840 he concluded that a simple historical pattern lay behind the origins of our present flora and fauna. In normally scarce environments, ones in which not all progeny can survive, some inherited and inheritable variations slightly enhance the chance for lucky individuals to survive and reproduce. In time, and in certain environments, cumulative variations may lead to major modifications. In a very long time such cumulative variations may account for so many modifications to one or a few original species as to lead to all present life forms.

Darwin identified not transformative laws, like those in Newtonian mechanics, but a historical pattern. Like most historians, he could look back and identify the necessary conditions for outcomes, but not identify sufficient conditions for any specific outcomes. Yet, misleadingly, he often talked about laws. What he identified were certain dynamic aspects within nature that assure cumulative or designlike, but not designed, outcomes. These outcomes include simple organisms almost perfectly specialized to fit a given environment, or more complex, internally specialized, and centrally coordinated organisms able to adapt to many environments. Such adaptation and complexity made possible the rich ecologies of today, when almost every conceivable niche in nature supports many forms of life. Unfortunately, Darwin used a very misleading metaphor—natural selection—to label a process that had no cause, reflected no agency, and thus involved no selection. The random nature of variations precluded any predictions about the exact characteristic of future emergents. Darwin assumed unknown but determinant physical processes behind observed variations. He assumed wrongly. We now know that copying errors in strands of DNA in cell division, and cuts in strands of DNA that allow multiple recombinations in the production of sex cells, are random and unpredictable. We know the molecular foundations of reproduction, yet no exact prediction is possible.

But Darwin's importance at Dayton lay not in his explanation of speciation, but what he said about the status of humans in his second major book, *The Descent of Man*. In one of the few references to Darwin in the trial, William Jennings Bryan took Darwin to task for his explanation of human origins. What Darwin had argued was that the enormous functional gap between humans and even other primates involved many relatively small, cumulatively inherited changes in parts of the brain and in the larynx. These changes enabled complex signaling systems to evolve into a symbolic language, and language made possible human self-consciousness and culture. Self-consciousness encompassed what people in the past had meant by "mind" or "soul," and mind, in this sense, was a very recent emergent, not some cause behind the material world. Darwin thus naturalized mental phenomena. And in so doing he posed a threat, not to theories about specific creation, but to almost all forms of traditional theism.

To the trial. In March 1925 the governor of Tennessee, Austin Peay, very reluctantly signed a bill approved by both houses of the legislature. The poorly drafted bill had only one operative provision: No teacher in any school or college supported by the Tennessee public school fund could teach "any theory that denies the story of the Divine Creation of man as taught in the Bible, and to teach instead that man has descended from a lower order of animals." Unlike earlier anti-evolution legislation, this act criminalized such teaching, with a prescribed fine from one hundred to five hundred dollars. The wording was inept. Every version of the Christian Bible contained not one but two quite different stories about divine creation. Many avowed Christians believed that the biblical stories were consistent with certain types of theistic evolution. It was not clear what "teach" meant. Did it mean that a teacher could not even answer student questions about theories of descent, or did it mean that teachers could not teach that such theories were true? In order to violate the law, did a teacher have to deny divine creation *and* support descent, or was either of these sufficient for conviction? Such unanswered questions led one of four state supreme court judges to find the act unconstitutionally vague.

The author of the act was a genial, good-willed farmer from north central Tennessee, John W. Butler. He was a Primitive Baptist, and thus, contrary to all newspaper accounts, neither an Evangelical nor a Fundamentalist Christian (his small sect repudiated mission activity, revivals, and even Sunday schools). Some legislators voted for the bill out of conviction, others out of fear of constituents. As the bill was worded, an overwhelming majority of Tennesseans, most of whom had not been involved in any fundamentalist crusades, agreed with its intent. The governor saw the bill as an affirmation of deeply held religious convictions, not something the state should enforce. Both the legislators and governor feared bad publicity for Tennessee and thus preferred to keep the bill out of the limelight.

The young and aggressive American Civil Liberties Union sabotaged such hopes. Fearing more anti-evolutionary legislation, the union sought an early test of the Butler Act and advertised for teachers in Tennessee willing to challenge it. The ACLU promised to pay all court costs. In the small county-seat town of Dayton, north of Chattanooga, a handful of local businessmen decided to accept the ACLU offer, to the dismay of most Tennesseans. A trial promised to put Dayton on the map and attract many well-paying visitors. The conspirators, one of whom disliked the Butler Act on principle, were able to persuade a young science teacher in the local high school, John Scopes, to be the guinea pig. He was reluctant but finally agreed. He taught general science, not biology, knew little about evolutionary theories, but had substituted briefly for the biology teacher. He did not remember ever mentioning the word "evolution," but the text that he helped students review had a section on Darwin and evolution. This was enough. Compliant high school students, after careful briefing, said the right words, and a jury indicted Scopes, making possible the test case, which lasted eight days, spread over two weeks, in the wilting heat of August 1925.

Without recounting many of the details here, I can briefly give only a synopsis: The trial became famous because of the outside lawyers present. William Jennings Bryan, in the last month of his life, volunteered his support for the prosecution; the ACLU reluctantly accepted the help of a notorious labor lawyer, Clarence Darrow, and a prominent New York divorce lawyer, Dudley Malone. A jury, made up mainly of local farmers, had to miss most of the trial, which largely involved one major procedural issue: Could the defense introduce the testimony of over a dozen expert witnesses who had in each case come to Dayton at their own expense? These included some religious leaders or theologians, and several prominent scientists. The defense lawyers conceded that Scopes had taught that humans did in fact, in some sense, descend from lower animals. What they wanted to prove was that human evolution, as a historical fact, totally apart from any theory about how it happened, was consistent with an enlightened understanding of the Bible.

The presiding judge sided with the prosecution and, after days of tedious arguments, denied the admissibility of expert testimony about either the Bible or evolutionary theories. Yet in order to assist the defense in its contemplated appeal to the Tennessee Supreme Court, and possibly also to extend and make more exciting the famous trial, he allowed the defense to read into the record statements from each of the experts, statements clarifying what they would have testified had they had the chance to do so. It was at the very end of this process that a gullible judge allowed Darrow to call Bryan as a purported expert on the Bible. This led to the most disgraceful part of the trial. Neither Bryan nor Darrow were biblical scholars, and the interchange between them was unedifying at best. During this exchange Bryan, following the lead of most Evangelical Christians of his day, admitted that the six days of creation in the first Genesis account did not necessarily mean six twenty-four-hour days.

Without the expert witnesses, the defense had no case. Besides, the ACLU wanted to appeal the case. Thus, when the jury finally was able to return to the courtroom, both the prosecution and the defense asked it to return a guilty verdict, which it promptly did. The judge, consistent with earlier moonshine cases, assessed the one-hudred-dollar fine, despite the fact that the state constitution required that a jury assess any fines over fifty dollars. The ACLU appealed. Before the Tennessee Supreme Court, the defense almost prevailed on the merits of its case. Two of the four judges voted to overturn Scopes's conviction on substantive grounds; two voted to uphold it, but on very narrow grounds. More important, the court as a whole correctly overturned the conviction because of a technicality, the misassessment of the fine, and asked the state not to retry the case (Scopes was no longer a state employee and no longer in Tennessee). This precluded an appeal to the United States Supreme Court, an appeal which, in any case, would have had small chance of acceptance. No clear federal constitutional issues were at stake.

Let me clarify why this was so. In 1925 Tennessee had a mild religious establishment. State laws required all teachers to read ten verses from the Bible each day. Opening prayers were universal. The state constitution required one to believe in a god and immortality in order to hold any state office. Yet the constitution guaranteed freedom of worship and precluded state favoritism to any one religious sect. In the perspective of today these provisions might seem incoherent, even contradictory. Not so for most Tennesseans.

The federal Constitution of 1787 delegated no powers to the new central government involving religion. The First Amendment made it clear that the Congress of the United States could not enact any laws respecting a religious establishment. This left the issue of religion up to the states. In the nineteenth century most states chose some elements of a state establishment. Tennessee was not alone in 1925. Only in 1947, in the landmark Everson case, did the federal Supreme Court, under the authority of the equal protection and due process clauses of the Fourteenth Amendment, extend the provisions of the First Amendment establishment clause to the states. This prefigured controversial decisions that banned religious instruction, school-approved prayers, and Bible readings in public schools. Thus, after 1947 it was clear that Tennessee's Butler Act was by then unconstitutional, but no one challenged it in federal courts before the Tennessee legislature repealed it in 1967. My point here is that, in 1925, the Butler Act did not violate any federal law, and nothing in the record indicates that the Supreme Court, in 1925, was open to an appeal based upon what later became its own doctrine.

What about the no favoritism clause in the Tennessee constitution? Here the defense had its strongest case, the one that most challenged state attorneys. The Butler Act did favor orthodox or traditional Christians over modernists, even as it clearly favored avowedly religious people as against those with no religion. In fact, this favoritism for religion, and the morality that purportedly depended upon religious belief, were key elements in the state case. Consistently, the state attorneys argued that no real or authentic religion could accommodate descent. Humans were special creations of a god. Thus, if the state were to continue to defend religious belief, and make God and immortality a test for office holding, the state had to keep from the schools any beliefs that undermined these constitutionally sanctioned beliefs. Descent theories were prime examples of such beliefs. They also would, in time, lead children toward agnosticism and atheism.

These arguments by the state were parochial and naive, yet probably well expressed the predominant view of the citizens of Tennessee. The state attorneys sensed that a whole worldview was at stake. From their perspective all the imported experts simply had to be wrong, else all the verities accepted by a vast majority of Tennesseans were in jeopardy. They argued that no really great or outstanding scientist had ever advocated the idea of descent. No one had ever established, or would ever be able to prove, that humans descended from animals. The only ones to take exception to this made up a small, superficial group of would-be scientists, or well-intentioned, would-be rescuers of religion—scientific dilettantes, near scientists, self-styled intellectuals, blindly partisan propagandists. The Butler Act was a defense against "the systematic, disturbing, misleading, uncritical, unscholarly, unhelpful and untrue intrusion of such half-baked and ill-considered" ideas. Those who used such cant were part of an ultramodern intelligentsia with sinister goals. They were against all religions, or what was the only hope for the world. Above all, they were subversive, in the sense that they used their sophistry to wean children away from all respect for authority, away from belief in a god and the moral constraints such a belief entailed. They supported an amoral, brutelike ethic, one that meant social anarchy.

As I understand it, the conflict at Dayton was not between any rigorous or new scientific knowledge and any priesthood or church. By 1925 the fact of organic evolution, if not the exact conditions that made it possible, was part and parcel of cosmopolitan understanding. In fact, it was all but truistic. The quite general fact of descent was over a century old, and thus commonplace. This understanding was comparable with the understanding that exists today, when almost every educated person makes assumptions about the natural universe, and about human history, that are radically inconsistent with any literal understanding of parts of the Bible. This is documented by almost every textbook taught in public schools, by every television program on natural history, even by popular fiction or movies. Children grow up with some conception of the antiquity of the earth, of its relative position in a galaxy and in the ever-expanding universe, of theories about the Big Bang as an elusive explanation of the origins of our universe, with a fascination with dinosaurs and other extinct species, with some grasp of the enormous variety of religions and religiously based scriptures, as well as with a belief that, in some sense, later and higher species have a genetic connection to earlier and at times more primitive ones. This is all common knowledge, not thereby infallible or beyond challenge and revision, but so much a part of self-understanding as to be basic to individual identity. That this is so, that the understanding of the world absorbed by most people in our society has changed so dramatically in the last two hundred years, is a fact of life.

But the question in 1925, and today, is, How far downward into the broader population has such seemingly commonplace knowledge penetrated? More critical, to what extent have millions of people, not necessarily provincial or uneducated people, been able to assimilate such knowledge and find a way to make it consistent with more traditional beliefs, many of which are rooted in various Christian traditions? In 1925 most of the protagonists at Dayton had, to some extent, struggled with this issue. Notably, the avowedly liberal and modernist Christians who came to offer expert testimony had made such accommodations, but in retrospect almost pitifully self-serving and incoherent accommodations. Local Christians even in Dayton could not have been unaware of some of the challenges, most of all those posed by evolutionary theories, but they had remained part of a provincial, strongly Evangelical culture. In the showdown, the Semitic cosmology of Genesis was still almost beyond doubt, however it related to the products coming from the theological and scientific workshops. However one understood the origin of humans, that understanding had to be consistent with divine creation, with a divinely established order of being, and with a special human status willed by the creator. It was clear to orthodox Christians at Dayton that the trimming and compromising represented by modernists struck at the heart of the older faith. The experts sounded like Christians, used some of the same language, but really believed in a quite different religion, one that involved new and very different gods. They were correct in this assessment.

On one level the Scopes trial vividly illustrated a developing clash between intellectuals and the larger public. This was not new. Tensions had always existed between the views of ordinary people and those of the few exceptionally gifted or well-educated people who probed the frontiers of thought and expression. But the gap in understanding and taste had broadened by the 1920s. This was evident in literature, in the plastic arts, in new philosophical schools, in the revolutionary shifts in physics, in music, in changing moral standards, but perhaps above all in the intense battles over religious belief.

At Dayton a local, regional culture suffered a type of invasion from the outside. Highly educated, cosmopolitan elites descended upon the village. Some were arrogant. Almost all were unintentionally patronizing. They found what they perceived as ignorance, or an unfortunate cultural lag, and with good intentions they wanted to begin an educational process, to bring the local citizens up-to-date on the complex issues involving evolution. They were quickly frustrated. They found a few local cheerleaders, some support from professors at Vanderbilt University, but no support from most ruling elites in Tennessee. They ran into a still homogeneous Protestant culture—not a monolithic culture, but one that still exhibited a type of solidarity when under attack. Lawyers, judges, and politicians rallied to its defense, and in so doing made the state seem hopelessly backward and parochial to the visiting outside observers or witnesses who came to Dayton, whether theologians, scientists, or journalists.

For most Tennesseans what happened at Dayton had to be disturbing. Eminent people from the outside, and educated elites within Tennessee, made two points over and over again: Organic evolution and the descent of humans was by then an accepted fact not only for biologists but for educated people generally; and a growing number of professed Christians not only accepted some form of evolution as verified beyond doubt but also argued that it was consistent with Christian belief and a correct or enlightened understanding of the Bible. In other words, only unenlightened, uneducated, or intellectually closed minds still said otherwise. Maybe, by strict constitutional standards, Tennessee had the right to preclude the teaching of descent even if it were true, but if this meant that it prevented its own children from learning the best of contemporary knowledge, knowledge accepted among the educated people of the world, knowledge that might soon be necessary for professional acceptance or even certain jobs, then the state was in an embarrassing situation. And those who came to Dayton to defend Scopes did all they could to create such embarrassment.

Scopes, beloved in Dayton, a willing and almost sacrificial volunteer who enabled the town to host the trial it wanted, assumed a role that soon made him seem, for the outside experts at the trial, a martyr to the cause of personal and academic freedom. From the perspective of most reporters, as depicted to the larger world, Scopes had defied not just the new Butler Act but the whole conformist mentality of village or province. He was a part of the revolt against the village, one who tried to escape Main Street. He tried, but failed, to bring enlightenment, a wider perspective, to an orthodox, even totalitarian society. Of course, the local ortho-doxy prevailed. The almost mythic fundamentalists, whom reporters found lurking everywhere in Dayton or even in Tennessee, became the devils of the piece, the epitome of mass society, the ignorant peasantry, the agents of popular repression. In the language of journalist H. L. Mencken, these Baptists and Methodists (sneer words to him) made up the vulgar democracy of America. Even as perceptive a critic as Walter Lippmann described them as ignoramuses and struggled to find a means of recon-ciliation between enlightened elites and the unwashed multitudes.

In a sense, whether humans had in fact descended from lower orders of life was not the issue. Neither legislatures nor courts are in a position to adjudicate issues of truth and falseness in biology or in any other disci-pline. Even if descent is an established fact, true in the sense that other empirically established hypotheses are true, the people of Tennessee might still decide that they did not want this "truth" taught to their chil-dren. The state, in its brief to the supreme court, made this point—that the legislature could rightly reflect the common understanding of the people of Tennessee, even if by some other standard the common wisdom was completely mistaken. But the attorneys for the state would not concede that descent was a fact and thus defended a Tennessee statute that only kept certain highly speculative theories out of classrooms.

From the perspective of today, three generations removed from the Scopes trial, what is evident is how many assumptions and beliefs were still shared by local citizens and the visiting experts. Both remained com-mitted theists. Even the most extreme modernists believed in a purpose-ful universe, in some ultimate cause behind natural phenomena. In fact, in retrospect the experts at Dayton seemed almost desperate to deny any ultimate conflict between what they called evolution and their upgraded or revised Christianity. It was as if most members of a cosmopolitan or elite American establishment, out of fear, had to deny any conflict. They feared the orthodox who seemed blind to the truth, even as they were deeply threatened by a growing number of intellectuals who had rejected any gods, any final cause operative in the universe.

One such "establishmentarian" compromise gained the most publicity. In 1923 Robert Millikan, the physicist and Nobelist, helped gather forty-five scientists, theologians (loosely defined), and public intellectuals to mediate the developing cultural wars. They signed a proclamation, or peace treaty, and did it to correct popular misapprehensions. The theolo-gians celebrated the work of scientists and, in a sense, gave them their divine blessing. The scientists repudiated the materialistic or naturalistic or irreligious position often attributed to them. This Washington agree-ment was, in retrospect, a near parody of modernist assumptions. The agreement opened with an unexceptional statement about the goal of scientists—to develop, without prejudice, the facts, laws, and processes of nature. It followed with the purpose of what it called religion—to develop the conscience, the ideals, and the aspiration of humans. Both functions were necessary for the progress and happiness of the human race. It ended with a muddy reference to the sublime conception of "God" furnished by what they called "science," a god consonant with the highest ideals of humans. This god had revealed himself, or itself, through countless ages in the development of the earth as an abode of man (a typical, immanent view of god), and in "the age-long inbreathing of life" into matter, culminating in man with a spiritual nature and godlike powers (a vague version of theistic evolution). What a nice god. It is hard to read such flabby intellectual junk today, but it had abundant appeal in 1923, despite ridicule from orthodox Christians and, above all, from nontheistic intellectuals such as Walter Lippmann.

It is good to remember that, for so many of the protagonists in the twenties, the challenges to older certainties were new. They were the first generation of thoughtful Americans to face up to them. Almost all the experts at Dayton had grown up in Christian homes and in evangelical churches. A few remained orthodox and tried desperately to hold on to the older religion as they understood it. Liberals and modernists tried to salvage as much of the older religion as they could. Rebels such as Darrow or H. L. Mencken exhibited a type of sophomoric rebellion and, with an often arrogant pride in their own liberation, spent much of their energies in caricaturing and vilifying those who still affirmed the beliefs they had "escaped." More perceptive and more brilliant intellectuals, such as John Dewey and Lippmann, accepted the loss of the old gods, glimpsed the human costs if not the tragedy of such a loss, and tried to find new, non-supernatural beliefs that could sustain moral engagement and communal solidarity. Others, such as John Crowe Ransom or George Santayana, revealed a more tragic reaction. They still loved the myths, and the wisdom, present in traditional forms of Christianity. But in no literal sense could they affirm the foundational beliefs of the Church. Their lack of belief reflected not a choice, but an existential fact. They had regrets. They envied those who still, in innocence, believed the older doctrines. They knew that only older certainties, and above all the old, fearful gods of the past, would ever have broad popular appeal. Above all, they celebrated the human truths that remained within the myths.

As this century ends, we are fully three generations beyond the twenties. The Evangelical Christians who won their case against Scopes have remained the most vital element within American Christianity. They adhere to the old cosmology. But theirs is today, more than ever before, a minority and a beleaguered subculture. On the other side, what was new and unsettling to intellectuals in the twenties is now commonplace. Those who struggled to accommodate new knowledge in the twenties knew, from experience, what it had been like to live in a structured and purposeful universe. They remembered the awe, the fear, and at times the comfort, of living in a world inhabited by gods. Thus they experienced the insecurity, and at times the elation, of knowing that the gods were all dying. The dying gods in their emergent new world were nonetheless still a vital part of their identity. For those who had for a time believed, then found themselves not believing (it was never a choice) in such a god, the most important fact of their existence was the god who was absent. His authority, his love and support, were gone. It was like the loss of a father. Indeed, such a loss opens up new areas of freedom and personal responsibility. But this is small comfort to one in the immediate aftermath of death.

Today fewer and fewer intellectuals confront such an experience. For them the gods of the twenties are long gone, forgotten and irrelevant. They live in a world beyond full understanding. They have to take full responsibility for their moral standards. They cannot appeal to any authority. They live in a world that, from their perspective, is without providential guidance, a world full of not only irony but tragedy, for it is a world that exhibits no purpose, moves toward no preordained goal, and provides no promise of human redemption. Thus, few contemporary intellectuals know the poignancy, the tragic sense of irreparable loss, that their grandparents suffered. Few can grasp the depth and vital significance of the issues at stake in a small Tennessee town in 1925.

American Religious Pluralism and Public Policy

It is part of conventional wisdom that the United States is a very diverse or pluralistic country. It may well be on the road to such, but it has not traveled that road nearly so far as a few other countries. Most of the movement in that direction has occurred in the last fifty years. Even for religion one has to qualify an at times smug, at times uneasy, image of an open, tolerant, and inclusive America. Even today the vast majority of Americans, if actively religious, are in the Judeo-Christian tradition. We have representatives of the three or four main branches of Judaism, and, if one counts very small denominations, literally hundreds of Christian sects. But compared to really diverse countries, such as India, we are still very homogeneous. Through most of our history the most divisive religious conflict has involved family quarrels, as between Roman Catholics and Protestants, or between Calvinist Baptists and Arminian Methodists. Nothing here compares to the deep cultural gaps that in India separate Hindus and Moslems, let alone Sikhs, Parsees, Jains, Catholic and Protestant Christians, Buddhists, and several tribal religions.

In most respects the British who colonized what is now the eastern United States were distinctive not for accommodating differences, but for the exact opposite—an enormous resistance to racial and cultural and religious differences. Unlike the Spanish, the British in America rarely intermarried with the native population. Instead, they displaced them westward. Unlike Spanish Catholics, they did not allow Indian converts to retain any aspects of their native religions. When they imported African slaves, they stripped them of as much of their former languages and religious practices as possible. Until World War II Americans continually adopted polices to exclude non-Caucasians and non-Christians.

Having said all this, I have to acknowledge that, even by 1730, the English colonies in America, if viewed collectively, seemed religiously

134

diverse from a western European perspective. All the major state churches of western Europe, and most of the schismatic sects, had already found a home somewhere in these colonies. After the religious revivals that spread through all the colonies by 1740, after the need for concerted action against the French and Indians, after the development of numerous intercolonial trade networks, the colonies sought and gained some degree of cooperation and a sense of unity. But religious diversity threatened such unity and has continued to pose problems all the way to the present.

Colonial America offered two powerful lures for Europeans. One was cheap land and the opportunity for family heads to become proprietors and thus freemen. The other was the vast space that allowed resented or persecuted religious minorities to find their own enclaves, where they could form the kind of communal and church life denied them back home. In New York and from Virginia south, the early English settlers had primarily economic motives, for they were largely Anglicans who tried to duplicate the homeland in all their institutions, including an established church. But in the three Puritan colonies in New England—in Rhode Island, in Maryland, and most of all in what became both Pennsylvania and Delaware—religious goals were paramount.

Imperial policy often supported the migration of resented minorities. It was James I who granted a charter to the Separatists or Pilgrims who came to Plymouth in 1620, and then Charles I to Puritans who came to Massachusetts Bay and Connecticut after 1629. Charles I arranged for Roman Catholics to settle in Maryland in 1634; Charles II gave a charter to a Quaker, William Penn, in 1681 for what became the colonies of Pennsylvania and Delaware. Such generosity to resented but often enterprising religious minorities served two goals—ridding Britain of sources of discontent and possible rebellion, and encouraging economic development in America. Thus, by 1750 the religious mosaic already included Roman Catholics, Anglicans, Lutherans, Moravians, German and Dutch Reformed, Scottish and Ulster Presbyterians, Congregationalists, Quakers, Anabaptists, and several smaller sects.

This diversity did not mean any acceptance of a pluralistic social order. And with the exception of Rhode Island and Pennsylvania, no such order existed at a local or even provincial level. In the seventeenth century the social order was fragile, a rule of law hard to maintain. This meant that local governments jealously tried to secure a homogeneous culture and severely limited all expressive freedoms. Tight and exclusive communities were the norm. These communities expelled or punished internal dissidents and rigorously excluded outsiders with different beliefs and values. The shared beliefs and values made possible close and supportive communities. The famous Puritan towns were excellent examples of a type of village totalitarianism. Repressive and exclusive, they were also very democratic, in the sense of broad political participation.

Such communal solidarity remained the norm throughout the eighteenth century. But with each passing year it was much more difficult to attain or preserve. Local religious communities had to find some way to coexist with very different neighbors, if not in their own colony at least in neighboring ones. Even the very exclusive Puritans, who imprisoned and at one point hanged resented Quakers who came to witness in Massachusetts, were happy for them to settle in a nearby and tolerant Rhode Island. When British policies threatened local interests, Puritans gladly joined with Quakers in Rhode Island and Anglicans in Virginia to resist. After all, in Britain the Puritans had been resented dissidents themselves.

I refer to this accommodation of differences, at a distance, as "distributive pluralism." It involved an increasing tolerance of diversity as one broadened the geographical boundaries. Locally, villages were usually exclusive. At the colony level they soon had to accept some degree of religious diversity. If they resisted this, as did Puritans in Massachusetts and Anglicans in Virginia, the 1689 Act of Toleration in Britain at least forced them to accommodate Quakers, although not yet Roman Catholics. After 1700, except for Roman Catholics, a type of often begrudging religious toleration prevailed in all the colonies. Not religious equality—far from it. Plenty of disabilities still burdened religious minorities. But no one could expel them or jail them. Only in Rhode Island and Pennsylvania did almost all Christian sects enjoy equality. These were the deviant colonies, but their very deviance provided a model for the new federal government after 1776.

What happened in Pennsylvania began as a principle with William Penn—to offer a refuge for persecuted minorities. It led, in time, to a more prudential accommodation of diversity. Given the large numbers of Scotch-Irish Presbyterians, Anabaptist sects, German Lutherans, Moravians, Reformed, and the older (but no longer a majority) Quakers, it seemed by the mid eighteenth century that public order, instead of requiring uniformity of belief, required just the opposite—a public tolerance of differences. Not that individuals in the various churches wanted, let alone appreciated, differences. They still largely lived in their local, isolated, and exclusive communities, as the Amish do today. Even Pennsylvania was a working federation of sectarian communities, but it was unique in offering no favoritism for any sect. When Britain forced it to enact several disabilities for Roman Catholics, it rarely enforced them.

After 1776 the new United States was in the position of an earlier Pennsylvania. It had to accommodate an already existing and irreversible level of at least Christian diversity. To describe how it did this is to essay one of the most complex issues in American history, and to enter an area that is so full of definitional traps that one can scarcely begin to clarify them all. I begin with a few.

Almost everyone who broaches the problems presented by religious diversity not only refers to the separation of church and state, but at times to the separation of government and religion, or even politics and religion. Begging the issue of what one means by "religion," an issue that has haunted the Supreme Court in adjudicating conscientious objection cases, let me boldly assert that it is impossible even to conceive of a complete separation of politics and religion, or even of government and religion. It may be possible to move a good ways, but never all the way, toward a separation of state institutions and organized religious bodies.

Almost all major religions involve not only beliefs, but various practices and strongly sanctioned moral codes. In some cases governments, in behalf of protecting life, or protecting citizens from esthetic or moral horrors, almost have to ban or regulate certain religious practices—such as human or animal sacrifices, the use of narcotics in worship, female circumcision, child marriages, or polygamy (remember the nineteenth-century Mormons). In other words, the exercise of police power will, sooner or later, in a religiously free context, conflict with what some people believe to be mandated religious practices, possibly even practices that they believe necessary for salvation. Thus, formerly the states, and since 1940 the federal government, have worked out all manner of compromises involving the free exercise of religion. Beliefs, of course, are beyond government control. Not so what one does as a consequence of beliefs, and here our governments have often intervened to limit religious practice, and they will continue to do so.

For most religious people norms of conduct have a religious grounding. For example, a god may command certain behavior. One of the most stupid statements that I have ever encountered is that governments cannot legislate morality. That is about all that governments do legislate. Laws are sanctioned modes of behavior, always predicated on some conception of what is right and wrong, beginning with laws against murder. If one argues that a government should never legislate the morality commanded by any religion, then governments could not legislate at all. Politics always involves people who see certain policies as consistent with, even mandated by, their religious beliefs. Such, for example, were the religiously motivated efforts that led to the emancipation of slaves and the passage of the 1964 Civil Rights Act. But any government, in almost any conceivable law that it passes and enforces, risks violating the religiously informed conscience of some citizens (look at abortion). This is inescapable, but the burden is lessened if something close to a moral consensus exists in a society. The greater the religious diversity, the less likely it is that a society will enjoy such a moral consensus.

In 1787 the delegates to the constitutional convention in Philadelphia made a wise decision. They would leave all issues directly affecting religious institutions to the states. Their reasons for seeking a tighter and more perfect union involved other issues—the need for centralized control over foreign policy and the military, over tariffs and international trade policies, and above all over the prerequisites of an internal common market (common currency, interstate comity, enforcement of contracts, common weights and measurements, postal services). Thus, a Constitution that very specifically defined the powers of the federal government delegated no powers to Congress relating to religion, as well as to other expressive freedoms. The new federal government simply could not legislate in this area. The Constitution contained no religious language; it mentioned no gods. And in article 6 it provided that "no religious test shall ever be required as a qualification to any Office or public Trust under the United States."

Our constitutional history would have been simpler, and quite different, if the first Congress had not approved, and the requisite states not ratified, the First Amendment. It begins with the elliptical phrase "Congress shall make no law respecting an establishment of religion, or prohibiting the free exercise thereof." This language was unneeded and redundant. It only reiterated what was already clear—Congress could not legislate on these issues. For some New England Congregationalists this redundant statement that the federal government could not do what it had no authority to do may have relieved concerns that the new federal government might somehow interfere with the type of church establishments that New Englanders loved. If not already clear, the amendment made it obvious that the states would continue to have a free hand in creating policies involving organized religious groups. This is what the states wanted.

From 1789 to 1940 the primary story of church-state relations in the United States involved the states. By the standards of the time, even the first state constitutions considerably expanded individual religious freedom from what existed before. In the sense that most then understood the meaning of a "religious establishment," all the states repudiated such, although briefly three southern states, and for an extended period three New England states, allowed or mandated a continuation of tax support for public worship. Yet by our present and much expanded legal understanding of what "establishment" can include, all the original thirteen states and Vermont endorsed a type of religious establishment.

This leads to the problem: What does one mean by a religious establishment? In 1787 most meant by "establishment" what England had—state recognition of and favoritism toward a specific Christian confession, with governmental funding of churches and a degree of governmental control over ecclesiastical policies. No one wanted this for America. A broader definition might include religious tests for citizenship or for office holding. Every early state constitution included such tests. Today, we also define as tending toward an establishment any policies that in any way favor one religion or family of religions over others, or favor all religions as against a secular social order.

For any extended period of time only Massachusetts (until 1833), New Hampshire (until 1819), and Connecticut (until 1818) came even close to an establishment of the stronger or traditional European sort. These states did provide tax support for public worship. This, in most towns, meant tax funds for Congregational or later Unitarian churches, but the three New England constitutions allowed other sects, if in a majority in a town, to have the same benefits. Only Massachusetts allowed towns to require attendance at public worship (compare to later compulsory attendance laws for public schools), but few towns ever enforced this. The purpose of such religious provisions were not, at least for most advocates, sectarian—an attempt to aid any one sect—but rather predicated on the need for public morality and political responsibility.

All the early states, as well as all later ones, adopted clauses that guaranteed freedom of worship. Except for the three New England states, all had articles that precluded favoritism either to any Christian sect or at least to any Protestant sect. Yet all had religious tests for office holding. Pennsylvania, as one might expect, was the mildest, requiring only a belief in a god (not any specified god). Four states (New Jersey, New York, and North and South Carolina) restricted office holding to Protestants. Delaware and the new state of Vermont required a belief in the Trinity (disabling both Jews and Unitarians) and a belief in the Old and New Testaments (disabling Jews), while Maryland and Massachusetts required only that one be a Christian. Tennessee, in 1796, first denied office to those who did not believe in God or a future state of rewards and punishments, a wording eventually adopted by five southern states and continued into the twentieth century. Yet, in what may seem an inconsistency today, these states all included a clause that provided that no civil rights or privileges could be denied or endangered because of religion. All early state constitutions included theistic language. They all appealed to divine wisdom or offered thanks for divine providence.

Changes came rather quickly, in part reflecting an accommodation with new immigrants. By 1868 the states had all removed Protestant and Trinity requirements, and thus constitutional disabilities for Catholics, Unitarians, and Jews. Outside the South few religious tests remained after 1860. From the beginning most states were very concerned about the rights of such minorities as Quakers and Mennonites, exempting them from normal oaths, and even providing for exemptions from militia duties on the basis of conscientious objection. Yet, in the other direction, an increasing number of states began offering tax exemptions for church property. Other states began to prohibit the use of tax funds for private schools (an anti-Catholic provision). By their understanding all the states, including even the five southern states with their god and future punishments provisions, believed that they had provided for complete freedom of worship and for at least a nonpreferential position respecting competing religious denominations. In other words, the states had gradually accepted language that seemed to assure almost as much neutrality, or as much separation, as the First Amendment mandated for the federal government.

Not so in practice. What actually prevailed was a type of informal Christian, Protestant, or even Evangelical establishment. State officials assumed as normative a belief in some version of the Christian god, in future rewards and punishments, in the critical importance of worship, and in the authority of the Christian Bible. The states required Bible readings in the new public schools, endorsed prayers at all public occasions, employed legislative chaplains, enforced blasphemy laws, enacted what they called Sabbath laws (really Sunday laws), and offered tax exemption to churches. These issues all directly involved religious beliefs or practices, not merely religiously based moral codes. Minorities suffered, whether Catholics, whose children could not use the Catholic Bible in school, Seventh-day Adventists and Jews, who could not work on Sunday but had to on the Sabbath, Universalists, who were not allowed to testify in courts because they did not believe in future punishments, and nontheists, who, if they dared reveal their atheism, could not testify in courts or, in any of the original states, even hold public office.

The federal government, with no constitutional leeway at all, was nonetheless complicit in such a loose Christian establishment. Presidents proclaimed thanksgiving days or days of fasting and prayer, while Congress held religious services in the House chambers and employed a Christian chaplain. And all branches wrapped much that they did in theistic language. Presidents soon added the nonconstitutional "so help me God" to their oath of office, even as recent presidents end their speeches with "God bless America." By congressional consent our coins include "In God we trust." The pledge of allegiance places all of us under god. Notably, no one ever makes clear which god is involved. Since an undefined god may seem innocuous, empty of meaning, threatening to no one, one might argue that these civic gestures are essentially meaningless. I suspect just the opposite and will return to this American civic god later.

Well into the nineteenth century most small villages or towns remained reasonably homogeneous. Informally, a local orthodoxy prevailed. State constitutional guarantees often meant little. No one enforced them against local majority opinion. Freedom of speech and press was severely limited; due process protections never fully honored; and parochial religious convictions dominant and exclusive. In the South such uniformity, and such repression of minorities, was often statewide, in areas where almost all Christians, white and black, were Baptists and Methodists, and where a type of localism was deeply entrenched. But such uniformity gradually broke down in larger cities and in areas of diverse immigrant populations. Here diversity was a fact of life. Formerly dominant elites lost power to enfranchised and often immigrant workers, and a growing intelligentsia embraced cosmopolitan values. Just as Pennsylvania presaged the formal or legal accommodations adopted at the national level in 1787, so such cosmopolitan and culturally diverse regions presaged the type of pluralism we now enjoy, or suffer, at the end of the twentieth century.

At a nongovernmental level such a pluralism has entailed the invasion of local, provincial, and exclusive communities by the values espoused by a cosmopolitan elite. Such a revolt against the village, against conformity and local prejudices, against most forms of religious orthodoxy, or what Sinclair Lewis summarized as Main Street America, first peaked in the twenties. Against great resistance this inclusive pluralism is now the official norm.

It is also the law of the land. Beginning in 1925, with free speech, the federal courts gradually so broadened their interpretation of the equal protection and due process clauses of the Fourteenth Amendment as to force states to accept the same First Amendment restrictions as did the federal government. This soon involved religion. In 1940 the Supreme Court (*Cantwell v. Connecticut*) ruled that states had to accept the "free exercise" clause of the First Amendment. Then, in the landmark Everson case of 1947, it incorporated the establishment clause. This led to a series of highly controversial decisions: a 1948 ruling that barred any religious instruction in public schools, the famous and still much resisted 1962 decision that barred school-sponsored or approved prayers in public schools, and a 1963 decision barring school-mandated or -approved Bible readings.

Since this expanded, and now irreversible, interpretation of the Fourteenth Amendment, the federal courts have been forced to render a series of often shifting and confused judgments about both free exercise and establishment. If one seeks some guiding theory, some precise test, then the courts have been in a confused muddle. They will remain so, for it is literally impossible for the federal courts to develop a precise and consistent formula for adjudicating complex cases involving religion. Above all, they cannot move all the way to complete neutrality or separation. If the courts tried to do this, they would lose a dangerous amount of public respect and invite a series of constitutional amendments. The Supreme

Court probed its limits in the 1962 prayer decision. In some cases litigants, with a clear standing, have forced the courts to rule on what many people (not the litigants) see as rather trivial issues (Christian symbols in public Christmas displays), while the Supreme Court has refused to get involved with what would seem to be major issues. For example, it has allowed the federal government to continue what amounts to major subsidies for churches and synagogues (because pledges paid to religious organizations qualify as contributions under our tax laws, the government indirectly contributes up to 20 percent of the income of middle-class congregations). It has never dared challenge chaplains in the Congress.

Quite often free exercise conflicts with separation. Look at military chaplains. At great expense the government pays for chaplains and thus provides direct aid to those troops with a specific religious allegiance. It favors religion as against nonreligion. Yet military personnel, in many wartime conditions, would have no realistic opportunity to exercise their religious convictions freely without some government effort on their behalf. Does not the right of free exercise require access to a clergy and to worship?

The most controversial religious decisions have involved local and parochial practices. Here the federal courts have had the support of cosmopolitan Americans, or an educated and politically powerful elite. In fact, most litigants claiming harm from a religious establishment have been outsiders who moved into formerly exclusive or repressive communities—such as Jews or atheists or homosexuals in near monolithic Southern Baptist villages. On the side of free expression the courts have tried to protect the practices of what most local people have seen as deviant and unwanted sects, such as Jehovah's Witnesses or the Unification Church. The effect, locally, has been intense resistance, for such successful litigation has disrupted old and traditional patterns of life and, indeed, threatened the type of close, familial, and comforting communities that such people value. Plaintively, such locals protest over and over again—Why do not such people go elsewhere, where they would be welcome?—meaning either a place where their values predominate, or to cosmopolitan urban areas bereft of any communal solidarity at all (New York, San Francisco).

To me the most interesting pattern in all the muddle has been the refusal of federal courts to tackle the issues related to a civic god. Here the courts confront a larger and more nearly national constituency. Also—and this may be critical—this civic god may be one of the few symbols that still tie some aggrieved or threatened provincials to a broader national culture.

The word "god" is not a proper name. It refers to any and all divine or supernatural persons, or even in some uses to a nonpersonal but higher reality. But such has been the depth of monotheistic assumptions in the

Judeo-Christian tradition that most Americans use this generic term, capitalized, as if it were a proper name. I find this use very confusing. When students use the generic as a name, I always ask what god they have in mind, what his or her or its name is, and what the dominant features are of this god. The response usually begins with confusion and ends with a great deal of imprecision. In fact, Christians vary enormously in what they intend by the word. Collectively, American Christians honor many gods, some scarcely related to each other in any of their characteristics. The fully corporeal god of Adventists seems unrelated to the divine spirit of Christian Science. But those in each tradition assume that only one god is real or existent, and thus they easily use the singular and capitalized term. An overwhelming majority of Americans—over 90 percent in most polls—profess a belief in some god. Only very refined surveys reveal how enormously varied these gods are.

At the time of our founding, theism was deeply entrenched, doubted by very few. The images of a god were not nearly as varied as today. Of the founding fathers Jefferson and Adams were among the few who had moved a long way from any form of Christian orthodoxy. They did not believe in Jesus as messiah or savior, in any of the doctrines related to his atonement, in any of his purported miracles, or in his resurrection. But both did believe in a creator god and in future rewards and punishments. They believed these two beliefs were common to all religions (they were wrong), and that the American republic could scarcely endure if the masses of people did not share these minimalist beliefs. As Jefferson put it, our liberties could not be secure unless people believed they were from God. As Adams lamented, our moral order would decay if people lost their belief in divine justice. Our truth claims would evaporate if people did not believe that a divine architect built an ordered and knowable world.

Thus, even for these two religious radicals, the new republic required some obeisance to divine authority. They hoped Americans would all gravitate to these few, essential beliefs and also follow the moral teachings of the man Jesus. All else in historic Christianity—all the miracles, abstruse doctrine, and vaporous spirits—had been as divisive as they were delusive. They hoped the sectarian Christian superstructure would soon drop away, leaving the religious distillate they thought all rational people could affirm. But they recognized that sectarian loyalties would not fade very quickly and took solace in the fact that even superstitious Catholics and Calvinists at least shared the minimal or essential religious beliefs.

In the early state constitutions it is remarkable how uniformly the theistic language was very general, even Jeffersonian, in flavor. The two leading appeals were to an Almighty God or to a Supreme Being. Other references

were to a creator, the great legislator of the universe, the creator and pre-
server of the universe, or the creator and governor of the universe. Despite
frequent references to Christianity, neither Jesus nor Christ were present in
any of the constitutions. Rarely does one find any gendered language in the
references to a god. Thus, the civic god began as a being who created and
governed the universe, but without any further specification. Undoubtedly,
individuals filled in the ellipses with the characteristics, with the more specific images, that fit the god of their own confessional tradition. I assume,
even yet, that it is this vague creator and governor of the universe that is
recognized on our coins and in the pledge of allegiance.

Along with this generalized god came what was soon a distinctively
American form of public religion. Tocqueville was amazed at this. At Sing
Sing prison, in 1831, the supervisors invited ministers, from varied neighboring congregations, to preach each Sunday. No one seemed to mind the
shifting denominational or confessional content in such sermons. Everyone attended. Why were Protestants not offended by Catholic priests? It
seemed, to Tocqueville, as absurd as having a rabbi give the invocation at
a graduation ceremony and a Catholic priest offer the benediction. What
type of doctrinal ignorance, or undiscriminating tolerance, or sheer
hypocrisy, supported such an unusual practice? Tocqueville wondered if
anyone in America cared about correct beliefs. In France they would soon
be fighting over such vital issues. In the early House of Representatives,
Sunday religious services, although nominally Christian, involved the
broadest possible spectrum of preachers, from a Unitarian to a Roman
Catholic. Long before they could obtain proper ordination, women
preachers also gave sermons. Blessing all this, even perhaps explaining it,
was the bland, featureless civic god.

Unlike in 1787, or even when Tocqueville visited in 1831, this civic god
is no longer consensual. The polls may be most misleading here. Many
people who profess a belief in a god do not refer to a creative and providential deity; up to half do not believe in future punishments. New Asian
immigrants usually do not believe in any version of the Semitic god. An
increasing share of intellectuals are not theists in any plausible sense of
that word. Thus, the civic god is now offensive to many people—to the
orthodox, who are horrified at its undemanding vagueness, and to all
nontheists, many of whom are deeply religious. Personally, I am offended
by this vague god. I will not repeat that part of the pledge of allegiance. I
cringe when presidents, not distinguished by clear and firm doctrinal
commitments let alone exemplary churchmanship, such as Reagan or
Clinton, appeal over and over again to this vaporous god. Such verbal
gestures seemed honest and fitting only for Jimmy Carter. Note that governmental sponsorship of such a civic god clearly tends toward an establishment of religion—it favors theistic religions over nontheistic ones,

such as forms of Buddhism or religious humanism, and over those who profess no religion at all.

Yet despite this fact and my own personal repugnance, I have to admit that this vague god may serve a constructive political role. Politicians are, or at least try to sound, conventional in their beliefs and values. Today, in what some refer to as "cultural wars," a widening gap separates an intellectual and artistic elite from most Americans. Very radical forms of skepticism, or new knowledge, have helped to undermine almost all the ancient verities. Some sense of a knowable order in our universe, some sense of universal values or at least the possibility of effective moral dialogue across enormous differences of culture, remains vitally important for most Americans. Such beliefs undergird the moral limits that Americans presume any legitimate government must accept. In an insecure Hellenistic age, with a greater and greater diversity of competing cultures, Americans may need symbols that provide some minimal glue to hold at least most of us together.

The United States has accepted an unprecedented challenge, one not assured of success—to try to sustain a more perfect union that finally embraces all races, all genders, all cultures, all religions or secular creeds. We are finally moving close to real diversity. Maybe a few icons that seem to have a religious or sacred content, such as that capitalized generic that is our civic god, are necessary. If so, maybe it would be unwise for offended Americans, like me, to make principled objections or to seek relief in the federal courts. And when a few do just this, such as Madeline Murray, maybe the courts have been wise, so far, in rejecting their legally persuasive claims. Maybe, in other words, we should continue to accept such obvious and illogical compromises with the principle of separation. Even Jefferson, who first used the misleading metaphor "wall of separation," frequently compromised the principle himself.

7

The South

I have never considered myself a southern historian. I have not written about the themes that have most dominated the well-developed and self-conscious field of southern history. Yet I have written books on Vanderbilt University, on Lyndon Johnson, on the Cane Ridge revival in Kentucky, and on the Southern Agrarians. These all would seem to involve the South, although each in a certain sense is peripheral to what most would consider the heart of the southern experience. But what does one mean by the loaded word "South"?

Problems of definition and identity are central to the following two essays. The first represents a copy of a lecture I gave somewhere, and sometime, at Vanderbilt. I found it in my file cabinet. It dates from just after I had published a book, *The Southern Agrarians* (University of Tennessee Press, 1988). It drew from a more formal lecture—"The South in Southern Agrarianism"—which I presented at the University of Georgia in the fall of 1985, as part of a symposium on southern culture. Numan V. Bartley edited these lectures and published them as *The Evolution of Southern Culture* (University of Georgia Press, 1988).

To my own surprise, since I did not consider myself a southern historian, the Southern Historical Association honored me with its presidency in 1996–97. This position required, among other duties, the preparation of a presidential address, to be presented at the annual convention in 1997, in this case in Atlanta, Georgia. Appropriately, I took this assignment very seriously, and did more work for this essay than any other I ever wrote. From long drafts, I finally reduced it to a suitable length. It includes some personal confessions but is also a sweeping, even epic, interpretation of southern history.

What Is a Bright Southern Boy to Do?

Most people do not have the time, or the information, to agonize about regional identity. This has been particularly true of southerners, who have been, as a whole, less mobile, more rooted in place, than people in any other section of the United States. They have been more provincial. Polls show, therefore, that they are usually proud of their communities, happy to live where they do, loyal to their home state, and not very critical of local institutions. This includes blacks as well as whites. Most welcome the label "southern." They either do not understand more cosmopolitan values or simply reject them out of hand. Instead of feeling inferior, backward, or oppressed, they are often boastful and innocently proud—not necessarily chauvinistic, for chauvinism usually reflects defensiveness, a form of fighting back, tied to a keen awareness of differences and the powerful lure of alien values. Whenever individuals in the South have become involved in sectional controversy, when they have been forced either to defend home values or capitulate to outside ones, then innocent pride has often turned into defensive and often ugly chauvinism.

As I have worked with the Vanderbilt Agrarians, I have come to realize that a critical issue for all, the most critical issue for some, was self-identity. Who am I? In my book on Southern Agrarianism, in which I focused on the ten men most involved in the movement, I tried to do justice to the Agrarians as reformers, to deal in detail with their programmatic crusades. In this lecture I will slight policies and more often talk about identity. I easily relate, personally, to this issue. At times autobiography may creep into my lecture.

We all have a compelling need to be respected, taken seriously, valued for our achievements, respected for our beliefs and preferences. We also need to have a sense of worth, to be morally complacent, else we lose confidence and even sanity. Loose tags like "insecurity," "inferiority complex," and "moral confusion" suggest the terrible consequences of a besieged and vulnerable ego. Of course, the foundations of identity are numerous, with most tied to individual experience and family dynamics. But part of the sense of who we are is rooted in larger affiliations—the church we belong to, the town or county or state or region or nation we live in. At times one or another of these communities can become focal in our awareness. The context determines. Southern boys, who never thought much about, or worried about, being southern, often became intensely aware of this mark of identity when they matriculated in a northern university or went off to the army. No one would let them forget it.

For bright, white, college-educated, privileged southern boys, the 1920s and early 1930s invited regional or sectional self-consciousness—most of all when they left the South, but even at home if they became intellectuals, if they joined in critical and ideological dialogues. At times the South was a topic of such dialogues. More often values widely shared and affirmed in the South were objects of intense criticism or open ridicule. Thus, intellectual engagement almost demanded a keen awareness of a South whose culture few nonsoutherners seemed to respect, as well as a section that lagged behind the rest of the country in almost every accepted measure of human achievement.

The larger South (all slave states of 1860 save for Missouri) from 1865 to 1930 remained impoverished by national standards. Not so before 1860, when incomes in this South, even including slaves in the computation, equaled those in the Midwest and were above 80 percent of incomes in the Northeast. In addition, the antebellum South contained pockets of great wealth. In the best cotton counties of the delta, per capita incomes led the nation. After the war southern incomes ranged around 50 percent of national averages, with some gains in the twenties that were quickly lost during the early depression. But even such a harsh ratio as this conceals the plight of the South, because southern incomes so reduced national averages, and because the eleven former Confederate states were even worse off, on average, than the larger South, which indeed included a poor West Virginia but a comparatively affluent Maryland and Delaware. Compared to wealthier states, such as Connecticut, southern incomes were scarcely above 30 percent. The gap was equally visible in agriculture, where productivity and incomes paled by comparison with the Midwest, and in manufacturing, where wages remained well below those in the Northeast in largely low-skill, labor-intensive, and nonunionized industries. Such comparative poverty accounted, in large part, for an even more dramatic lag in education and other services. It probably helped account for a South that made almost no contribution to the fine arts except in literature, and even then often by expatriate southerners. The South, apart from Baltimore and Washington, D.C., had no first-class universities, no great newspapers, no major publishers, no leading museums, no major symphonies, and on and on one could extend this list.

The South also lacked the degree of social order enjoyed in the North; violence seemed endemic, crime rates high. In spite of the puritanical code preached in the churches (prohibition and Sunday laws, and all that), a paradoxical and almost feudal code of personal honor yielded up its feuds and horrible lynchings. Culturally, the South, if anything, seemed to lag more with each generation. Economic progress did not translate into cultural gains. In religion the South had become the Bible Belt by the era of the Scopes trial, with a preponderance of its churches fundamentalist and evangelical in an age when northern intellectuals either embraced modernist, esthetic, or socially active forms of Christianity or, more often, rejected all forms of organized religion. For many northern intellectuals "Methodist" and "Baptist" became sneer words.

Hovering over all these marks of provincial backwardness was the tangled problem of race. In all areas, from literacy to crime, blacks helped account for the southern lag. The separation of the races, and tensions between them, placed major obstacles in the way of economic progress. Legalized segregation and disfranchisement had indeed made possible increases in white paternalism and some black progress, even in education. But the cost was high. Just as with slavery, this new racial settlement involved such flagrant injustices, such inequalities, that it was already, by the twenties, drawing the condemnation of advanced moral opinion around the world. And the external critique was sure to grow exponentially, as was obvious to almost any perceptive southern intellectual. This meant that the South, as a whole, still had to live under a type of moral stigma and to suffer a type of guilt.

Given these hard facts, how could a bright southern white boy, possibly the grandson of Confederate soldiers, gain any sense of pride? He could flee the South, find opportunities in the North. Many did. But a bright southern white boy who made this choice carried with him an unerasable fact—he was from the South. Shaped by it. Warped by it. Like provincials everywhere, he carried, even in his accent, a mark of inferiority. Even when they did not intend it, host Yankees exuded a sense of social confidence and moral superiority. They were relaxed winners; white southerners, sensitive losers.

Of course, despite a lack of opportunities, a southern boy could stay at home. There he could try to cure the South's problems. But according to what model? It was easy to absorb the values of northern critics and thus to work to make the South like the North, help it catch up. Implied in this was a repudiation of the existing South, and thus an affirmation of an essentially nonsouthern identity. It was another way of fleeing the South, spiritually. Thus, it meant a type of alienation, an alienation felt by so many educated, morally sensitive southern boys. In the South but not of it. Ashamed of it.

Finally, one could remain in the South, either physically or spiritually, and try to find in its history or culture something distinctive yet ennobling or redeeming. One could affirm southernness, yet without necessarily becoming blind to the region's quite real economic and social problems. The ten young men who make up my subject for this lecture all took this option, although not until they had at least flirted with alien gods. Each, in a sense, fled the South but then came home to reclaim it, in some sense redefine it, perhaps even create it. Each found in the South a cultural ideal, even though one often tarnished or unrealized in the besieged present. Each found a slightly different ideal, celebrated the reality or at least promise of a slightly different South, but persuaded themselves, by 1930, that they shared enough of a common identity, affirmed enough similar ideals, that they should endorse a common platform or manifesto. This prefaced a poorly planned and very uneven collection of essays published as *I'll Take My Stand*. Although twelve authors contributed essays to this book, I will not include two—Stark Young and Ralph Blue Kline—in the following analysis. Neither made a full commitment to the Agrarian cause, or remained a part of the Agrarian circle.

All ten of the committed Agrarians except Lyle Lanier had lived for a time outside the South. Many became most aware of their southernness while in alien lands. Lanier, of the ten, alone stayed home and possibly for this reason seemed least clearly involved with issues of southern identity. Two young historians from Alabama plantations, Frank Owsley and H. C. Nixon, moved from Auburn, where they had attained their M.A.'s, to Ph.D. work at the University of Chicago. Each suffered problems of adjustment. In Arkansas an overly sensitive and vulnerable boy from a wealthy Little Rock family—John Gould Fletcher—went to the prewar Harvard under family pressure, was there an utterly miserable misfit, dropped out just before graduation, and fled to London, where he flirted with Fabian socialism and became an imagist poet. In Georgia, John Donald Wade left his beloved home in Marshallville to begin graduate work in English at Harvard. He served in the Army during World War I, then, as an instructor at the University of Georgia, left to complete a Ph.D. at Columbia University, not clearly because he wanted to go north but because the South offered no comparable training. A precocious and rebellious and confused Allen Tate matriculated at Vanderbilt. From northern Kentucky, with maternal roots in Virginia, he at first detested the South, never really felt at home in it, and gladly fled to the Bohemias of New York City after graduation, glad to escape southern provincialism and ignorance.

The other four young men were from the Cumberland basin. John Crowe Ransom, son of a Methodist minister, a brilliant student at Vanderbilt, won a Rhodes scholarship, in Britain immersed himself in classical philosophy and English country life, and only reluctantly returned to a position at the pre–World War I Vanderbilt when he failed to gain a job in a prestigious northern university. Donald Davidson, son of a public school teacher in middle Tennessee, struggled to get a decent grammar school education, worked to pay his way almost through Vanderbilt, and then, with his teacher, Ransom, served in France in the war. He returned, with home loyalties, yet married an Ohio woman and contemplated a career in journalism in Cleveland. Robert Penn Warren, from nearby Guthrie, Kentucky, came to postwar Vanderbilt to study English. There he almost floundered, suffering a mental breakdown in the heady days of the Fugitive poets. He gladly fled to graduate work at Berkeley and then Yale, won a Rhodes scholarship, and at Oxford began his loving but always in some sense detached analysis of his southern heritage. Andrew Lytle was a fellow student, from an affluent Murfreesboro family with land in Alabama. He came at the end of the Fugitive period, loved poetry, but moved to a graduate program in theater at Yale and, for a time, aspired to a career as a playwright and actor in New York City.

By the late twenties each of these ten young or almost young men were intensely conscious of their southernness, and each was by now anxious to affirm and defend some version of southern culture. None wanted to create a new South in the northern image, although their reasons for this varied. None wanted to sink into nostalgia, exploit local color, or embrace the myths of a lost cause. They wanted nothing of the pathetic, imitative gentility of a southern upper class, of debutantes and country clubs. But in different ways they all realized that the Confederate South since 1865, a sixty-year period that their own parents and grandparents suffered through, made up an aberrant, distorted, exceptional interlude in southern history. The South of their day, defeated, economically exploited, politically marginal, did not offer a fair basis for cultural evaluation. Thus, they had to look back to the pre–Civil War South to gain some sense of southern possibilities, to glimpse a culture not yet embarrassed by defeat, not under siege, and one with the material foundations and political strength needed to support cultural integrity.

What type of South existed before the war? What cultural possibilities did it suggest had the war not intervened? Here the ten Agrarians offered a range of answers, but along a continuum between two poles. On one side was an image of the old South best articulated by Owsley, but echoed in whole or part by Lytle, Davidson, Nixon, and Warren. This was a South made up, primarily, of small family farms, managed by owners, and serviced by small merchants and artisans. Such a South did not significantly differ from rural areas of the Midwest and even New England. This was the yeoman South, one idealized by Owsley in his *Plain Folk of the Old South*. It entailed families who owned land and enjoyed independence, class harmony, simple folk arts, respect for nature, and religious piety. Large planters with many slaves made up an exception to this pattern, but they never dominated the South.

Such a yeoman and egalitarian society always faced a threat from large merchants, bankers, and factory owners, or people the Agrarians referred to as industrial capitalists. Good Jeffersonians had always been besieged by all those evil Hamiltonians, who had hypocritically used the issue of slavery as an excuse for subduing, then exploiting, the South. No Agrarian doubted this view of a capitalist conspiracy behind most of the reverses in southern history, a view they shared with most Marxist historians in the twenties and thirties. After the horrors of Reconstruction, after redemption, the South suffered a continued colonial status. Northern economic policies—monetary restraint, high tariffs, corporate subsidies, tax policy, unequal rail rates—all discriminated against the South, against farmers, and against most small-scale producers. Images of the war prevented the natural alliance of South and Midwest. And, slowly, even conscientious Southerners, desperate to break from the bonds of poverty, began to flirt with the industrial ideal, to sell out their own heritage. However mistaken, the New South movement was at least understandable, for the South paid a dear price for its undying dream of proprietorship and freedom. Yet the dream lived on, more compelling in the South than in any other section. Much of the supportive economic order remained. In 1930 approximately 60 percent of southerners lived in villages and rural areas, approximately 40 percent worked in agriculture, with perhaps another 20 percent in services or first-level processing directly tied to agriculture.

The other Agrarian image of the old South reflected European, aristocratic, antimodernist, precapitalist sources. Ransom, Tate, and Fletcher first defended it, although each backed away from this view in the depression. Wade, with his portrait of Cousin Lucius, seemed to support it. From this perspective the old South was a near copy of rural England, with a leisurely or aristocratic gentry, a hierarchical social order, nonconsumptive values, and at least the foundations for artistic creativity and an ordered religious life. The enemies of such an organic society were the perennial Yankees—hurried, practical, anxious to subdue nature, in favor of progress, addicted to consumer values, committed to efficiency, and without refined taste or religious awe. By 1933, as economic distress replaced cultural resentment as the primary focus of agrarian writing, the yeoman image all but replaced the aristocratic one among all the Agrarians, including Ransom.

In an attempt to provide some unity to a rather haphazard collection of essays, Ransom composed the manifesto that gave some focus to *I'll Take My Stand.* In it he tried to blend some of the yeoman-populistic themes with the aristocratic bent that still dominated his thinking. This 1930 manifesto remains a powerful statement, loaded in language, deliberately polemical in form. It was a call to arms for southerners threatened by "industrialism," a label that most Agrarians changed after 1930 to "corporate capitalism" or just "capitalism." Briefly, "industrialism" referred to all collectivized forms of production, even those in agriculture. An industrial economy is made up of large accumulations of capital, directed by a few managers, and is dependent on the labor of nonpropertied, dependent, and thus servile wage laborers. The manifesto remained distinctive in Agrarian literature because of the philosophical nuances contributed by Ransom. Central to his argument—one shared with Marxists—was the primacy of productive arrangements in determining all facets of a culture. Thus, an agricultural economy fostered a respect for nature, a flowering of the arts of good living, and an openness to religious myth, all either precluded or distorted by industrialism. In an industrial society the main victims are the workers, those who groan under the system, who have no intrinsic involvement with the ends of work, who suffer from insecurity and a hurried, even frantic industrial regimen, who know only the brutalizing effects and none of the joys of work, and who gain the satisfaction only of an almost mindless consumption.

The manifesto was most distinctive in its wholehearted rejection of any further collectivism as a cure for modern problems. The socialist goal of worker ownership was delusive, for it threatened not only less economic efficiency (not yet a major concern of Agrarians) but ever less freedom, dignity, and artistry for workers. Yet to Ransom a communist society was a logical, even an inevitable, outcome of industrialism, simply a further extension of existing forms of corporate collectivism. Almost perversely, but suggestively, he made capitalism and communism synonymous terms. Tate later argued that capitalism and socialism were both names for an attack upon property. At the same time, Ransom and Tate argued that ameliorative reforms could not repair the fundamental evils of industrialism. The countervailing power of unions, state regulation, and welfare transfers were all only ways of rearranging the economic foliage, said Tate. These could not touch the root of the problem, which required a revolutionary answer. And, in Tate's view, only reaction could be truly revolutionary.

By making something called industrialism their main target, the Agrarians could link their protest to more than a century of defensive southern arguments. The charge of wage slavery went back to southern critiques of the first northern factories. So did images of an overly frantic, hurried, anxious, impious social order. Such indictments at least glanced off enough targets, touched upon enough personal insecurities or resentments, to be perennially persuasive, perhaps most of all in the North, or in cities. Attacks on commercialism or consumerism or alienating types of ownership and work have dominated a large share of social criticism in America. Thus, such targets proved very useful for the Agrarians. It allowed them to argue, at least in a broad way, that the South still nourished, in its soul, a set of values much more appealing than those increasingly dominant in the North. The South, despite all its problems, stood for leisurely and artful work, family integrity, religious and natural piety, and the simple but well-integrated arts of living. Of course, the language was loaded, the arguments as contrived as vague, but this was part of the game. Southern boys, with a brilliance that matched any social criticism in the North, and with an unrivaled eloquence, were able to proclaim: We are as good as you, perhaps better. It is the game of cultural nationalism, played most earnestly by captive peoples or by regional intellectuals rejected or ridiculed by the dominant arbiters of taste in cosmopolitan centers.

The Great Depression made the early Agrarians prophets in ways they never expected in 1930. The industrial machine, which they had castigated for its dehumanizing effects, now seemed tarnished by its economic failures. The Agrarians had applauded, above all else, a nonacquisitive economy, one that allowed leisure. Leisure meant not idleness, but artful work pursued for humane ends at a leisurely pace without the discipline of bosses or time clocks. In the prosperous twenties they had identified the primary evil of modernity as employment. Suddenly, the great perceived malady was unemployment. To them it was simply the other side of the coin—an inevitable, always potential consequence of employment and its insecurities.

After 1933 "property" replaced "leisure" as the key word in the Agrarian vocabulary. These southerners joined New Humanists and English distributists in a true Agrarian crusade, one largely publicized in a new review journal launched by Seward Collins with Agrarian help, the *American Review*. They now embraced the radical implications of land reform, of taking property from monopolistic owners and opening up access to nature for everyone. Tate, the most radical, wanted to confiscate all the wealth of what he called the "money power." The southern Agrarians now realized that what industrialism had meant all along was the gradual destruction of property, along with manageable, personalized, household forms of production. The modern corporation had slowly destroyed property and free enterprise, even as it reduced the majority of humankind to wage dependency and a type of slavery. Obviously, by property they meant not consumer goods or investment paper but the means of production—land and tools. Only a secure access to these allowed people to escape servile dependency, to gain independence and freedom, even the freedom requisite to responsible citizenship. Tate tried to disabuse Americans of their corrupted uses of the word "property." Any ownership apart from management, from a personal and moral responsibility for the use of land and capital, did not qualify as property. From the same perspective, Ransom referred to modern investors as economic geldings, emasculated and irresponsible owners with no effective control over what happened to their so-called property. And corporate managers, like overseers on antebellum southern plantations, did not own land and capital and had no personal responsibility for its humane use and no paternal regard for workers. As powerful but irresponsible hirelings, they served only two urgent goals—maximizing the profits of owners and protecting or increasing their own salaries and power.

This understanding of a corporate or collective economy clarified the reform goals of the Agrarians. They wanted to preserve the remnants of a proprietary society, a society everywhere threatened but still dominant in agriculture. But farmers, particularly those in the South, suffered from deep maladies, some rooted in national policy, some in their own capitulation to the values of an industrial order. Thus, at one level, the Agrarians tried to find solutions to the economic disabilities of farmers in the thirties. Beyond this they tried to motivate farmers to turn away, in part, from commercial, commodity production, away from their vulnerability to competitive prices and world markets, and back far enough toward self-providence to bring market production in line with demand. Thus, in their practical essays, the Agrarians supported the use of absentee land or overly large plantations for a new homestead plan, urged controls over land use, applauded farm credit relief, speculated about institutional changes that would allow more regional autonomy, and celebrated local, artisanal crafts and folk arts.

From a contemporary perspective the historically most distinctive characteristic of almost any South had to be its biracial makeup. Despite Texas Hispanics, Louisiana Creoles and Cajuns, and widespread clusters of Germans, the South was mostly settled, its culture largely shaped, by several tribes from Britain and Africa. African Americans were, in a sense, omnipresent in Agrarian images of the South. So was what they called the "Negro problem," which so divided the individual Agrarians that they could never agree on any but generalized economic solutions for blacks. But from a present perspective, what is surprising is how much even those such as Lanier, Ransom, and Warren, who would later embrace complete black equality, still viewed blacks as an unwanted burden, as cultural appendages. They revealed little appreciation of how much British and African cultures mixed and merged in the South, of how much blacks influenced southern religion, cuisine, music, and literature. Only Nixon reflected any broad appreciation of black culture, and only he among the Agrarians in the thirties worked for black equality. At the other extreme, Davidson, Owsley, and Lytle not only slighted black contributions but put blacks down with nasty, racist statements.

How correct were the Agrarians in their views of the South, past and present? I have no answer. They never agreed on these issues. And each view begs too many empirical issues, issues that scholars can hardly yet sort out, let alone address. Certainly, half-truths informed both their historical and their cultural myths. In a sense, what is remarkable about the early thirties is how little anyone knew about the South. In the absence of knowledge, impressions had to guide. Yet in the face of a rural South blighted by economic inefficiency, underemployed workers, undercapitalized farms, backward or ignorant farming practices, insecure ownership, tenancy rates approaching 50 percent, terrible public services, ill-funded schools, meager public health facilities, monotonous and unhealthy diets, widespread violence, and racial fears and resentments, how could anyone idealize the existing South? It is therefore no wonder that the Agrarians always, in a sense, wrote with the haunting sense of what might have been, or what should have been.

By 1937 the southern Agrarians began to slip into silence. Most had left Nashville. Their alliance with the distributists fell apart early in 1937. The *American Review*, embarrassed by the increasingly fascist views of its editor, stopped publication in 1938. The golden moment had clearly passed.

Before ending my remarks about the Agrarians as a semiorganized group, I want to return to the issue of identity. In my book I have tried to show how much individuals invested in Agrarianism, how vital and important were the friendships and associations of the brethren in the early thirties. But I also have tried to trace what happened to individual Agrarians after the breakup of the community and the end of any coherent movement. In these years of retreat, the internal differences that always lay, like a time bomb, beneath the Agrarian crusade, finally exploded. In some sense each Agrarian found redemptive content in some aspects of the South, old or new. But the content varied immensely. And as the South changed, as new crises came along, the differences divided these individuals into three or four distinguishable subgroups. A word on these.

Three Agrarians kept the faith as they understood it. Owsley, Davidson, and Lytle, more than any of the others, defined themselves by their southern loyalties. They made a commitment not to certain ideals concretized in the South, but to their homeland. They became southern loyalists and, in later times of adversity, overly defensive chauvinists. They resented all criticism from the outside, became bitter and churlish in their denunciation of the North, and tried, with small success, to build another defensive movement in the fifties and sixties to resist what they saw as a second reconstruction by invading Yankees. As race replaced economic and cultural issues as the center of conflict, they became part of the defensive southern effort to retain segregation. Wade, sympathetic with their views, did not have the stomach for political conflict and suffered the early civil rights movement with sadness and puzzlement.

Ransom and Tate never repudiated the cultural themes that they saw as the heart of Agrarianism. Ransom moved to Kenyon, transferred his loyalties to a "new criticism," and looked back on the political programs that he so fervently embraced in the mid-thirties as unrealistic and mistaken. He said so, the only Agrarian openly to repudiate any part of the earlier crusade. Tate, as time passed, denied that he ever saw Agrarianism as anything other than a philosophical and religious protest, a vehicle for resisting, unsuccessfully, the inroads of a successful but hated modernism. With Agrarianism so perceived, he had no need to recant. Lanier probably agreed with Ransom, but he never expressed any open disillusionment. His career simply took him to the North and confronted him with very different challenges. Notably, from their northern perspectives, both Ransom and Lanier embraced integration, while a more reluctant Tate, guided by the policies of the Roman Catholic Church, urged Southern compliance, with good grace.

The other three—Warren, Fletcher, and Nixon—flesh out the great diversity among Agrarians. Warren never clearly committed himself to an Agrarian program but, with a degree of detachment, tried to understand the South, which provided the setting for most of his novels. With compassion and love, aware of the ultimate meaninglessness of human existence, he explored the nuances of southern identity and, in the fifties, became an eloquent spokesman for racial justice. Fletcher defies any coherent analysis. At times a belligerent southerner, he never had the personal stability to adhere to any ideology or program and thus seemed to vacillate wildly. In one of his frequent bouts of near insanity, he publicly resigned from Agrarianism in 1935 over an exaggerated point of principle and eventually ended his life in suicide. Nixon shared the economic concerns of Owsley and deeply loved aspects of southern life. Yet, at first alone among the Agrarians, he identified many of the problems of the South as rooted in a vicious class system and saw as victims of that system most southern blacks. As an old, unreconstructed populist, he wanted to build an effective political alliance among exploited groups in the South. Like all the Agrarians, he at first placed great faith in the New Deal but by 1937 was alone among the group in supporting New Deal social legislation, and in his open, often courageous, advocacy of black equality. In a sense he burned himself out in radical politics, retreating to Vanderbilt as a nontenured professor of political science.

Even as the Agrarians suffered their own personal fates, the depression interlude gave way to a new prosperity. The depression proved to be a detour in American history, not the opening of a new era of retrenchment and stability. The intellectual openness of the early thirties, the luxuriant sprouting of all manner of strange ideological plants, gave way to the orthodoxy of a regulatory-welfare state and a corporate economy. In Tate's language, we only rearranged some foliage, made cosmetic changes. To his despair Americans came to accept, if not love, the new look. They certainly did not want to dig at any of the roots. American farmers, instead of seeking a secure refuge from the insecurities of an international market, soon began their desperate love affair with efficiency, effecting after World War II the clearest industrial revolution in all of our history. Instead of accommodating new people, supporting a move back to subsistence, a highly capitalized agriculture in only fifty years would eliminate approximately 75 percent of the family farm units that existed in 1930.

The South accommodated the agricultural revolution more slowly than the North and suffered some of the consequences in lower incomes. But today, except in some favored areas such as the Mississippi Delta, agriculture has become a minor source of jobs and incomes, and close to being a hobby or a tax dodge for people employed in nonagricultural industries. In few areas of the South can one find even one family whose total income derives from farming. Instead, the South is the new manufacturing capital of the country. Despite a closing gap in incomes, despite the Sun Belt phenomenon, despite the miracle of air-conditioning, the industrial foliage has not changed that much. Wages remain below national averages, fewer workers enjoy the protection of union representation and bargaining, state regulations tend to be more lax than those in the North, state-shared welfare transfers are well below national averages, and a whole array of public services remain ill funded in comparison to those in the North. Thus, not only has industrialism conquered the South, but has done so in its worst possible dress.

The main bent of the Agrarians was openly, even boastfully, reactionary. They wanted to reverse existing trends, repudiate progress, go back to earlier ideals, restore values now all but lost. And whatever the oversimplifications in their descriptions of American society, the mythical content of their historical and cultural judgments, they were correct in one sense. An earlier America, whatever the compensatory costs, had realized, as perhaps no other society in modern history, the proprietary ideal. Nowhere else had small owners enjoyed, or suffered, as much control over land and tools as did American farmers and artisans in the early nineteenth century. No more. And few are the echoes of the Agrarian critique today. Almost unnoticed, in the late sixties and early seventies a few scattered groups joined in efforts to expand ownership, in language that sounded like that of the Agrarians. But, as one might suspect, the latter-day advocates of wider ownership have often included home ownership, even corporate stock, as authentic examples of property. They have also joined with movements in behalf of more social responsibility on the part of large corporations. One can hear the Agrarians groaning in their graves. For whatever else they were, they were radicals, not accommodationists. They tried to get at the roots of modern ills and wanted drastic structural changes in our modern corporate economy.

They accepted the high risks. They knew it was not easy to restore property even to a majority of American families. Drastically lower living standards was only the first of many possible costs. The perceived rewards, as so eloquently advertised by the Agrarians, may have briefly seemed worth the sacrifice in the midst of a depression. Not for long. Independence, leisure, piety, and a taste for poetry are, as I gauge contemporary values, well down the list, trivial beside career success, expressive freedoms, and a heady dose of consumptive pleasures, all gained by a productive system legally stripped of the worst abuses and indignities of the past. As a despairing Owsley put it, without a realistic chance of regaining property, most Americans will continue to vote for policies that maintain them as well-fed hirelings. As one of those who so votes, I cannot help but feel a twinge of guilt. I am not sure I like myself for going along with the existing system. To the accusing Agrarians, I have sold my soul to the devil for a good mess of porridge.

Hot, Humid, and Sad

Sometime, probably in high school, I first learned that I was a southerner. No one told me that as a child. As I learned what characteristics purportedly fit the South, I was not very pleased with my newly discovered identity. It did not seem to fit very well. All but one of my ancestors involved in the Civil War fought for the Union, and Andrew Johnson was the only hero from my home county. I did know something firsthand about a one-party political system, but the party was Republican, in a congressional district that has not elected a Democrat since 1865. I had never seen cotton grow, never tasted hominy grits, and only one black family lived in or even anywhere near my rural village. Yet by accident of geography I found myself a part of the South, and thus in my subsequent reflections I will speak as a somewhat reluctant southerner.

For me the word "South," however many images and associations it evokes, always triggers a feeling of great sadness. Like people everywhere, southerners are almost completely captive to the lingering and often unanticipated consequences of past choices. Some of the choices that make the story of the South so sad go back to the earliest Europeans who conquered, displaced, and almost eliminated the original people who had lived on this continent for at least twelve thousand years. Of course, the invading interlopers often mistakenly believed that they were settling in a virtual state of nature. We know better. Thus, we look back and cry. They looked forward with hope.

Among these colonizing Europeans, some settled in what we now refer to as the South. But which South? In both popular and scholarly contexts, the word "South" refers variously, even when references partially overlap. I think that the least ambiguous South is one defined as the humid subtropical zone of North America (see map). The world's three major humid subtropical zones are on the east coasts of continents. They are distinguished by heavy precipitation (over thirty inches) distributed throughout the year (thus humid), with winter frosts (thus not tropical), but with mean temperatures never below freezing during any month (thus subtropical).

161

Map 7.1 The Humid Subtropical Zone of North America (The Climatological South).

In many respects, the North American humid subtropical zone caters to human needs. It has a quite varied terrain, and includes, in its highly productive belt of pines, the world's only subtropical conifer forest. Its hot and long summers abet the rapid maturation of frost-sensitive but long-season vegetation, including several of the world's most important crops—maize, cotton, tobacco, soybeans, rice, peanuts, and, at its southern extremity, sugar cane and citrus. Yet its summer heat and humidity is not only debilitating but also friendly to parasites, fungi, and bacteria that attack both plants and animals. Summer rainfall, though plentiful on average, is highly variable, with both destructive storms and occasional extended droughts.

Unfortunately, no one has ever tried to collect data specific to this climate-based South. Political boundaries do not coincide. The two best approximations are the slave South (the area with legal slavery in 1860) and the standard statistical South, as used by the Census Bureau. The slave South includes Missouri; the census South does not. I have chosen to work with the census South, which at least contains most of the hot and humid South. It includes sixteen states and the District of Columbia.

Other Souths stray farther from the immensities of geography, climate, and economic resources. The most conventional of these is the Confederate South, which is very important for political analysis but arbitrary for most economic and cultural uses. One can further reduce the South—to the lower South (where the average daily low temperature in January is above 32 degrees), and, in popular imagination, to a South largely defined by Alabama and Mississippi, or even to a literary South confined to the area around Oxford, Mississippi. Among social scientists I find a fascinating but often unselfconscious choice—to make low indices of human welfare definitional for a South. If an area is not poor, it is not southern. In this perspective the South is now disappearing, and prosperous states like Delaware and Maryland have not fit their definition during the twentieth century.

All the early English colonists sought profitable exports back home. Only these could procure needed imports of finished goods and exotic foods necessary for a decent livelihood. Conditions in the colonies favored primary production, not only agriculture but the harvesting of forest, ocean, and mineral resources. So the first southerners, in the greater Chesapeake area, did what was obvious and rational. They soon found a crop that was in great demand in Europe—tobacco—and organized their economy around it. It is only recently that we know the deadly effect of this noxious weed. Later, in coastal South Carolina and Georgia, the growing of swamp and then tidewater rice involved even greater locational advantages. At least a few colonial tobacco and rice farmers became, for the time, comparably wealthy. No other economic choice would have served them as well.

In a time when all crops were labor intensive, tobacco was exceptionally so. It still is. In low-rent America the cost of free labor was often prohibitive. Thus, any large-scale tobacco or rice production, necessary for the accumulation of great wealth, required servile laborers, those bound to masters by law, not free to seek their own land. Indentured servants worked well for a time; enslaved Indians did not. But as everyone knows, during the mid-seventeenth century large farmers in the Chesapeake, and later in the low country, turned to imported Africans, who after about 1690 became the main component of servile labor. Colonial governments gradually developed the legal mechanisms for perpetual servility. Here was the first terrible trap they set for the future South.

In most areas of tobacco, rice, and, after the Louisiana purchase, sugarcane cultivation, the plantation-slave system became deeply entrenched. The most affluent white southerners became inured to it, dependent upon it. Some planters in favored areas enjoyed the highest incomes in America. Charleston remains a monument to their wealth and excess.

After 1790 an industrial revolution helped seal the destiny of the South. By an industrial revolution I mean something quite specific—such changes in tools and techniques of production as to insure, in an economic sector or in major industries within sectors, increases of productivity on the order of 100 percent in one generation. These productivity surges are rare. One occurred from 1790 to 1820 in both the agricultural and manufacturing enterprises tied to the production of cloth. The cotton gin, the spinning jenny, and power looms, joined with pooled and specialized labor on plantations and in mills, quickly increased productivity, lowered unit costs of cloth, and dramatically increased living standards in most of the world. In the early boom, favored producers became rich.

Many of these were in the American South. For growing, ginning, and marketing cotton, about half the South was favored because of climate and soils, legally protected slave labor, and available credit. England, and soon New England, used mobilized capital and wage laborers to exploit the secondary processing of cotton. Indirectly, the cotton boom benefited all regions of the United States.

The long-term costs of the cotton boom in the South were very high. As do all heavy-foliage, nonlegume crops, cotton quickly drained the nutrients from the thin upland soils of the Piedmont and invited serious erosion. Soil exhaustion required a continued clearing of forests for new ground and spurred the movement of planters and their prime capital, slaves, ever farther west, with disruptive environmental and human costs. Cotton profits disproportionately benefited large producers, who enjoyed economies of scale through the more efficient use of slave labor and easier access to credit. This meant a small slave-owning elite, with affluence and luxuries, but much lower incomes for the majority of non-slave-owning farmers.

Most important of all, the cotton boom solidified southern support for slavery. Slave labor discouraged new immigrants from Europe, as did low wages after the Civil War. Thus, the South's population remained largely British and African, despite the French-African mix in southern Louisiana and significant Hispanic and German minorities in Texas. The South missed many of the cultural innovations of new ethnic groups, particularly in religion. Up to half of its British population, and eventually its African also, embraced an internally splintered, evangelical form of Christianity, with Methodists and Baptists dominant. Although average incomes in the South were near parity with the non-South, such were their distribution, and such the political climate, that social services lagged well behind those in the North, most of all in public education.

By 1860 an accounting time was near for the cotton half of the South, even without a war. The unpaid environmental costs were already staggering. In much of the nondelta Southeast the soils were close to exhaustion. But most of the problems related to slavery. Moral outrage had made the South a pariah area, under constant attack, and increasingly vulnerable politically. Slaves were skilled not only in agricultural but in various trades, but they represented a large, mostly illiterate population. Among whites, the level of human capital was also much below that in the North.

The chickens all came home to roost after 1865. Wartime destruction was only part of the story. Emancipation eliminated slave property, formerly the most secure and mobile form of capital and the most reliable tax base. Emancipation created an impossible burden of needed but largely denied social services, particularly for propertyless freed people. Public education declined to the point of extinction. Even white illiteracy increased, as the South witnessed a massive decline in human capital. In the worst of times cotton and other agricultural prices vacillated but then moved downward in the seventies, a normal evolution in maturing industries, but one so timed that the South could not begin to gain the new efficiencies in production needed to sustain prewar farm incomes. National monetary, tariff, tax, and transportation policies generally penalized the South, while a one-party Democratic South lacked leverage in national politics. For a half century it suffered from a paucity of federal patronage.

The trap, set by two centuries of choices, now closed. For eighty years the South suffered its nadir, a dark, gloomy, and violent period unrivaled in any other section of the country. From 1860 to 1880, per capita incomes in the South plummeted to less than 50 percent of national levels. With some small fluctuations, they remained at only 50–60 percent until 1940, and no more than one-third of incomes in the most wealthy northeastern states. Here we have a clear case of an industrial devolution followed by sixty years of relative stagnation. I say relative, because the South did enjoy some periods of rather impressive growth after 1880, but at an average pace that only matched growth in the non-South.

Some commentators attributed the lag to a heavily rural, agriculturally based economy. This was misleading. The problem was not agriculture (today the most efficient sector of both the American and the southern economy), but the inefficient agriculture and low wages that prevailed in most of the South. That agriculture absorbed half the labor force as late as 1920 was an excellent measure of inefficient production. For most of the year this meant a redundant labor force, one made necessary by high labor demands in peak periods for cotton, tobacco, and sugar. Because of population pressures and fractional inheritance, the size of farms decreased until 1930.

This left only one avenue for growth—in productivity per worker and per acre farmed. Warring against this was exhausted soils, low land prices, fragmented and very expensive sources of credit, low levels of human skill tied to a paucity of governmental services, inefficiencies of scale tied to fragmented and small tenant and cropping units, and the economic inelasticities and social costs of southern racial policy. Farm productivity in the South would increase scarcely at all over a sixty-year period (per acre cotton production even declined).

In spite of these realities, a century ago many southern politicians and entrepreneurs at least honestly believed that the South was entering a great era of growth. Celebrations of progress in both agriculture and manufacturing marked a series of expositions in New Orleans, Atlanta, Louisville, Nashville, Charleston, and Norfolk. This sense of progress and growth was based on some realities.

The rapid acceptance of chemical fertilizers after 1880 gave a temporary reprieve to pre-boll-weevil cotton production east of the Delta. Midwestern grain farmers came south and developed a mechanized and efficient form of rice culture in Louisiana, Arkansas, and Texas. Gradually, the southern states did restore a weak, underfunded, and racially unequal public education system, with literacy increasing after 1890 even for blacks. Low-wage manufacturing, largely in textiles but also in tobacco and furniture, grew rapidly in the Piedmont, today the largest manufacturing belt in the world. The Baltimore-Washington area gradually became an integral part of the east coast manufacturing and commercial belt. Coal and iron created a boom in Birmingham; Coca-Cola began a whole new industry in Atlanta. Extractive industries boomed, as largely outside investors exploited southern resources first in timber, then coal, and eventually petroleum. Finally, from 1897 until 1919, international conditions facilitated a period of high agricultural prices.

Southern boosters also cited as a positive factor the rapid waning of class-based populism. They applauded a new racial settlement perfected early in the new century, one that solidified racial separation, practically ended black voting, and thus gave legal content to an already quite rigid caste system. But unnoted by all the cheerleaders was the concomitant growth outside the South, small relative gains in southern incomes, and a gradually accelerating migration of southerners to the north and west. The image of exceptional southern growth was, in part, a mirage.

Yet, in retrospect, with our vision colored a bit by nostalgia and shaped by our knowledge of today's intractable social problems, it is easy to celebrate aspects of this impoverished South. Blacks, given the harsh restrictions upon them, took advantage of bargaining power tied to mobility. They rejected the close supervision involved in wage labor, withdrew some female field labor, and gained a semiproprietary status as tenants. They had no better option. Given the lack of skilled laborers and the difficulty of attracting investment, local entrepreneurs had to turn to very labor-intensive forms of manufacturing. Meager incomes created all manner of tensions, frustrations, and human suffering. We know that story— malaria and yellow fever epidemics, shacks for housing, parasitic infections tied to poor hygiene and to poverty, and above all the terror of lynching. In every measure of human progress and welfare, the South lagged far behind the rest of the nation. Even as late as the 1930s Howard Odum and Rupert Vance cataloged, in depressing detail, all the disabilities. These accompanied some meager blessings. Although half the share-croppers seemed to move every year, most, whether black or white, remained in the same communities. Small evangelical churches, black and white, offered comfort and, for blacks, a rare sanctuary almost fully under their own control. Even the most impoverished croppers had a role, a place, even some aspects of proprietary independence. And in places, and in good times, some upward mobility was possible. Until 1900 blacks steadily increased their ownership of often marginal farm land. Schooling, however inadequate, opened new vistas for the more gifted white students, who in many cases subsequently left the South. However low the wages and the productivity in southern manufacturing (up to one-third less than in the North), the new mills in the Piedmont provided living wages if several family members worked. By southern standards the mill towns and early Appalachian mining towns both provided better housing and better schools than such workers had known in the past. In hilly areas of the upper South, small farmers resisted debt, made home subsistence their first goal, and sold a variety of products in regional markets, but were not dependent for their livelihood upon such markets. Incomes were small, needs limited, but communal life often rich and supportive.

After the boom of World War I gave way to lower or unstable agricultural and land prices in the twenties, the South seemed as deeply mired as ever in its economic doldrums. It even lost the limited income gains of the preceding two decades. All the factors that precluded exceptional growth remained in place, including inherent obstacles to mechanization for cotton and tobacco. Then came the Great Depression, and everyone seemed poor.

In ways hard to measure, one could see the first hint of changed fortunes for the South in the very midst of the depression. The political realignment that began in 1932 soon made the federal government not an impediment to, but an ally of, southern economic development. Patronage now flowed south, and for the next half century southern states enjoyed a positive balance in federal payments. Both work-relief programs and wage legislation narrowed the sectional wage gap. New farm policies doomed plantation agriculture.

Perhaps of equal importance, the plight of the South became a national obsession. Officials in several federal agencies, plus documentary movie makers and photographers, helped put the spotlight on a sad South, the number one problem area of America. This concern began to pay off in World War II, when the South gained a majority of military bases and more defense contracts than its small manufacturing base would have indicated, all abetted by climate, federal agency commitments to southern growth, abundant electricity, and a willing body of redundant agricultural laborers.

Thus began what seemed like an economic miracle. From 1940 to 1980 the South closed most of the gap that had made it the underdeveloped region of the nation. This rapid shift of economic fortunes for such a large region was unprecedented in American history, an almost perfect inversion of the devolution from 1860 to 1880. No one can fully explain this turnaround, in the sense of sufficient conditions, but one can easily list many necessary conditions.

Most important, I believe, and the evidence seems almost conclusive, was a second industrial revolution, one involving agriculture. It affected the American economy and even the world economy but had particular significance for the South. It helped to double incomes in developed countries and populations in underdeveloped ones. This was the only sectorial revolution in American history. In a period largely concentrated between 1950 and 1975, American agricultural productivity more than doubled. According to one estimate, from 1948 to 1972 farm output per hour of work almost quadrupled. Food prices as a proportion of family incomes fell precipitously, to around 10 percent, or the lowest level ever recorded in human history. Anticipations of such an agricultural revolution had come incrementally in the Midwest before 1950, but not in most of the South. In the cotton belt, only 8 percent of farms had tractors by 1940; few had electricity. Thus, the transformation of agriculture was more radical in the South than in any other region. Many concomitant economic changes occurred in the South, but none of these was so revolutionary. Productivity growth in nonagricultural industries was gradual, incremental.

This industrial revolution was by far the most significant in American and possibly in world history. It reflected the cumulative results of federal agricultural policies (subsidies for agricultural education and for extensive research and development, and beginning in the thirties a detailed regulation of production and prices). Acreage reduction programs and price supports for major crops, beginning in 1933, encouraged not only a reduced product but more efficiency in production. Such shifts led to a displacement of 25 percent of southern tenants and croppers from 1935 to 1940. Federal policies joined an explosion of new knowledge in several agriculturally related sciences, the rapid shift from human and horse labor to petroleum-powered machines, and expanded and better-informed uses of chemical fertilizers, insecticides, fungicides, herbicides, and defoliants. This revolution increased the size of commercially important farms and drastically reduced the southern agricultural workforce from almost 50 percent of the total in 1920 to under 3 percent today. From 1950 to 1970 alone, farm jobs in the South declined by almost 2.5 million, affecting a population of over 10 million. Commercial farming moved to the better soils, leaving much of the formerly cropped South in pasture or new forests. In this brief period southern agricultural productivity, which had so lagged behind that of the Midwest, almost caught up with the national average, with the mechanical cotton picker the most significant new tool. The old agricultural South is no more. The old type of sharecropping and tenancy is a memory. Southern blacks have almost completely deserted agriculture (less than 3 percent now work the soil). The rural South now enjoys more forest cover, more pastureland, less erosion, and clearer if not chemically purer streams than in over a century—the fescue belt. Until World War II most southern farms differed only in slight ways from those of the nineteenth century. The mule and the hoe were omnipresent. I know from personal experience. Now hoes rust in corners of smokehouses that no longer store any hams, while rotting harnesses remain in the gear rooms of the slowly disappearing all-purpose barns that once dotted the South.

According to the agricultural census of 1992, the still declining number of southern farms has fallen to below eight hundred thousand, and this number includes those with sales as low as one thousand dollars a year. The operators of such farms make up less than 2 percent of the workforce, and over half of these have outside jobs. By 1992 only ninety thousand southern farms had annual sales of over one hundred thousand dollars; these accounted for at least 80 percent of the total southern product. In states such as North Carolina, manufacturing firms exceed the number of full-time farmers. Yet, contrary to widespread assumptions, almost all of these large farms are family owned, even when families form corporations, and by all indications they will remain so. It is a surprise for many to learn that the most productive sector of the American economy is one still dominated by individual proprietors, and is the one sector most carefully regulated and coordinated by government.

Southern agriculture is not declining, despite major structural changes. The product continues to go up. The South leads the nation in cotton, rice, tobacco, poultry, sugarcane, citrus, peanuts, and several small crops. North Carolina is now second in hog production. Texas leads in cattle, with one-sixth of the total. Arkansas leads the nation in poultry, and four of the top five poultry states are in the chicken belt that stretches from Delaware to Arkansas. Poultry and livestock exceed in value all row crops.

This great transformation of southern agriculture, so rapid and so disruptive, forced former agricultural laborers to move to manufacturing or service jobs, if they could find them. At first they found them either in the North or in labor-intensive southern manufacturing or low-wage services (domestic servants, retail clerks, secretaries). The human costs of this structural change, of this displacement and migration of millions of families, is beyond calculation, as Pete Daniel has so sympathetically demonstrated. Before World War II a steady stream of displaced agricultural workers, or stranded extraction workers, left the underdeveloped South, which had retained the highest birthrate of any region. The flow continued for whites until 1960 and for blacks until 1975. Then it reversed, with a return migration that has almost matched the former exodus. The great out-migration of blacks began in 1916. It peaked during World War II and the fifties (over 2.5 million in two decades), and continued with another 1.2 million in the turbulent sixties, but in that decade these fleeing blacks were more than replaced by nearly 2 million whites, most skilled and prosperous. From the overwhelming majority of blacks who lived in the South (90 percent in 1900), only 55 percent remain today, with less than half in the Confederate South. The migrants from the South and their descendants now make up the most desperate underclasses of northern cities. The South lost its least competitive, least educated, citizens. By 1969 only eighteen thousand black sharecroppers remained in the South. The Census Bureau stopped counting such an anachronism.

In the sixties the South became a magnet for entrepreneurs and investors. The agricultural revolution created a reservoir of cheap, docile, and nonunionized workers, a labor surplus that curtailed employment opportunities for many of the now fleeing blacks. Low wages joined with low taxes, plenty of subsidies and promotions by state governments, and what, at least after air-conditioning, became a favored climate continued to lure outside investors. Such economic development both contributed to and then fed upon the civil rights movement, which led eventually to a unified southern labor market. Federal subsidies remained vital in a dozen areas. Because of federal mandates and incentives or subsidies, the level of social services in most southern states converged by 1970 toward the national average, including expenses for education when adjusted to incomes. Racial integration made possible, for the first time, southern colleges and universities that could aspire to national eminence.

These shifts began to repair the long-standing deficit in human capital. Since 1970 improving skills have helped lure capital-intensive manufacturing and higher-wage service industries to the South. Southern productivity and wages have slowly converged toward those in the North. The now dominant southern service sector has provided the economic base for six nationally significant metropolitan areas, plus eight other regionally significant metropolitan areas with over a million people (one-third of America's million-plus metropolitan areas are now in the South). But the upgrading of skills has eliminated formerly unskilled jobs, leading to greater inequalities in income in the South than in the nation as a whole.

How closely has the South gained economic parity with the rest of the country? I do not have time to do more than summarize some of the data. The South has 35 percent of the nation's population, up from 30 percent in 1930. It is only slightly more rural than other sections, with 75 percent of its population now in standard metropolitan statistical areas. In labor allocation it is very close to the national pattern, except for an unusual concentration of manufacturing in the Piedmont (North Carolina leads the nation). On most measures of human welfare, the South is close but still below the national average. In many areas—infant mortality, poverty levels, educational attainment—the lag largely reflects the continuing but now decreasing gap between blacks and whites.

Perhaps the single most revealing pattern of convergence has been in income per capita. From 60 percent of the national average in 1940, the South rose to 88 percent in 1980 (the miracle years). It has continued a slow rise to 93 percent today, with the most significant national income increases since 1990 in the South. Because of lower living costs, some economists believe real southern incomes match, or even slightly exceed, the national average. They clearly do so for whites, but the incomes of blacks in the South are proportionally slightly higher than those outside the South.

Such aggregate data conceal major internal and regional differences. Delaware, Maryland, the District of Columbia, and Virginia all enjoy incomes above the national average; Florida is at the average. Georgia, North Carolina, Texas, and Tennessee, all above 90 percent, will gain income parity early in the next century if present trends continue. South Carolina may come close. But some Deep South states—Alabama, Mississippi, and Louisiana—will remain well below the average, as will the upper South states of Oklahoma, Arkansas, Kentucky, and West Virginia. The three poorest states are all in the South—Mississippi, Arkansas, and West Virginia. The South still has more pockets of poverty than any other section.

I want to emphasize what may already be obvious—the federal role in this southern renaissance, and a major internal transfer of wealth from the rest of the country to the South. The people of the South, or state governments that have reflected their caution, could not, or would not, so raise local taxes as to pay for the social services required for this transformation. The contemporary South is a product of a regulatory and welfare state and of war and cold war military expenditures. This is not a firm rule, but in most free societies today high living standards correlate positively with a high level of public expenditures, and thus high taxes. Governments either provide, or carefully supervise, a wide range of needed services, beginning with education and medical care. They own or subsidize and regulate transportation facilities, communications, and utilities.

They use various redistributive polices to provide minimum incomes, closely regulate the conditions of employment, and protect fragile environments. When southern states would or could not tax to provide these needed services, the federal government either did it for them or through grants or bribes induced southern states to do it for themselves (for example, 40 percent of funds authorized by the Elementary and Secondary Education Act of 1964 flowed into southern school districts). But above all, the Civil Rights Acts of 1964 and 1965 forced the South to accept equal opportunities for blacks.

The virtual disappearance of a distinctive statistical South does not mean that the South has solved all its problems. Income disparities remain greatest here. The South's exceptional leverage in national politics depends on the survival of a new but increasingly fragile two-party system. In almost all indices of human welfare, African Americans are at the bottom and so pull down averages as largely to account for the lag in states such as Mississippi. But even this gap has narrowed, and in some areas, such as high school completion rates and salaries for beginning skilled and professional workers, it has closed completely.

Culturally, the South is still distinct, possibly more self-consciously so than ever before. It is now a bit more diverse ethnically, because of migrants from the North, and Hispanic immigrants in Texas and Florida. Yet it remains predominantly British and African. After a long decline the 20 percent black population is now growing, in part because of a high rate of in-migration. Because of the population mix, and traditions, the South still has its Bible Belt and still largely hosts the NASCAR circuit. Blacks and whites have their own distinctive musical forms. The South has inspired, and now glories in, a distinctive literary tradition. Its religious mix is still largely evangelical, but with deep divisions within the older mainline denominations. An evangelical tone encompasses both blacks and whites, and unites them in opposition to many new shifts in moral values and modes of life, even as they remain deeply divided on economic and social policies. The South predictably leads the nation in church membership and attendance and in traditional cultural values.

Does convergence mean that one can be sad about the prior history of the South, but glad about the present South? Is the ordeal over? Can southerners now rejoice? Not at all. In the past southerners at least had clear goals because they faced so many intractable economic and social problems. Now, in the very midst of dramatic achievements, achievements for which they can no more take full credit than they should have to assume full responsibility for past injustices, the sadness of the story is ever more apparent. We have to live with a heritage, and the psychological fallout possesses us still, and will for generations to come. Soul erosion is harder to cure than soil erosion.

We do not choose our past. We inherit it. Thus, in all our most essential traits, we do not choose our identity. We have to live with it. To some extent, the past is a burden to everyone. But not equally so. I became more aware of this in an extended trip to India, where the burden of the past is so omnipresent and so depressing. In the immediate background is British rule. From railroads to government forms, India lives in the shadow of what the British created. This has left a deep ambivalence. On one hand, Indians blame most present problems on British imperialism. On the other, they boast of a parliamentary system based on the British model and a Western-style constitution, even as they flock to cricket matches or, if wealthy, to polo fields. The British pushed economic rationalism and universalist moral standards on a caste-ridden and parochial India. By self-righteous judgment, or by example, the British devalued most aspects of Indic culture, and in the case of the caste system labeled it immoral and unjust. The path to success, for Indians, required a capitulation to British standards. The English language became a symbol of achievement, even as it remains a prerequisite for business or professional success.

I do not want to argue for exact analogies, although some are at least suggestive. In India two very different cultures, each with an ancient heritage, confronted each other. In the United States no such cultural differences separated North and South. But a sense of inferiority, a lack of a confident identity, equally haunts both black and white southerners. Both Indians and southerners have been the object of either moral censure or patronizing concern by cosmopolitan, affluent, and socially secure outside elites. Both have tried to deal with a caste system. And despite the outlawing of castes, caste remains at the heart of Indian society, embedded in the identity of people at all levels. Indian intellectuals are embarrassed by such historic anachronisms, but not totally immune to their legacy. Socially secure Brahmans still have a disproportionate amount of wealth and political clout. They know this, and feel an appropriate but futile guilt. Members of the lower castes, as a whole, have not risen very rapidly in occupations and incomes, probably because no legal changes can undo the corrosive impact of the past upon their own sense of identity.

White southerners know some of the guilt of upper-caste Indians. Black southerners know some of the insecurities of former Indian untouchables, although even during slavery their status was never so low. And all southerners, black and white, know that either today or not so long ago, they were on average poorer, less healthy, more violent, less educated, and less cosmopolitan in culture than other Americans. Thus, should Emory University gain all the strengths of Harvard, it would not feel like Harvard. Such trivial traits as regional accents still stigmatize. Southerners as a whole, when they travel or become self-conscious about sectional differences, suffer from this perception. And however much nonsoutherners, often morally complacent because of their generous intent and benevolent motives, try to be fair to rednecks or blacks, they end up patronizing their inferiors. When they become self-conscious about such attitudes, they feel guilty. They then celebrate one or another token of southern culture, be it cuisine, religion, or music. And southerners can only curse their fate and pray for the gods to rid them of well-meaning patrons.

Of course, the burden of this past rests most heavily on blacks, but not much less so than on poor, economically insecure whites. Blacks are doubly victims, of racial bias and a bias against southern culture with its complicated mixture of British and African roots. And no easy or early answers are possible for blacks. They were servile, then low caste, and even now, when legally liberated, still without the secure historical tradition and sense of self-worth that typifies those southern whites who formerly monopolized knowledge, ownership, and power. For some blacks, insecurity has propelled them into a competitive frenzy, as the middle class moves rapidly to equality in income and wealth. For others it has meant frustration, alienation, and all types of pathology, in crime, family decay, and poverty. The burden has been greatest for males, a burden not always lessened by occupational success, which has often accompanied depression and even suicide. Self-doubt is pervasive, and at times reinforced by the patronizing efforts of whites to assuage their own guilt. Suspicion and even paranoia thrive. This is tragic, in the most literal sense. Southerners are in a trap, created by past choices, and without any early way out.

The sadness has a personal dimension. I have traveled a long way from home—from a small cabin in east Tennessee, from the year-round discipline of tobacco culture, from depression poverty, poor schools, and evangelical churches. I am one of the Appalachian refugees. My own self-concept, the deepest images I have about who I am, have never kept up with my geographical and cultural moves. I have always felt awkward, out of place, undeserving, even overpaid. My being here tonight, in this honored role, before this audience, is beyond my comprehension, fraught with self-doubt and tinges of guilt.

Thus I end with some unanswerable questions: How many years, how many generations, will it take southerners to escape the ego-shattering fallout from their past? How much achievement, even compensatory overachievement, will finally allow southerners, black and white, wherever they now live, to relax and accept as normal what is now so much more open to them than ever before—economic opportunity, cultural attainment, and, above all, moral complacency? How soon can acknowledged guilt bestow on former oppressors a sense of forgiveness? How soon can the past suffering of victims eventuate in some measure of redemption? How soon?

8

✛

Communal Memory and Historical Piety

In some sense almost all stories about the past are biographical. The stories are about individuals or groups of people. Such stories, as told and retold by each generation, help shape the identity of people still living. It is such shared memories, such commonalities, that, more than anything else, give people a sense of roots and communal identity. I have long been fascinated with the role of biography, both of individuals and groups. What follows is an essay I wrote on this subject for a faculty seminar here at Vanderbilt. I have used the same themes in various contexts. The present essay dates from 1998.

Now Let Us
Praise Famous Men

This is not a sermon. At least, most of it is not. Yet I want to begin with a long selection from the Bible. I take it from the Wisdom of Jesus Son of Sirach (Ecclesiasticus), possibly the first person on record who offered a rather detailed commentary on biographical writing.

> Let us now sing the praises of famous men, the heroes of our nation's history, through whom the Lord established his renown, and revealed his majesty in each succeeding age. Some held sway over kingdoms and made themselves a name by their exploits. Others were sage counselors, who spoke out with prophetic power. Some led the people by their counsels and by their knowledge of the nation's law; out of their fund of wisdom they gave instruction. Some were composers of music and writers of poetry. Others were endowed with wealth and strength, living peacefully in their homes. All these won fame in their own generation and were the pride of their times. Some there are who have left a name behind them to be commemorated in story.
>
> There are others who are unremembered; they are dead, and it is as though they had never existed, as though they had never been born or left children to succeed them.
>
> Not so our forefathers; they were men of loyalty, whose good deeds have never been forgotten. Their prosperity is handed on to their descendants, and their inheritance to future generations. Thanks to them their children are within the covenants—the whole race of their descendants. Their line will endure for all time, and their fame will never be blotted out. Their bodies are buried in peace, but their names live for ever. Nations will recount their wisdom, and God's people will sing their praises. (Ecclesiasticus 44:1–15)

Jesus son of Sirach is not well-known by Protestants. His writings come down to us by way of the Septuagint, or the Hellenistic Greek version of Jewish sacred writing. Jerome translated these writings into Latin (the Vulgate) as the Christian Old Testament. It is still a fully integrated book in the Catholic Bible. Not so for Protestants. In about 90 C.E., after the fall of the second temple in 70, and at a time when the new Christian movement offered powerful competition, the Jewish teachers or rabbis (from the House of Hillel) who dominated the position of high priest and the Sanhedrin, gathered north of Jerusalem to approve a Jewish canon. They left out more recent books that had long circulated and were in the Septuagint, but which, in their estimation, lacked a prophetic authority. The longest omission was this book. Subsequently, Luther and Calvin adhered to the Jewish canon and segregated these rejected writings in a separate Apocrypha, usually bound between the two testaments. They appeared here in the all-important English or Authorized Bible (King James). In time, Protestant publishers increasingly left out these parts of the Bible, with the active support of anti-Catholic Evangelical denominations. Few Protestants fought to preserve them. Thus, knowledge of this fascinating literature tended to die out among Protestants and, to an extent, even among Jews.

A word about this Jesus. Internal evidence suggests that he wrote around or just after 200 B.C.E. His text has few references to historical events, but he ends his gallery of great men with an almost sycophantic essay on the high priest Simon, son of Onias II. Simon held his office under the early and mild Seleucid or Syrian rulers of Judea, and just before the terrible blasphemies of Antiochus IV, whose reign began in 175 B.C.E., when a son of this Simon was high priest. We cannot be sure, but it is likely that Jesus died before 175, or else he would have exhibited a much more pessimistic outlook in his wisdom.

It is almost certain that the references to Simon the high priest do not refer to a later Simon, the greatest of the Hasmonean kings in a newly liberated Judea, and a king who merged the monarchy with the office of high priest. Simon was the third son of Mattathias, of the Hasmon family, to rule and to suffer martyrdom in a Judea only finally and completely liberated from Syria during his reign (142–134 B.C.E.). The first taste of independence came under his brother Judas (the hammer, or Maccabee) in 164, when Jewish rebels captured and briefly held Jerusalem after a decade of desecrations by Antiochus IV. They cleansed the temple, beginning the festival of lights or Hanukkah. It was only in 140, under Simon, that Judea gained a recognition of its independence from a rapidly fragmenting Greek dynasty in Syria. Its independence would last less than a century, until 63 B.C.E., when Pompey established Roman jurisdiction over Palestine. Simon extended the boundaries of Judea to their greatest extent since the age of Solomon, helped expand the second temple, and seemed destined for a long reign when he was murdered in 134.

The writings of Jesus son of Sirach, whom Christians would later refer to as ben Sirach (from his Hebrew name, Joshua ben Sirach), fits within a genre of Jewish literature called wisdom writings. This genre flourished in the Hellenistic period, with some of the more ancient strands of wisdom bound in the eclectic book of Proverbs. Loosely, wisdom literature replaced prophetic writings and preceded, but overlapped, the later apocalyptic writings. Of all the wisdom books I prefer this one. This Jesus was an orthodox son of Israel, but not rigid in his interpretations of the law. His book largely contains a series of little sermons or homilies, which led the western Church to name it Ecclesiasticus, or church book. It has provided a gold mine for preachers. It has practical advice on wealth, on wives, on piety, on work and the professions, on various virtues, and ends with poetic eulogies to famous men. Not women. This Jesus gives brief vignettes of the heroes of Israel, from a formerly legendary Enoch (on his way to a new status among the heroes of Israel), through Abraham, Moses, David, and certain prophets, and ends with Simon the great high priest. Jesus refers to the great, legendary judges, but only to men. He ignores Deborah, as he ignores a later Esther. He probably died a century before Salome Alexandria, a woman who ruled Hasmonean Judea after 76. He would not have been happy with such an inversion of gender roles.

This Jesus lived just before the rapid ascendancy of the great rabbis or pharisees. He had not absorbed such newfangled ideas as the resurrection of the dead. He was always sensible and hopeful. He exhibited none of the world-weary moral cynicism and despair of a probable contemporary, the unknown author of Ecclesiastes. He reflected none of the soaring Platonism of the much later author of the Wisdom of Solomon, and neither did he so often personify a feminine Wisdom as the Spirit of God. In a brief interval of Jewish revival, he bared none of the apocalyptic pessimism that dominated Jewish literature a hundred years later. For our purposes, what is important is that he still relied on divine providence and believed in the possibility of great men, of true heroes.

The preface to his short biographies has a certain fame. American historians know it from a book by James Agee, who was familiar with this passage and used it as a completely ironic title for a story of three sharecropping families in Alabama in the depression thirties. Agee probably knew it because of its use as a text for All Saints Day (November 1). Protestants know All Saints Eve, or Halloween, much better than the day itself. The second paragraph of the passage quoted at the beginning often serves as a text for All Souls Day (November 2). I think inappropriately, as I will argue later.

The actual text does not make clear why Jesus wrote his brief biographies. His heroes were all men of renown, and much fuller details of their lives were present in the historical books of the already compiled Jewish scriptures. His brief poetic renditions seem to be ritualistic, a recalling of what his audience knew already. Thus, I suspect the point is not in the details, but in the use he makes of the vignettes, and the purpose for citing them all over again. For this reason I emphasize the preface, not the biographies. He may, in fact, have been seeking political favors from Simon and thus paraded the great heroes in order to flatter Simon by placing him in such an imposing lineup. But more likely, in a book of homilies, he had a didactic and a religious purpose.

Such a genre has two clear purposes. They are probably linked to the hidden origins of both history and biography, to the early stories of great ancestors told around the campfires of preliterate tribes. Language probably developed in a context of danger, as a means for coordination in a battle or in the hunt. But surely soon after its origin language served a less directly utilitarian function—as the basis of gossip and storytelling. By the time of this Jesus such stories had become the basis of moral homilies, guidelines as to one's duties. He wanted the youth to emulate such heroes. Closely connected, such stories helped cement loyalty to a tribe or nation or religion. They gave one a sense of roots, of a special identity, and of belonging to a group. By the nineteenth century, such uses usually converged on the idea of the good citizen. Either Jesus, or more likely subsequent editors, ended his series of vignettes with the following words, which reflect this didactic purpose: "In this book I have written lessons of good sense and understanding, I, Jesus, son of Sirach, of Jerusalem, whose mind was a fountain of wisdom. Happy the man who occupies himself with these lessons, who lays them to his heart and grows wise! If he lives by them, he will be equal to anything, with the light of the Lord shining on his path."

But more fascinating to me is not the didactic use of such writing, but another reason why Jesus, and other Jews, kept telling the stories of famous men and, on occasion, famous women. I want to return to the middle paragraph in the opening quote, to the "unremembered" others. I see this not as a backhanded recognition of the forgotten multitudes of simple folk, but as an implied indictment of nations and peoples unlike Israel. Jesus makes clear that Israel will not let its progenitors be forgotten. Israel, the people of the covenant, will always remember. He recalls the great names, those who contributed so much to the nation. He expects people at the local level, in a tribe or a patriarchal family, to remember the lesser men, to tell their own local stories. These national heroes had special importance, for they were the chosen agents of the Most High God. They helped Jehovah carry out his mighty plans. They had cosmic as well as national significance. Not so even the heroes of other nations, for people who did not live in the perspective of a covenant, of a great mission. Non-Jews do not remember, do not maintain a tradition.

This raises, for me, the most elusive yet most important reason for biography and history. I call it historical piety. The word "piety" often means respect for, or fear of, the gods. It entails a recognition, and an acknowledgment, that we owe our lives, and all our successes, to powers beyond ourselves. It is an ever-present warning against self-satisfaction and pride. We do not choose to be born. Life is a gift from without. And the choices we make, the successes we realize, as well as some of our failures and frustrations, always ride piggyback on what came before, on the choices made by our progenitors. Jesus son of Sirach wants the children of Israel to acknowledge this dependence, this living in a present always colored and informed by the past. He insists that it is the duty of Jews to be historical. It is a matter of justice, and thus of duty, to honor those who came before and who deserve our praise. We thus have a growing debt that is always due. The costs of forgetting may, or may not, be mistakes in the present. This is not the point, for it is almost irrelevant to our duty to honor famous men and women.

Even if such remembrance has no impact on our own growing identity, even if it does not help shape our ideals or values (it is inconceivable that it will not), I think Jesus would still command us to praise famous men. This duty rests on a type of moral or esthetic imperative. To the extent we forget, to the extent that we take too much credit, to the extent that we become blinded to the past, we are to that extent less human. We forget the ancient covenant, lose the purposes that dignify our collective life, and are fated to become as the unremembered. It is important that this Jesus, unlike his better known namesake, did not believe in a life after death. Thus, we who forget, who lose our sense of dependence, are like the animals. No one will remember us if we do not keep alive this type of piety. This is why historical forgetfulness is the unpardonable sin—it means that we die as though we never existed, or had never been born. It cuts us off from all chances of immortality.

Although it provided a precedent for later hagiography, what Jesus commended was not such. He did not write about saints. He knew the warts that marred his heroes, although it was not part of his purpose to recall those. He knew about David's Bathsheba. Only Enoch had no known flaws, and that is because no one knew any details about the life of Enoch, only that Jehovah had taken him into the heavens without the penalty of death. The correct label for this type of biography is eulogistic. By definition it is selective, not critical. I am sure Jesus believed what he included in his poetic stories to be true, but he knew it was far from the whole truth. I submit that, for most people even today, their only frequent contact with biography is in the form of eulogies. When we honor our dead friends or colleagues in memorial services, we compose such eulogies. We hear them at funerals and family reunions. In the most sketchy form, we read them in obituaries. And at least in those moments we experience some of the piety that Jesus felt before the great heroes of Israel. It is a context of appreciation, a celebration of the enduring achievements and contributions of a person. It is not a proper time to enumerate weaknesses and failures. In death, if not in life, these are all forgiven. In life our criticism, our condemnation, may effect a reformation. It is in order. Not so at death. If rehearsing the failures of the dead help us focus our moral judgment, then critical biography has its own peculiar use, but it takes us beyond the range of proper piety.

Jesus son of Sirach lived within the assured providence of Jehovah. All events reflected his certain although often concealed purposes. The heroes of Israel served his goals. Nothing was ultimately in vain. All history was, in some sense, providential history. Proximate causes might not be clear, but ultimate causes were clear. This outlook almost precludes either irony or a sense of tragedy. All people receive their due, in the form either of deserved punishment or rewards. Outcomes may not make sense to us, but God knows. Our futility, our frustrations, our failures are products of our impiety or disobedience, and thus always earned. This Jesus never confronted the dilemmas of Job, who seriously doubted not the existence of a god but his justice. For this Jesus justice always prevails, sooner or later. The larger meaning, the plan at work, made less critical any detailed investigation of human motives, or any careful attention to exact details. Jewish histories and biographies were thus appropriately epochal or poetic.

Two hundred years before Jesus son of Sirach wrote his wisdom, a retired and disgraced Greek warrior, Thucydides, essayed a different type of history and biography. He had no sense of an ancient covenant, no belief in an all-controlling divine providence. His complex stories about the ongoing Peloponnesian wars are full of irony and reveal trapped humans, caught up in a great, tragic, almost endless war. In this context Thucydides wanted to go beyond epics and poems—they are almost always fantastic, even though flattering to the side that invents them. Thucydides displayed his own version of piety—those involved, on both sides, were caught up in truly momentous events, displayed a wide range of talents and virtues, and thus deserved a true account, down to their exact motives, so that Greeks would remember. It is not always clear why they should remember. He hints at certain regularities in human affairs, perhaps nourished a belief in some common human nature, and thus may have believed that future statesmen could learn valuable lessons from his account, an account checked against his own observations or the testimony of reliable witnesses. Implied is that only such critically verified accounts could be reliable. But such a practical purpose is not a dominating motif in his stories. He was not the first social scientist. He did begin a tradition that appeals to modern academics much more than the providential and poetic history told by Jesus. Contemporary historians, by and large, do not believe in an all-controlling providence, and perhaps few believe in heroes.

I suspect eulogistic biography has the deepest roots in our past, and possibly fulfills deeper psychological needs than any other genre. It remains the most pervasive popular form of biography, even in our cynical age. But I can distinguish several other types of biography, each with their own special appeal and uses. At the far extreme from eulogy are iconoclastic biographies. They have come into their own in the twentieth century. We identify them with such people as Lytton Strachey and the Bloomsbury circle. Such biographies often involve famous people, former heroes. But, on close observation, they all fall off their pedestals, reveal the flaws behind the public mask. Whatever the purpose of such biographers, such debunking studies have a compelling appeal to readers. It is as consoling as disillusioning to find all the blemishes that mar the rich or the powerful or the purported righteous. It is not only realistic, but liberating, to realize, with Emerson, that this old earth has no real heroes, that should the angels come to earth to chant the chorus of the heavens, they would end up eating too much gingerbread. When duty nags, or guilt overwhelms, it is quite a relief to read about Martin Luther King's or John F. Kennedy's fatal disrespect for the women they used for their own pleasure. They were weak like all of us. Bringing the icons down is a very egalitarian tactic. This is the basis, and the universal appeal, of gossip. Those of us at the bottom seem to rise a notch with every fallen hero. Other people's foibles and failures lessen our sense of impotence or of guilt. Such biographies may not encourage moral engagement, or great courage, but they may boost our beleaguered egos.

Iconoclastic biographies take two forms. One is based on disappointment, the other on disillusionment. They have a very different impact. Those who become bitterly disappointed with a hero continue to reflect a belief in the possibility of great achievement. They are often the supreme moralists. I have flirted with this form of biography myself. I have known such biographers, most of all Rexford G. Tugwell, whose hero, Franklin D. Roosevelt, had the power to do enormous good but, in Tugwell's perspective, flubbed it. His limited successes paled when compared to what might have been, had Roosevelt seized the opportunity and, of course, followed Tugwell's advice. Robert Caro exploits the theme of disappointment in his biography of Lyndon Johnson. He expected so much and found so little. Johnson betrayed all of us, despite his achievements. And behind it all was a horribly flawed person. But the sense of betrayal reveals the continued hope for great deeds. In fact, this type of biography tends to scapegoat, to place preternatural powers in the hands of individuals, to see almost unlimited room for change if the leader will only take charge and do the right thing. In other words, they make unrealistic demands upon individuals, often ignore contextual constraints, and display a type of moral outrage. Woodrow Wilson is perhaps the one American president who has most often lent himself to this treatment. This is a proper form of biography for committed but defeated radicals, those who still believe we can make it to the kingdom if we are not betrayed by one or more apostates. At its extreme, this biography of disappointment becomes conspiratorial. Someone, or some group—be it capitalists, or Jews, or Communists—always subverts the cause, loses the great victory.

A biography of disillusionment is very different. Literally, one who is disillusioned has lost all illusions. This world has no heroes. Virtue is mere convention. The mood is cynical or resigned, not angry. The proper response is not glee at the fall of the mighty, but a type of compassion or pity. Whereas a biography of disappointment rests on exaggerated hopes of human achievement, biographies of disillusionment rest on few hopes and low expectations. In some cases they reflect the belief that humans have no effective choices at all over the course of events, that they are captive to factors beyond their control. Circumstances rule. Then what seems heroic is merely accidental. Few take this extreme view, but aspects of disillusionment are present in most contemporary biography, which is above all highly ironic. The egalitarian bent of this type of biography may match that of the biography of disappointment. It too consoles small people with limited aspirations. It may help reconcile all of us to our fate. If it has heroes, they are in the image of a Sisyphus or a Don Quixote.

Finally, and at some length, I want to explore another form of unselfconscious and ironic biography, but one that is not at all iconoclastic. It is based not on disillusionment but on a lack of high expectations. This might be called the Lake Wobegon model of biography.

In 1988 I volunteered to write a history of my boyhood church—a Cumberland Presbyterian congregation in rural upper east Tennessee. At the time of the building of the 1888 church building, I was able to identify twenty-eight families (almost all) who then lived in the community. Incidentally, one of the wealthiest families by 1900 was black (he has the second-tallest tomb in the county), one of two local black families (none survive). What I ended up with was a forty-page essay, one that included the names of almost three hundred residents of the village from 1795 to the recent past. It is a thin collective biography of the valley. As one might expect, older residents, and in particular people who grew up in the village and then moved away, were enthused about the essay. Requests for copies still come to the church. But younger people seemed less interested. They could not understand why I went to all the effort, ending up with the names of people they had never heard of. But the effort did create some genealogical interest. On homecoming Sunday several families posted numerous old photographs of nineteenth-century ancestors on the back wall of the church. The essay revealed more extended kinship networks than anyone knew about; distant cousins finally became aware of the connection.

For the pre–Civil War families in the valley I could learn little more than their names and the inexact sites of their farms and houses. In no sense could I write biographies; I knew nothing about them, and for the antebellum period no memories have survived in any of the existing families. Just names. As I will note shortly, this poverty of information slowly changed for people born in the late nineteenth century, but not because villagers shared the piety of Jesus son of Sirach. I found almost no compelling sense of connections, or indebtedness, to those ancestors. In some cases, as villagers made clear, they would rather forget most of them. As it turns out, the village has no heroes. At least, they do not honor any such, and clearly they know of no famous men or women.

In a conventional sense they do honor heroes from the past, including the heroes of Jesus son of Sirach. The hagiography of Sunday schools and grade schools has had its impact. Moses and George Washington are both heroes, at least by acknowledgment. But they are distant, detached, not part of focal awareness. They have little tie to any local sense of identity. All the sermons or eulogistic stories about them do not have much effect. I think these distant heroes, as I assiduously read about them as a child, must have helped shape my values, orient my conscience, and thus both fund my ambition and sustain my guilt. But I do not believe it had much effect on the people who remained in the village. When I return I am always surprised, in some cases appalled, by a certain flexibility of conscience, and a tolerance for deviance, so long as one does not run aground on what neighbors think. Conventional and often inflexible in belief, the villagers are quite opportunistic in conduct.

This village as I knew it as a boy in the 1930s had no airs, no pretensions. It was even then, in the terms of a Vanderbilt University sociologist, a so-so community. Everyone was just tolerable. Leadership was almost nonexistent. No one pushed ahead very much; if you did, you left. To be ambitious was to be uppity, a fatal sin in the local scale of values. Most forms of achievement, including leadership roles, were accepted but not particularly valued, unless they allowed one to gain money and possibly not have to work so hard. Work was a necessity, not an art, and had low value. Thus, in the countless stories I heard as a youth, about contemporaries or progenitors, these issues were rarely prominent. I learned almost nothing about the achievements of my ancestors. It is as if they achieved nothing at all, at least by the terms of preferment in the larger culture. Not much was expected or desired. At times the village even seemed to mock, or flaunt, the official values of the local culture. For many years it helped elect as its county commissioner an able man who everyone knew was a homosexual.

Yet having said all this, I still grew up in the midst of a constant input of stories about the dead. I heard endless details about earlier uncles, cousins, or neighbors. This talk competed successfully with gossip about living people. Crops and people were the only really important topics of conversation. Gossip was the key form of entertainment. What surprised me when I compiled the families present in 1888 was how many of them I felt I knew. Most died before I was born. A few lived on into my childhood. But often I could not distinguish the difference. I thought I knew Ike Good very well. My father had told a hundred stories about him. But he died when I was four years old. All I can really remember is his long white beard. But I know him very well. He almost kept us from retiring a mortgage on our farm, not by intent but because he thought he could figure mortgage interest and he really could not, as my mother finally demonstrated. Most of the citizens of 1888 were all still alive in living memory when I was a boy, which allowed me to record them in my essay with a sense of some degree of familiarity. I had really heard, and absorbed, all those stories about them. My sister tells me that she always found such stories tiresome and thus cannot remember any of them. Maybe I was already destined to be a historian.

I cannot remember any stories about really great men in my village, or not even many righteous ones. But I did hear of a few righteous women. Thus, no one had to knock anyone off pedestals. We had no local icons to break. What I learned was a great deal about personality traits, eccentricities, about who was sane and who crazy, who generous and who stingy. The stories were often whimsical, embellished I am sure by the telling, and always about flawed people, many of whom were complete misfits. In fact, as a subject of both gossip and later biography, it seems that one of the few enduring gifts people ever made in my community was their own unconcealed weaknesses. They provided juicy tidbits for the gossips (all of us).

At the least the village must have been interesting. As my parents told about the early part of the century, it often seemed twice as exciting as in my day. In the tales almost everyone, dead or alive, seemed to provide content for scandal or for humor. Some examples: It seemed that half the first babies in good, often pious, families were conceived before marriage, and everyone knew who they were and joked about it. On one of my visits my mother gave me a detailed list of young women, early in the century, who were notoriously promiscuous (all are now dead). Several families had a long history of perennial insanity. One of my childhood companions, an old man who played checkers superbly, had to take periodic trips to the state asylum. Once, before I was born, he ran off, and neighbors—soon even the law (their term)—searched frantically for him for a week. They found him hiding in a hollow tree, one of the more memorable events in village history. When I was ten, my father and I took this same man to the county jail for safekeeping, but just at the door he broke loose and my father and a policeman spent a half hour running him down. Old Archibald Baxter lived up on the ridge, apparently had a charming personality, but had at best a meager farm. But when an outsider came in and established an academy and industrial school, he became instructor in agriculture. The school soon folded, but from then on he carried himself with the dignity of having been a professor. This was in 1907. I learned about this much later, long after old Arch died. I use these incidents to suggest the flavor of cherished memories. I hope they remind you of Lake Wobegon. For note that those who told these stories were not angry, not disappointed, not disillusioned, but in fact full of love and affection.

This is an example, I suspect, of the biography told by common people throughout the ages, people without great aspirations. They are at an opposite pole from Jesus son of Sirach. Because none were heroes, they rarely served as role models for children, although a few very pious church members did play that role. My parents had no didactic purpose in telling these stories. Some, in fact, had a moral impact because of precautionary warnings. Do not do as they did. But these people, in lingering memory, retained a type of vitality. They never achieved very much. Some lost their farms. Many declined into what we called poor whites. They were conspicuously flawed people, in need of forgiveness. And the stories about them, without intent, were full of just this—compassion and forgiveness. We honored them because of, not in spite of, their weaknesses.

My father was a great storyteller. He made these people come alive for me, and thus my sense of obligation was fulfilled when I finally wrote a bit of their history. Maybe that accounts for my absorption. Maybe it is simply the approach of old age, and a growing sense of both piety and nostalgia. My father embellished his stories. He never tried to conceal that. I soon knew most of the best stories by heart. My mother would not let him tell them over and over again in her presence. With the passage of time each story acquired a title or a name. I could call them up, have Daddy retell them. A year before he died, I visited home with a tape recorder. He was flattered, anxious to perform. Characteristically, he asked which stories I wanted him to tell. I made the selections and, although his health was poor, he rose to the occasion; they were longer than ever before, more detailed, more dramatic. And all about people and their escapades. It is in this sense that I grew up in the past, with a special type of heritage. Without a covenant, without great heroes, without a sense of providential importance in any of these flawed lives, but nonetheless with a vital connection to, and appreciation for, those who came before. I sometimes wonder if my children will have a similar heritage.

9

✢

Scholarship

I end this series of essays with a subject that does not clearly relate to beleaguered villages. It does express some of my convictions about learning and inquiry, and about the relationships, at times the tension, among truth, beauty, and the good. At first I had intended to include some much longer essays on higher education. After writing a very long history of Vanderbilt University in 1985 (*Gone with the Ivy*), I received numerous invitations to lecture on Vanderbilt, a subject I did understand, and on higher education, a subject about which I was in no sense an expert. But what I have included, in part because it is brief, is an address I recently gave to a group of undergraduates at Belmont University, after they had successfully completed special research projects.

Students and Scholars

I am happy to address a group of undergraduates involved in research efforts. Congratulations on the completion of your projects. I know you have searched diligently and in some small area added new truth to some discipline. You may now, on the basis of such achievement, call yourself a scholar or a scientist. This also means that you have become a more rounded and accomplished student. For I refuse to so define either "student" or "scholar" as to place them at odds with each other. That would be as distorting as setting teaching and scholarship in opposition to each other.

I am old. I may easily fall into lamentations, which implies nostalgia. I am a philosopher. As such, I will attend constantly to definitions and distinctions. I am, at times, a preacher, and I will therefore add some sermons, but ones more attuned to grace than to choice or achievement.

When I was a boy (the nostalgia comes early), in a rural community of east Tennessee, an older, perhaps Victorian vocabulary still prevailed. Everyone referred to children, when they began school, as "young scholars." Our old-fashioned desks were scholars' desks. And at least high school teachers still gained the title of professor. Then the words "student" and "scholar" were synonymous. By most uses they are not so today. But use is far from uniform, and definitions go begging in this area as in most issues touching upon education. By necessity I will offer some of my own arbitrary definitions. All definitions are arbitrary, matters of stipulation or convention, as they are not based on any external authority.

I offer the following definition of a student, one that may seem very idealistic. First, a student is a person who wants to know something, about any subject, and is willing to take the needed steps to satisfy this desire. But not all people who want to know are students. For the student the desire to know always results from personal curiosity. To complete a task, one may need to know a great deal, and on behalf of the task go to extraordinary effort to learn, but otherwise not have any compelling interest in the subject. This person is not a student. His goal, his end in view, has nothing to do with satisfying one's curiosity. For the curious the gain-

188

ing of knowledge is an end in itself, fulfilling in the achievement. The knowledge gained may be very useful and lead to other good experiences, but to be a student, one must seek knowledge as a good in itself. Thus, by my definition, a student is one who craves knowledge for his own personal and immediate satisfaction, who finds delight and fulfillment in the knowing.

Every three-year-old child is, by this definition, a student. A child has an omnivorous curiosity. She wants to know everything about an exciting world around her. She asks endless questions, listens intently, observes acutely, and experiments with objects to see how they work. My mother tells me that as a child I almost drove her mad by taking things apart, including a clock I could not put back together. Later, with literacy, curious children read continuously. It is so much fun to know. The nagging practicalities of life are still ahead, such as making a living, or getting good grades in order to get into medical school. Lamentably (I promised you some lamentations), by the age of eighteen, so many people seem to have lost such delight in knowing, such catholic interests, such unrestricted curiosity. Few people who take my courses are students. They sit, listen, and respond because of instrumental reasons, to get some relished good that has no tie to the delights of knowing. At times they are bored. I am sad. I wonder what happened along the way to dull or narrow their interests. I try to present to them a feast of information, hoping that something will revive the childish wonder. This rarely works. The problem is deep, not open to manipulation. Curiosity is a gift, not an acquisition.

Students will use any method to satisfy curiosity. They will consult authorities, read books, enroll in lecture courses. But because of their curiosity, their desire to know, they will soon refuse to accept any information uncritically. They will question all received opinion. And, at least in informal ways, they will observe, put hypotheses to a test, carry out simple experiments. Eventually, they may become acutely self-conscious about the credentials of received knowledge even in the most refined scholarly and scientific fields. They will then ask questions about methods, about how scientists establish their truth claims, about the foundations or justifications of such methods. That is, a student is already, by the fact of being a student, not only an incipient scientist but a latent philosopher of science, one concerned about the criteria of meaning and truthfulness that prevail in any discipline. Only those who seek instrumental knowledge, who have no lively curiosity, who do not appreciate knowledge as a wonderful good in itself, will never glimpse the compelling lure of inquiry and become absorbed in the aggravating but inescapable problems of philosophy.

Here I do want to make a distinction—one between the often artless inquiry of a child and the disciplined, rule-governed inquiry of the developed scientific and scholarly professions. Those of you honored tonight have begun your apprenticeship in such disciplines. The criteria of meaningfulness and of truth in such disciplines are challengeable. In fact, nothing has been more fashionable in our recent intellectual history than a whole series of challenges to the truth claims of scientists and scholars. I will not address these complex, often muddy issues this evening. Suffice it to say that, if you choose to become adept in one of these disciplines, you must learn the well-established conventions or methods that are now sanctioned by a profession. Call them mere conventions, or social practices, or favored hermeneutics. It does not matter. These are the skills that one must use to gain recognition and certification. I doubt that anyone will ever find any formal way to justify any of the rules or methods that we use in any discipline to establish truth claims. But acceptance of these rules does provide us with reliable and useful knowledge, and maybe that is justification enough. What I want to argue now is that an apprenticeship in such a sophisticated or refined discipline means that students such as you have moved a good way from the informal and often trial-and-error inquiry of the child. You have embraced a very skilled and artful form of inquiry. In the sense that we now use the words, this makes you practicing scientists and scholars, artists at work in one of our local knowledge shops—Belmont University.

For the student, truth is a compelling goal. For the artist, so is beauty. For the moralist, so is the good. Thus I engage the Platonic trinity all over again—the true, good, and beautiful. I now want, very carefully, to relate beauty and good to truth, artistry and political involvement to the quest for knowledge.

By "art" I refer to a type of doing, or the product of such doing. An artist makes something. He takes raw material, whether clay or pigment or musical notes or words or even other people, and combines them in such a way as to achieve some esthetic goal, some vision of unity, harmony, or symmetry. But I use the word "art" not for all doing, but only for very imaginative and skilled achievement. An artist begins with a vision of a completed object and then successfully manages the raw materials that come together in the finished object, whether this be a house, a painting, a garden, a poem, a musical composition, or some new and unifying scientific hypothesis. Art demands talent and much training. It requires concentration and much effort. It can monopolize our time and our attention. It requires types of knowledge. But it is not knowledge. In the midst of her creation an artist may seek needed knowledge, even carry out some inquiries, but often, blinded by the vision she is trying to fulfill, she may not value or find any delight in the knowledge itself. She is not then a student. And because of the monopolistic demands of her mistress, art, she may have little time to indulge her curiosity. In fact, many types of work, whether creative or not, help stifle childish curiosity. But, despite this tension, note one similarity between the artist and the student—both are motivated by something good in itself, something wonderful in the having. It is a special quality of experience that permeates the creative process and graces the completed object for all those who experience and enjoy it. A work of art, like knowledge, may serve other goals. But what motivates it is a quality of experience realized. It is an end, however much it is also a means to gain something else.

The process of inquiry is a means to get knowledge, to satisfy curiosity. Thus inquiry is the one art form most congenial to the ever curious student. Disciplined inquiry involves not only creative thinking, but observing, testing, validating or falsifying. It may lead to the discovery of heretofore unnoticed relationships, or to the imposition upon nature of relationships never heretofore present. It structures the world as well as records existing structures. It is in this sense very creative. It is conceivable, in developed professions, that one may conduct experiments, or search in archives, from habit, to earn a living or a promotion, without any compelling intellectual interest or esthetic yearnings. By conventional definitions such bored workers may gain the title of scientist or scholar, but not by my definition. I do not think a mere lab technician is a scientist, any more than an antiquarian is a historian. Of course, and this is my sermon, I hope (I am not sure inspiration works here, and I know that commands are counterproductive) you will always remain students motivated by the sheer delight of knowing, and that as maturing scholars you will continue to respond to the esthetic delights that attend artful inquiry. I hope you never lose the excitement of discovery, the fulfillment of creativity.

If you realize these, my highest hopes for you, you will join an eminent crowd. For I truly believe that all the really brilliant or pioneer work in the formal and empirical disciplines has always been motivated by intellectual and esthetic goals. Only those who have a lively and wide-ranging curiosity, and who perfect the skills of inquiry to the level of a rewarding art, have contributed in major ways to human understanding. Like Einstein, they have all been perennial students, all gifted artists.

One might argue that, so far, I have offered an indulgent or irresponsible portrait of both students and scholars. I seem to have legitimated mere curiosity, and thus types of knowledge that may serve no extrinsic goals, or types of artistry unrelated to social need. I have pointed to the obvious fact that scholars and artists respond to purely intellectual and esthetic goals. These goals, in themselves, are not in opposition to the moral use of knowledge. The same knowledge that satisfies curiosity may cure cancer. Without the delight of knowing, the compelling lure of curiosity, I simply doubt that the more rigorous and dedicated cancer research would ever take place. In this sense society has a compelling need for curious intellectuals and inspired artists, even though, at times, both curiosity and inspiration may lead to knowledge that has no clear practical uses. That is, it may not be the means for the attainment of other goals. The ones who discover, or create, knowledge may often not know whether the product of their inquiry will be useful or not. It is not always easy to predict this. When Riemann developed his non-Euclidian geometry in the late nineteenth century, he had no intimation that it would provide the mechanical equations for the general theory of relativity.

I want to say a kind word for goods in themselves, even for a type of self-indulgence. As an almost congenital Puritan, I am able to understand those people who are always working toward goals, but who never have time for a holiday. Or those who are so busy growing roses that they never pause to smell their fragrance (only today I picked the first roses of this beautiful springtime; I smelled them). Or those who spend a lifetime preparing for heaven with no time to enjoy the heaven that is all around them. I pity them, even as at times I pity myself. When one thinks about it, why do we work so hard to gain future goals? Is it not to be able, at least some time, to relax and enjoy life's experiences for what they are in themselves? Are not all justified and eventual goals also final goals, things good in the having, self-justifying? If this is so, then why deprecate the joys of the moment, the types of experience that beg no further justification? In one sense they are indeed useless, if use always implies something in the future. But why should we so restrict our conception of "useful"?

Maybe good experience, at least for someone, not necessarily for oneself, is the only worthy goal that one can ever pursue. Think about it. What are the alternatives? If there are none, then one has no reason to depreciate moments of sheer delight, or to dismiss them as indulgent. Rather, one has a compelling reason to help secure such moments for as many people (possibly also as many animals, or as many gods) as possible, and to prolong them as long as possible. I want other people to share my delight in knowing, and hope to guide them to such experiences. That is one of the primary reasons I teach, an often enjoyable art in itself, but one full of such nondelightful and purely instrumental tasks as grading papers. I want other artists to share my delights in creativity, particularly the joy of writing, and hope that I can share with them some of the vision, or some of the needed knowledge, that will help them perfect their own unique creations, cognitive or otherwise.

But to so validate intellectual and esthetic pursuits is not to settle the issue of moral responsibility. Note that I refer to pursuits, not achievements, for in inquiry, as in all developed arts, the fulfillment always has unexpected elements, delightful spontaneity, something more than what one envisioned or planned; as much grace—that is, undeserved and unsought gifts—as planned outcomes. But in our world one cannot ignore the social costs and consequences of learning and inquiry. Many people have a stake in what I do to satisfy my curiosity or feed my artistry. Someone paid for your college education. It is costly. Those who paid are not able to share in the delights of your knowledge, or at times even experience the beauty of your new theories. It is not that they are lost in instrumental pursuits. They may have their own self-justifying experiences, and these may or may not involve both inquiry and artistry (do not deprecate the artistry of cooking, the self-justifying joy of eating). But they are different experiences, and in the larger context of a society we are morally compelled to so allocate resources as to make such goods available to all citizens. Those who provide an education expect contributions from the recipients of such subsidies—work that will serve the ends of the society. They have a right to demand such. And even apart from the demands of a larger society, individuals know that if they do not contribute to the welfare of others, they will lose any sense of moral complacency and feel miserable. Truth and beauty, however much they are goods in themselves, must, at least part of the time, contribute to a broader public good, else they are indeed indulgent and irresponsible. Scholars and artists are human, subject to moral, which is also to say political, obligations.

Is this a limitation upon one's intellectual and artistic freedom? It is at least a constraint. We cannot play all day, even if we are into the knowledge game. It is too easy to console ourselves with the prospects that almost any knowledge may prove, sometime, to be useful. Society has compelling needs in the present. And we have a duty to address those needs. If we have a wide-ranging curiosity, it need not crimp our style too much if we feel morally obligated to seek knowledge that is critical to other people. If, in a scarce society, we have to indulge our creativity in making beautiful hoe handles rather than a sculpture to rest in a museum, what have we lost? Nothing esthetically, and we have gained the possibility of moments of self-fulfilling experience for all those who suffer the drudgery of cultivation. To stress the self-justifying aspects of learning is not at all to argue that noninstrumental knowledge qua knowledge, is superior to useful knowledge, or that instrumental arts are esthetically inferior to what some refer to, with ill-concealed snobbery, as the fine arts.

My point is not to argue some equivalence between beauty, truth, and good, but the possibility of complementarity. It is not indulgent to note, and to certify, the immediate goods involved in searching and making. It is only honest to point to how these goals inspire and motivate, to the point that without them most inquiry would not take place. But it is indulgent to argue that one can use the resources of society to search and create only in areas that cater to private whim and fancy. Some types of beauty may inspire others, inform great goals, help people shape new identities. Insofar as one can anticipate such a fruitful form of beauty, then we have a moral obligation to use our gifts, at least part of the time, to attain such beauty. I know it is often hard to predict. I know that social demands may become dictatorial or lead to a form of censorship. But my point is that students and artists are also citizens. They have to balance these roles. In extreme situations a society may have to censor certain forms of creativity or enlist scientists in unwanted inquiry (one thinks of the Manhattan Project). In a peaceful and affluent society we can afford almost unlimited freedom in these areas, knowing that in the long run we will all benefit. But as an individual, one cannot escape responsibility for what one does with one's life. Thus I rejoice in those types of knowledge, those forms of artistry, that contribute to long-term goals that help feed and clothe people, that help mature the strongest character in individuals, that make equity and justice more likely in a well-ordered society. I especially value the political arts.

An unattainable, never fully definable goal, is a proper mix of social purpose, individual curiosity, and esthetic sensibility. But to aspire to such a mix is not to deny the tensions among these goals. A single-minded and very specialized artistry can squelch almost all curiosity. A morally blind curiosity may lead one into useless or even socially harmful fields of inquiry. An excess of puritanical zeal may restrict creativity to a few narrowly sanctioned subjects or to one prescribed style.

I want to end with a brief survey of the three main areas of knowledge—formal, practical, and humanistic. They demand different skills and serve different social goals. By "formal knowledge" I refer to essentially tautological and abstract systems, with no empirical content and no necessary empirical reference. Examples are mathematical systems, types of logic, or dynamic models. In each of these areas inventive humans, over time, have legislated the manipulative rules for working within such abstract systems. A student wants to learn such rules, beginning with first-grade arithmetic. Learning to navigate in such abstract fields can be great fun. Such abstract systems can also be very useful, even essential in classifying and relating experienced phenomena. Inquiry, in these abstract fields, involves the expansion or refinements of existing systems or models, or the invention of new ones. Here social usefulness is the most difficult to assess or predict, and here, as a mark of wisdom, society is most willing to leave curiosity and creativity completely free. Some people, in a very misleading and pretentious way, refer to these as pure sciences.

The practical or generalizing sciences involve testable claims about what we bump into. They reference the experienced world. Here inquiry has led to the most highly refined bodies of knowledge, and the most carefully developed methods of inquiry. Here our focus is usually restricted to areas of rhythmic repetition, to regularities in behavior, to relatively closed systems, and not to the even more numerous experiences that are chaotic. Here we discover, or induce, invariant relationships. These allow us to cite fully sufficient conditions for events, to predict into the future or retrodict into the past, and often to exercise minute control over the course of events. Such knowledge is both predictive and very useful. It not only allows humans to control an environment, but it also sets clear boundaries to what is possible, and thus helps orient moral vision. Insofar as such regularities prevail in human affairs, and they never do without qualification, we try to gain such knowledge in what we call the social sciences, but a knowledge usually restricted to probabilities, which allows only statistical prediction, and which permits less than full control over events.

The third type of knowledge involves human culture or meaning systems. Here we find no generalizations or perfect regularities. After all, humans use language to formulate or create the regularities in the generalizing sciences. In cultural studies we never find fully sufficient conditions for culturally shaped events, and thus never gain full predictability. What we can do is find patterns in past events, isolate rather stable customs or preferences, and thus often identify necessary conditions for what has already happened. Our perspective is then toward the past, and thus historical or anthropological. Such cultural understanding, whether historical or critical, can provide useful guidelines about the near future, thus lending a degree of confidence to policy choices. But more often than not, we develop cultural knowledge in order not to direct events, not to gain practical mastery, but to gain knowledge about ourselves. We find out the meanings, the beliefs, the preferences that constitute our personal or group identities. The purpose of such identity-oriented disciplines is to clarify or reinforce communal loyalties, to provide us with a sense of roots, and at other times to force us to make critical judgments about ourselves and the beliefs and preferences that characterize our culture. It is by such a dialogue with beliefs and preferences that we change, grow, adopt new identities. Because of this the humanistic disciplines are most closely tied to moral philosophy, and thus to the values and goals that orient policy choices.

To one final observation. Even if it is conceivable that in mathematics and physics a person might maintain a relatively clear demarcation between learning about a subject—a student—and becoming personally involved with expanding such knowledge—a scholar or scientist—this is all but impossible in the humanities. Because self-reflection is at the heart of cultural studies, one necessarily moves back and forth between received knowledge and critical engagement. Maybe it is because I am a historian that I have chosen this evening to so emphasize the overlap, and thus the fluid boundaries, between being a student , a scholar, and a good citizen.

10

Endings

In clearing out old files, I recently found some scribbled words, on yellow, lined paper, that I wrote in 1978. It was at a conference on local history at Appalachian State University in Boone, North Carolina. I not only agreed to give the opening keynote address (see chapter 1), but at a final luncheon to offer summary remarks on the conference. I took notes during the sessions, and in less than an hour wrote down some concluding remarks. The audience expected words of great wisdom. They received only the following. Note that, except for my father, I have changed the names of all people referred to who live in my home village.

Good-bye

For me this conference has been a homecoming. Much more than I anticipated, but consistent with the announced theme, the subject of the conference has been not so much the role of local history as the role of *our* local history. From music, to storytelling, to gravestones, to historic preservation, to town planning, the sessions that I have attended have all reflected an intense awareness of locality, of western Carolina, of the surrounding mountains. I have caught some contrasting nuances in this emphasis—authentic pride, apologies, concern, criticism—but it is all in the family.

As you know, homecomings are often joyful in anticipation, terribly disturbing in fact. When we are away for a long time, or even a short time, we cannot come home again, not fully. We do not fit as well as we anticipated. We have changed. Our home folk have changed, and so quickly we fall into confusion. Our identities become jumbled and disoriented, just at the very time we thought they would finally all fit together. For me, so much at this conference has been familiar. It has jarred all but forgotten memories. Yet I cannot quite sort out what of this past, of childhood and youth, is essential to my present self, how much only a curious souvenir. In any case this conference stands out from any I have attended. It has been unique. It is rare for so many people to come together, some from a distance, and to share so much. Or so it seems to me.

Conferences and conventions create a small, isolated world. They detach us from our normal routines, cut us off from families and close friends. Temporarily, we move into a small society and orient ourselves to it. We distance ourselves from our normal life. This can be liberating, at least for a time. But conventions often end on a sad note. After inspiration, challenges, we face a letdown. We have to go back to unresolved problems, problems not related to the subject matter of the convention.

But I sense that our conference will not end the way most do. Most depend on the glue of shared professional interests. They bring together otherwise diverse people and, as all of us, vulnerable people. Competitive motifs tend to dominate, as we search for reassuring symbols of status and acceptance. Always, in the rat race, some are way ahead of us. People more able challenge us, but also indict us—Why have we lagged behind? God, I can't do all that. Or we turn to sour grapes: Has he not taken a tiny bit of ability, and with his promotional skills gone a long way? At least I deserve my position. On and on goes this internal dialogue, the nursing of bruised egos, the anxious search for confirmation of our competence, achievement, or worth. It is no wonder that we have a disproportionate number of suicides at the end of conferences.

I do not think such status anxieties have been important in this gathering. We have been more at ease, more relaxed. We expected to be heard and we knew we would be understood. Why the difference? I begin with a minor reason. We have indulged ourselves with all our memories. Nostalgia has haunted our sessions. This may be typical of conferences on local history, or conferences attended by people of age and maturity. Rejoice in the memories filtered and purified by time. Some of the sweetest returns of life come long after the fact. As one old man put it, Ain't it wonderful that our forgetter is stronger than our rememberer? I am only sorry we did not have more time to remember.

But the more profound reason for lessened anxiety, I suspect, is the local orientation, not to occupational achievement but to place and family. This is not unique to the mountains. It characterizes local communities everywhere. When Professor Ross introduced me at our opening dinner, I caught some perhaps unintended significance in what he said. He began with my birthplace, Chuckey, Tennessee. Not in ages have I sensed that this identity was important to an audience. But here it was perhaps more important than what followed—an academic pedigree. Tokens of professional status usually count most among historians. Not here. Even for nonhistorians it usually counts most. On an airplane, in a chance encounter almost anywhere in America, the big question is always, What do you do? An English exchange student at the University of Wisconsin came to me almost in tears. Wherever she went, and particularly among parents of roommates or college friends, she confronted one unwanted question. Often it came indirectly, even hesitantly. Back in England, what did her parents do? She was insulted, for she rightfully felt that people were unable to relate to her, as a person in her own right, until they knew the answer to this question. Somehow she had to assume the occupational status of her parents. I suspect, had she visited my parents, they would never have asked that question.

When I return to east Tennessee, as on this visit, I have to resume an older identity. Harry Conkin's boy. He works somewhere up north. He hasn't done too well. Look at that seven-year-old, rusted Plymouth. This orientation to family and place is not always easy for me to accept. My acculturation has gone too far in the other direction, as I recognize whenever I visit home. My parents, or neighbors, care nothing for academic achievement. They know where I came from, and, with a confidence that irks me, they know exactly where I belong.

My father reinforces that "democracy" of place, and of esteem. I tell him, with pride, that the new book is finished and will be out in October. Fine, he responds. But, "I hope this one finally earns enough money to make it worth the doing."

And then on to important issues. "Have you yet visited Glen down in Rockford? It is not far from Madison. He has a good job up there. He was home last month, driving a brand-new Buick."

I protest. "I do not really know Glen. He grew up after I left the Shed. We have nothing in common."

Dad can hardly restrain himself. "Nothing in common? Why, he grew up not a mile from here. And besides, he is your half second cousin. Uncle Andy Smith was his great-grandfather."

I give up, half to please him, half because I am slowly adjusting to a different role and self-image. I really do enjoy what follows.

"Daddy, how is it exactly that you are related to Uncle Andy?" As son, and now student, I may spend an hour listening to my father and teacher. With great patience—I should know this already—Daddy fills in all the family relationships, complicated by all the halves. So many women died young back then. Fortunately, my mother does not have as much feel for place or family. She moved about when young, and she has never tried to keep up with over one hundred first cousins. Her mother was one of twenty children. My mother is more oriented to vocation than to kin. I guess I took after her.

Still, I do enjoy the game. I assume another role, but not completely. I cannot go home. For, in spite of parents, kinfolk, and neighbors, I am no longer sure it is home. Usually, my home is where my job is, where I go to church, where my children go to school. It has been a floating home, tied not to place but to function, in a society largely oriented to function.

At this conference an orientation to place has trumped an orientation to function, although not completely. I have noted aspects of both. But more than at any other conference I ever attended, I have heard the searching questions back and forth: Where are you from? Surely, if we had had more time to explore that question, we could have moved on to who is related to whom. After all, it is very important that one knows where one came from, and who one's cousins are. What better foundation than that for local history?

In closing, may I say that I suspect most of you came from somewhere very close. And could we spend a bit more time, and trace back a few generations, I am sure most of us are kinfolk. But until we have more time for such explorations, good-bye.

Index

Adams, John, 21, 87, 143
affirmative action, 117, 118
Agee, James, 178
agrarian ideas, 65, 153–59
agriculture: changes after 1945, 66; in
  colonial America, 163; in
  communal colonies, 35, 38; in the
  South, 149, 153, 156, 159, 165, 167,
  168, 169; the post–World War II
  revolution in, 168–70; subsistence
  form of, 39–40, 41, 44–46, 47
Alabama, 37, 151, 152, 163, 171, 178
Alien and Sedition Acts, 82
American Association for the
  Advancement of Science, 121
American Civil Liberties Union, 125–27
American culture, models of, 111–12,
  115–16
American Friends Service Committee,
  39
*American Originals: Homemade Varieties
  of Christianity*, by 121
American Railroad Union, 32
American Review, 155, 157
American Socialist Party, 33
American values, 11–12, 14–15, 17–18,
  22–23
Amish, 136
Anabaptists, 135
Anglicans, 106, 135, 136

Antiochus IV, 177
anti-poverty legislation, 68
Appalachia, 1, 13, 14, 16, 167, 174
Appalachian State University, 1, 197
Aristotle, 87, 88
Arkansas, 151, 166, 169, 171
art, definitions of, 190–91
Arthurdale Colony, 20, 37–48
Australia, 69

Baker, Vaughan B., 52
Bancroft, George, 87
Bankhead, John H., 37
banking and credit, 56, 58–59
Baptists, 14, 131, 134, 141, 164
Bellamy, Edward, 23, 24, 26–31, 34, 65,
  66, 70
Berger, Victor, 32, 33
biblical canons, 176–77
Big Daddy from the Pedernales, 52
Bill of Rights, 82–85
biography, forms of, 178–86
Borland, W. P., 32
Brotherhood of the Cooperative
  Commonwealth, 32
Bryan, William Jennings, 124, 126
Buddhists, 134
Burley Colony, 33, 34, 35, 36
Butler, John W., 125
Butler Act, 123, 125–28, 130

Calvin, John, 76, 111, 177
Calvinists, 12, 143
Cane Ridge revival, 121, 147
Cantwell v. Connecticut, 141
Caro, Robert, 182
Carter, Jimmie, 144
Christian Commonwealth, 31
Christian Eucharist, 9
civic god, American conceptions of, 142–45
civil rights, 68, 69, 95, 105, 115, 137, 139, 158, 170, 172
Civil Rights Acts, 68, 137, 172
Clinton, William J., 144
collectivism, 26, 57, 65, 66, 67, 154
Columbia University, 151
Coming Nation, 32
community building, 19–20, 37, 47–48
Congregationalists, 135, 138
Connecticut, 106, 135, 139, 141, 149
Conrad, Glen R., 52
conservation legislation, 68
Constitution, Federal, 15, 29, 63–64, 75, 79, 82–84, 89, 91–94,107, 113, 127, 138–39, 140, 141
cooperation, 26, 34, 47, 135
Cooperative Brotherhood, 33
Cooperative Commonwealth, 21–34
cotton cultivation, 164–65, 166
Cuba, 70
cultural relativism, 119
cultural wars, 131, 145
culture, concepts of, 9
Cumberland Presbyterian Church, 11, 183

Daniel, Pete, 170
Darrow, Clarence, 122, 126, 132
Darwin, Charles, 100, 123–25, 126
Davidson, Donald, 74, 152, 157
Dayton, Tennessee, 122–26, 128, 129, 130, 131–32
Debs, Eugene, 32, 33, 34
Declaration of Independence, 15, 25, 64, 74, 79, 80, 93, 112
Delaware, 135, 139, 149, 163, 169, 171
democracy: definitions of, 87–88, 93–95, limits on, 89–90, relationship

to Federal Constitution of 1787, 91–92; relationship to political parties, 93
Denmark, 23
Descent of Man, 124
Deutscher, Isaac, 95
Dewey, John, 103, 132
divine rights, 80
Division of Rural Rehabilitation and Stranded Populations, 38
Division of Subsistence Homesteads, 37, 39–40
Dutch Reformed Church, 135

Eisenstadt, Abraham, 51
Emory University, 173
environmental legislation, 68, 92
Equality, 24
Everson Case, 127, 141
evolutionary theories, 123–25, 128–29, 130
Evolution of Southern Culture, The, 147
expressive freedoms, 82–86, 94–95, 106–7, 114
Extension Service, 44

Fabianism, 23
Farm Security Administration, 39, 52
FDR and the Origins of the Welfare State, 52
federal aid to education, 67, 68
Federal Emergency Relief Administration, 38, 39
Federalist, The, 82
Federal Reserve System, 60
Federal Trade Commission, 60
First Amendment, 75, 81–85, 94, 113, 114, 127, 138, 140, 141
Fourteenth Amendment, 84, 92, 114, 127, 141
fiscal policies, 57–58
Fletcher, John Gould, 151, 153, 158
Four Foundations of American Government, 74
Fourier, Francois, 64
France, 2, 20, 76, 82, 94, 144, 152
Franklin, John Hope, 51
freedom of the press, 81–83

free speech, 81–83
fundamentalism in religion, 102, 131

George, Henry, 22, 65, 66, 70
Germany, 55, 111
Gone With the Ivy, 187
Great Depression: origins, 55–59; references to, xvii, 27, 40, 43, 44, 52, 155, 167; why it was the last, 60–62
greenbelt cities, 19, 39
Gronlund, Lawrence, 23–24, 26–30, 31, 32

Hamilton, Alexander, 82
Harriman, Job, 34
Hegel, Georg Wilhelm, 29, 111
hermeneutic circle, 18
Hindus, 134
Hinton, Richard, 32, 33
History as a System, 7
history, the discipline of, 1, 3–5, 7–18
Hitler, Adolf, 56
Hobbes, Thomas, 29
Hoover, Herbert, 55, 56, 57, 61
housing reform, 67, 68
Howells, William Dean, 24–27, 28, 29, 35
Huguenots, 76
humid sub-tropical climates, 161–62
Hutterites, 19, 121

Idaho, 32
I'll Take My Stand, by Twelve Southerners, 151, 153
immigration patterns, 40, 41
India, 52, 97, 134, 173
Indiana, 32, 74
inquiry as an art, 191
Interstate Commerce Commission, 60

Jackson, Andrew, 87
Jacksonians, 64, 70
Jefferson, Thomas, 21, 64, 79, 82, 93, 112, 113, 143, 145
Jehovah's Witnesses, 142
Jesus son of Sirach, 176–81, 184
Jews, 139, 140, 142, 177, 179, 180, 183
Johnson, Andrew, 161

Johnson, Lyndon, 52, 60, 63, 66, 68–69, 147, 161, 182

Kennedy, John F., 68, 69, 182
Kentucky, 147, 151, 152, 171
Kenyon College, 158
King, Martin Luther, 182

labor unions, 22, 104
language, origins and nature of, 2–3, 8–9, 100
Lanier, Lyle, 151, 156, 158
Lewis, Sinclair, 141
libertarianism, 85, 86
liberty, concept of, 75–76, 81
Library of Congress, 121
Lippmann, Walter, 131, 132
Llano Colony, 19, 34, 35
Locke, John, 76, 77, 78, 79
Looking Backward, 23, 24, 31, 32, 34, 65
Louisiana, 19, 20, 21, 34, 35, 52, 55, 156, 163, 164, 166, 171
Louisiana Gothic: Recollections of the 1930s, 52
Luther, Martin, 111, 177
Lutherans, 135, 136
lynching, 150, 166
Lytle, Andrew, 152, 157

Maccabees, 177
Maine, 32
Malone, Dudley, 126
Marx, Karl, 65
Marxism, 23, 32, 65, 104, 153
Mason, George, 79, 80
Medicaid, 69
Medicare, 69
Mellon Foundation, 1
Mencken, H. L., 131, 132
Methodists, 131, 134, 141, 164
Millikan, Robert, 131
Mississippi, 108, 159, 163, 171
Missouri, 149, 162
mixed government, 89–90
money, definitions of, 78–79
Moravians, 135, 136
Mormons, 108, 137
Murray, Madelin, 145

National Recovery Administration, 60
Nationalist Clubs, 32
Native Americans, 77, 110, 134, 161
natural rights, 75–86, 89, 90, 94
neighborhood, concept of, 11–17
New Deal, 19, 20, 37, 39, 44, 48, 51, 52, 59, 60, 67, 158
New Deal community projects, 37–49
New Hampshire, 139
New Harmony, Indiana, 74
New Jersey, 139
New York City, 23, 24, 25, 31, 126, 142, 151, 152
New York state, 64, 135, 139
New Zealand, 69
Nixon, Herman C., 151, 152, 156, 158
North Carolina, 1, 31, 46, 106, 121, 169, 171

Okies, 45
Odum, Howard, 167
Ortega y Gasset, 7
Owsley, Frank, 151, 152, 157, 158, 160

Peay, Austin, 125
Penn, William, 135
Pennsylvania, 81, 85, 106, 107, 135, 136, 139, 141
Pickett, Clarence, 39
Plain Folk of the Old South, 152
pluralism: dilemmas of, 97–99; distributive models of, 85, 92, 107, 113–14, 116, 136, 140, 141; inclusive models of, 92, 95, 114–16, 117; religious, 134–45
Polybius, 88
polygamy, 108, 137
popular sovereignty, concepts of, 89
populism, 32, 166
Post Office Department, 44
prayer decision of 1962, 15, 105, 142
Presbyterians, 12, 135, 136
property: concepts of, 21–22, 66, 155–56; right to, 21, 76–80, 81
Prophets of Prosperity, 74
Protestantism, 113, 116
public schools, cultural role of, 116–17
Puritans, 51, 81, 84, 88, 106, 107, 135, 136
Puritans and Pragmatists, 51–52

Quakers, 85, 135, 136, 139

racial theories, 111–12
Ransom, John Crowe, 132, 151, 152, 153, 154, 156, 158
Rawls, John, 90
Reagan, Ronald, 66, 144
regionalism, 14
regulatory and welfare state, xvi, 22, 51–52, 60–61, 67–71, 171
religion, definitions of, 122
religious establishment, definition of, 138–39
religious freedom, 83, 86, 108, 111–12, 114
Resettlement Administration, 38, 39
Rhode Island, 81, 106, 135, 136
rice cultivation, 162, 163, 166, 169
Roman Catholics, 59, 116, 134, 135, 136, 139, 140, 143, 144, 158,176, 177, 189
Roosevelt coalition, 59–60
Roosevelt, Eleanor, 39, 44, 48
Roosevelt, Franklin D., 37, 38, 39, 40–41, 56, 59, 60, 182
rural relief, 38, 39
Ruskin Colony, 32, 34, 35

Santayana, George, 52, 100, 132
Schlesinger, Arthur, 98
science, definitions of, 123
Scopes, John, 126–27, 130, 132
Scopes Trial: cultural issues at stake, 129–33; constitutional issues, 127–29; details of trial, 126–27; intellectual background, 124–25, 126
Second Treatise of Government, 76
Self-Evident Truths, 73, 74
Semitic cosmology, 122–23, 124, 129
separation of church and state, 15–16, 17, 127–28, 134–45
separation of powers, 89–90
Seventh-day Adventists, 140
Sierra Club, 105
single tax theory, 27, 65
Skidmore, Thomas, 64
slavery, 22, 63, 76, 84, 93, 108, 111, 150, 162, 164, 173

Social Democracy (political party), 32, 33

Social Democratic Party, 33

Socialist Labor Party, 32, 33, 34

South: agriculture in, 149, 153, 157, 165–66, 172; boundaries of,161–63; cultural maladies of, 150, 152, 157, 165–66, 172; definitions of, 147–48; incomes in, 171–72; industrial revolution in, 163–64, 168; manufacturing in, 46,159, 165, 166, 167, 168–71; population shifts in, 169–70, 171; post-Civil War poverty, 149, 152, 157, 165; pre–Civil War wealth, 149; racial strife in, 150, 156–57, 158, 166–67, 172; references to, xvii, 45, 52, 59, 69, 135, 139, 141, 147, 148; religion in, 150, 164; role of slaves in, 163, 64, 174; Sun-Belt growth in, 167–72

South Carolina, 139, 163, 171

Southern Agrarians, 147, 151–60

Southern Historical Association, 147

Southwestern Louisiana, University of, 19, 20, 52, 55

Spence, Thomas, 65

Spencer, Herbert, 29, 31

Stock market crash of 1929, 54, 59

Strachey, Lytton, 182

Stromberg, Roland, 1

students, definition of, 188–89

subsistence farming, 39–41, 44, 45–47, 57–58

subsistence homesteads, 19, 37–47

sugar cane cultivation, 162

Tate, Allen, 151, 153, 154, 155, 158

Tennessee, 32, 33, 37, 54, 104, 105, 107, 122, 123, 125, 126, 127, 128, 130, 131, 139, 147, 152, 171, 174, 183, 188, 199

Tennessee Valley Authority, 105

Texas, 38, 156, 164, 166, 169, 171, 172

theism, 90, 112, 113, 125, 143

Thucydides, 181

tobacco culture, 42, 54, 162, 163, 165, 166, 167, 169, 174

Tocqueville, Alexis de, 87, 93, 94, 144

Tomorrow a New World, 19

totalitarian communities, 15, 84, 88, 104, 114, 130, 135–36

Traveler from Altruria, 24, 25

Truman, Harry, 67

Tugwell, Rexford G., 39, 182

Two Paths to Utopia, 19

Uneasy Center, The, 121

Unitarianism, 31, 139, 144

United States Information Agency, 52, 97

Universalists, 140

University of Chicago, 151

University of Georgia, 147, 151

University of Hartford, 97

University of Maryland, 51

University of Wisconsin, 36, 199

utopian experiments, 19–20, 23–35

Vance, Rupert, 167

Vanderbilt University, 1, 98, 130, 147, 148, 151, 152, 158, 184, 187

Vermont, 138, 139

Virginia, 39, 43, 79, 80, 135, 136, 149, 151, 171

Virginia Declaration of Independence, 79

Wade, John Donald, 151, 153, 158

Warren, Robert Penn, 152, 156, 158

Washington state, 33, 34

Washington Agreement of 1923, 131–32

Wayland, Julius A., 32

welfare programs, 22, 57, 60–61, 65–69

Westbrook, Lawrence, 38

West Virginia, 39, 43, 149, 171

When All the Gods Trembled, 121

Whig Party, 64

Wilson, Woodrow, 183

Winthrop, John, 88

women's rights, 30–31, 106, 114

Works Progress Administration, 39, 45

World War II, 39, 45, 48, 56, 61, 67, 111, 115, 134, 159, 167, 169, 170

Wycliff, John, 111

Young, Stark, 151

About the Author

Paul K. Conkin is Distinguished Professor of History at Vanderbilt University, where he received his Ph.D. in history in 1957. He has received numerous awards, including a John Simon Guggenheim Memorial Fellowship, a Senior Fellowship from the National Endowment for the Humanities, and a University Fellowhsip from the National Endowment for the Humanities. He was president of the Southern Historical Association in 1996–97. He is the author of many books, including *American Originals: Homemade Varieties of Christianity* and *When All the Gods Trembled: Darwinism, Scopes, and American Intellectuals.*